BAT BOMB

*Jack Couffer*

# BAT BOMB

## *World War II's Other Secret Weapon*

**University of Texas Press**
**Austin**

Library of Congress Cataloging-in-Publication Data

Couffer, Jack.
    Bat bomb : World War II's other secret weapon / Jack Couffer. —1st ed.
        p.   cm.
    Includes bibliographical references (p.   ) and index.
    ISBN 0-292-70790-8
    1. Bats—United States—War use—History—20th century. 2. World
War, 1939–1945. 3. Incendiary bombs—History—20th century.
4. Couffer, Jack. 5. World War, 1939–1945—Personal narratives, American. I. Title.
    UH100.5.B38C68   1992
    940.54'4—dc20                                                    92-11888
                                                                         CIP

Grateful acknowledgment is made to the following for permission to quote
from various materials and/or conversations: Ozro B. Wiswell for quotes from
a telephone conversation; Denny Constantine for material regarding rabies
and bats; *Harper's Magazine* for permission to reprint material from the article, "One Way to Cripple Japan" by Charles L. McNichols and Clayton D.
Carus, copyright © 1942 by *Harper's Magazine*. All rights reserved. Reprinted
from the June issue by special permission.

# Contents

PREFACE  vii

ACKNOWLEDGMENTS  ix

1. THIS MAN IS *NOT* A NUT  1
2. SECRECY IS OBVIOUSLY ESSENTIAL  10
3. THE SUGGESTION IS RETURNED AS IMPRACTICAL  15
4. THE ARMY AIR FORCES WILL COOPERATE  20
5. FLAMETHROWER  27
6. NO QUESTIONS WILL BE TOLERATED  35
7. THEY CAN FLY!  45
8. CHEMICAL WARFARE CONCLUDES  52
9. THE BAT-SHIT MAN  77
10. OZRO  84
11. OSAKA BAY  95
12. MUROC  98
13. CARLSBAD  113
14. BANDERA  126
15. PROJECT X-RAY  144
16. THE OTHER WAR  160
17. THE HIBERNATION EQUATION  169
18. THE FISTFIGHT  179
19. DUGWAY  202
20. IT'S A BIT "STICKY" IN EL CENTRO  217

*Photographs Following Page*  232

EPILOGUE  233

REFERENCES  241

INDEX  243

# *Preface*

SOME WHO WERE THERE may question details in my reminiscence, and through time's hazing parts of the story are admittedly knotty points in my memory. The quotes from documents are correct to the letter, and the places and situations are as true as time, the tide of recall, and the ebb and flow of keepsakes of the mind can ever be (sources for government documents are listed in the references). Some events, even certain conversations, flash back clearly, as if I'd tied a string around my finger to help hang on to them. Other mental souvenirs come back less clearly, sometimes helped by a nudge from my friends. I took no notes and the remarks and opinions are not presented as verbatim statements, but are rather intended to express the gist of what people had to say. If some of the original authors of these words find them garbled or unrecognizable, I apologize and admit the fault is probably mine.

When I started to jot down my recollections it was only as an exercise to record the rather curious history of yet another in a long list of oddball wartime operations. I didn't realize that there was a story woven into the tapestry of haphazard-seeming incidents and that lacing it all together would make a drama come clear. I didn't know that I had been cast in a skit of hardly earthshaking importance, but a story nonetheless of intrigues, double-crosses, loyalties, loves, of larger human strengths and weaknesses.

All of this happened nearly fifty years ago, so if I'm muddled here and there, I hope I can be excused. But this is the way I remember it.

# Acknowledgments

THANKS TO JIM CHESTER, whose researches have helped me to look back and separate myths from facts; and to Harry J. Fletcher, Ray Williams, Jack von Bloeker, and Devil Bill Adams, who helped me remember. To Denny Constantine, the real batman. To Doc Adams, Tim Holt, and Eddie Herold, now gone. And to the other members of the project team—I hope they can relive with me this experience of long ago with a wistful sense of purpose and fun.

BAT BOMB

# 1

# *This Man Is* Not *a Nut*

FOG CLUNG to the hills, wet with winter grass; vague shapes plowed through the mist. They could have been Pleistocene beasts, like the dwarf elephant whose bones I was assisting the senior field collector to excavate, but the shadows were only cattle. We worked on the sheer side of a clay-banked gully where the remains had lain for half a million years. The ivory tusk-tip had been exposed by the last rain, and with pick, trowel, and brush we slowly brought the entire skull to light. In a plaster jacket it would go into the research collection of the Los Angeles County Museum, where I was a part-time student assistant.

We had been camped for a week near the end of Santa Rosa Island off the coast of Santa Barbara, twenty miles from ranch head-quarters and the nearest people, or so we thought. Then the shapes of two riders materialized from the fog. They stopped at the arroyo edge above us, classic cowboys, with Mexican chaps and wide-brimmed hats dripping with fog.

"They told us to fetch you back to the ranch," the elder cowboy said. "We got horses at your camp."

"But I've just finished my survey and we've started to work," my boss said. "We've got another ten days."

"No, you ain't." The cowboy puffed his Camel (this was in a time before cowboys all smoked Marlboros) and swung one leg over his pony's neck, perching high with his boot in his lap. "The foreman said bring you back, so I gotta bring you back, ¿que no?"

"What's it all about?" my boss asked.

"¡Quién sabe! Maybe something to do with Pearl Harbor's been bombed?"

The offhand slouch, the cowpoke's long drag on his cigarillo, conscious mannerisms of nonchalance, contrasted effectively with this seemingly important information.

"Where's Pearl Harbor?" I asked.

In those first confused days of the war it was expected that the Japanese would follow up their success in Hawaii with attacks on the U.S. mainland. West coast harbors were closed with antisubmarine nets and all boat traffic was stopped. Our museum field party of seven scientists and helpers was stuck on the island. In my adolescent innocence I thought our situation was exciting, and the drama of being marooned and a week late in getting back to high school after the Christmas break made me the first one in my class with an honest-to-God war story.

I spent mornings in the structured classes of Glendale High School, afternoons as a student assistant in the labs at the museum, where I assisted the various biology curators and was now learning to collect, prepare, and catalog small mammals for the research collections in the Department of Mammalogy. My mentor in this, my favorite niche, was Jack C. von Bloeker, Jr., an authority on the order Chiroptera—bats. His enthusiasm for these flying mammals, so profoundly associated with spooks, ghosts, witches, evil, and all sorts of weird happenings of mysterious and supernatural kinds, was dangerously contagious. All of this dramatic symbolism associated with bats was romantically fetching. I soon became seriously infected with von Bloeker's disease.

Our collecting forays took us scuffing through the musty belfries of old churches. With flashlights poking under highway bridges in Los Angeles we searched out colonies of *Myotis*, and from abandoned mine shafts and rock cracks in the nearby desert we collected specimens of the sixty-five or so species and subspecies of bats then known in North America. One kind, the spotted bat, rarest of modern mammals, and to my bat-besotted mind the most beautiful of creatures, was known to science from only four specimens. All had been encountered as the result of some freakish accident, as if occult forces had caused the demise—one had drowned itself in a railway water tank, another had impaled its skull on the wicked spine of a barbed wire fence. I yearned to discover the hidden secrets of this extraordinary animal—where and how did it live? Why had so few been found over so wide a diversity of habitats?

My tutor in this compulsive study of flying animals was thirty-three when I was seventeen, and he treated me and my fellow student assistant, Harry Fletcher (who was as fascinated with fossils as I was with bats), with all the understanding and perhaps more worldly insights than if we were his own sons. V. B.'s son was only three, and his two daughters at the ages of eight and four seemed disappointingly disinclined to follow his passion for natural history. One girl had a pet white rat which she clothed in dresses and hats and thus showed some promise at an early age, but her interest soon turned more to the haberdashery than to the rodent.

Von Bloeker was comfortable in the laboratory, where most of a museum curator's time is spent, but he wouldn't have been happy there without the knowledge that working up the data and collections from one fieldtrip would lead to another. His true calling was in the field—v. B. was essentially a collector, one of that old-fashioned breed of naturalists to whom a new specimen of any category, so long as it came from the earth or was one of its living inhabitants, was a treasure. In this respect, I thought of him as a modern-day Charles Darwin.

Von Bloeker was a chain smoker. When I press myself to recall a picture of him, I see his fine-featured face—thin, pointed nose cocked away and brown eyes squinted nearly shut—trying to see through the bluish column curling up from the cigarette forever dangling from his lips. The index and middle fingers of his right hand were stained a sickly yellow-brown, and his clothes reeked with the pungent odor of tobacco.

Fletcher was a couple of years older than me. His most noticeable personal trait was the habit of regularly combing back his straight, sandy-colored hair. Fletch wore his locks in the style known as a ducktail, a coiffure in favor with the notorious zoot suiters, but that was his only connection with that curious cult of the times.

Fletch's hair-grooming habit was so deeply ingrained that he reached in his hip pocket every thirty minutes, brought forth his comb, and performed the customary four strokes whether his head needed it or not. This formalized routine, as unvarying and rote as blinking, was as much a part of Fletch as his pinkish complexion, an eternal blush that glowed like the tinted paraffin faces in a wax museum.

One evening after the long ride from the museum by trolley and hitchhike (in 1942, a boy could stand on the roadside with his thumb out and people would stop their cars to give him a lift, a practice now unfortunately considered dangerous for both driver and passenger), I arrived home to find an official letter headed "Greetings," the curiously euphemistic caption for this momentous correspondence from draft boards across the nation—my Notice of Induction.

This letter, coming as it did only a few weeks before my high school graduation and coupled with my fascination for bats, doubled my interest in the unexpected visitor who blew into the stuffy Laboratory of Mammalogy like a breath of fresh air. He looked like Santa Claus without a beard, cherubic and ruddy-faced, small and plump—his white hair stood out in wild disarray, and small, round piggy blue eyes never seemed to blink, but sparkled mischievously. It was not the guru of Yule: he announced that his name was Dr. Lytle S. Adams, that he represented "the War Department," and that everything he said, including even the fact of his visit, was a military secret.

Von Bloeker introduced me as his assistant and our visitor said, "Yes, I know about him."

Knew about me? A seventeen-year-old high school kid? The War Department was aware of my existence? Even before I knew him I felt a warm flush of good fellowship toward this jolly-looking little man. Later I would learn that I had merely been subjected to Doc's inimitable style. He had known nothing about me, of course, but merely reacted to the introduction in his usual disarming way, tossing off the winning allusion at the auspicious moment.

Adams untied a frayed rope from around a worn-out leather briefcase and dove into the interior, stuffed to bulging with dog-eared papers. He pulled forth a document and flashed its red stamped notice with the word "Secret" conspicuously emblazoned in the margin. "Can't let you read this," he mumbled, implying far more textual content than there was, "but it's my letter of authority from the Great Man himself."

In addition to the bold security classification he allowed a glimpse of the letterhead. We saw "The White House, Washington, D.C.," a gold seal, and the signature: Franklin D. Roosevelt.

Now, years later, in quest of the research to joggle my memory and fill in the blanks for this reminiscence, I was supplied with a copy of a letter by the FDR Library. It is a reply to Dr. Adams's original proposal to the president and is the only personal correspondence on file from FDR in reference to our subject, so it must be the paper Doc flashed for our cursory inspection that day. The message was surprisingly cryptic in view of its import.

MEMORANDUM FOR COLONEL WM. J. DONOVAN,
U.S. GOVERNMENT, COORDINATOR OF INFORMATION.

This man is *not* a nut. It sounds like a perfectly wild idea but is worth looking into. You might reply for me to Dr. Adams' letter.

FDR

The note was not only brief in words, it was short on character perception as well. Doc Adams definitely *was* a nut, but to give the old man his due, not in the dismissive context implied by President Roosevelt.

The correspondence that produced FDR's brief assessment of Lytle S. Adams and his idea was handed to the president by his wife, for Doc had a large circle of acquaintances in the higher echelons of society and government, among them, Senator Jennings Randolph, who had introduced him to Eleanor.

Adams was a practicing dentist and oral surgeon who dabbled seriously in inventions. He had learned to fly with Glenn Curtiss in the early days of aviation, and his most successful invention was a rural air mail pickup system that made it unnecessary for the pickup plane to touch down, thus obviating landing fields in remote areas. He had demonstrated the device by delivering and picking up mail off the deck of the *Leviathan* in the English Channel in 1929, and regular deliveries and pickups were made from the middle of the lagoon at the Chicago World's Fair in 1934. He sold a partnership in the system to Richard du Pont, who established pickup routes in Pennsylvania, West Virginia, Delaware, and Ohio. Tri-State Aviation, of which Adams was president, was the parent company of today's USAir.

The First Lady was interested in Adams's invention, and he had flown her around in his own plane to different presentations. She made it possible for Adams to get the president's ear and offer his idea for helping to win the war.

The colorful language which Adams used in his letter to the president was not typical of his writing style. It may have been Doc's attempt to set his missive apart, to draw attention to it. If that was the case, the device was not only effective but quite within the tactical precepts of his showmanship.

Irwin, Pennsylvania
January 12, 1942

My Dear Mr. President:

I attach hereto a proposal designed to frighten, demoralize, and excite the prejudices of the people of the Japanese Empire.

As fantastic as you may regard the idea, I am convinced it will work and I earnestly request that it receive the utmost careful consideration, lest our busy leaders overlook a practical, inexpensive, and effective plan to the disadvantage of our armed forces and to the sorrow of the mothers of America. It is one that might easily be used against us if the secret is not carefully guarded.

I urge you to appoint a committee to study thoroughly and promptly all the possibilities of this plan and that its members shall consist of civilians eminently qualified to not only pass upon, but solve all technical matters and recommend methods for the execution of the raids.

Dr. Adams's letter went on to nominate a number of well-known scholars and businessmen to head the various departments that would be involved. Then he attached the following description of his scheme:

Proposal for surprise attack
"REMEMBER PEARL HARBOR"

Shall the sun set quickly over "the land of the rising sun"? I would return the call of the Japanese at Pearl Harbor on December 7, 1941, with a dawn visit at a convenient time in an appropriate way. . . .

The . . . lowest form of animal life is the BAT, associated in history with the underworld and regions of darkness and evil. Until now reasons for its creation have remained unexplained.

As I vision it the millions of bats that have for ages inhabited our belfries, tunnels and caverns were placed there by God to await this hour to play their part in the scheme of free human existence, and to frustrate any attempt of those who dare desecrate our way of life.

This lowly creature, the bat, is capable of carrying in flight a sufficient quantity of incendiary material to ignite a fire.

The letter makes the point that if millions of bats carrying small firebombs were released an hour before daybreak over a Japanese industrial city they would fly down to roost in factories, attics, munition dumps, lumber piles, power plants—all the structures of a community—and the hundreds of thousands of fires ignited simultaneously in inaccessible places would be impossible to control. His letter continues:

> The effect of the destruction from such a mysterious source would be a shock to the morale of the Japanese people as no amount of [ordinary] bombing could accomplish. . . . It would render the Japanese people homeless and their industries useless, yet the innocent could escape with their lives. . . .
> If the use of bats in this all-out war can rid us of the Japanese pests, we will, as the Mormons did for the gull at Salt Lake City, erect a monument to their everlasting memory.

Adams's letter goes on to point out that bats hibernate during winter and in this state of lethargy could be easily collected, fitted with tiny incendiaries, and transported without feeding or care other than to maintain the conditions necessary for hibernation. Just prior to release the bats could be made active again by warming.

> An important consideration is that a bat weighs less than one-half ounce, or about 35 to the pound, which means that approximately 200,000 bats could be transported in one four-motored stratoliner type airplane, and still allow one-half the payload capacity to permit free air circulation and increased gasoline load. Ten such planes would carry 2,000,000 fire starters.
> In submitting this proposal it is with a fervent prayer that the plan will effectively be used to the everlasting benefit of mankind.
>
> Yours humbly,
> Lytle S. Adams

It was essentially this incredible scheme, which already had tentative government approval, that Adams proposed to von Bloeker that day in the museum lab. In retrospect, one thing seems nearly as extraordinary as the concept of the plan itself. At no time, either in our preliminary discussions or later on as the project developed, did anyone challenge the idea from an ecological or moralistic point of view. No one addressed the issue "What about the bats?" In this day of animal rights activism and the conservation ethic such a project could probably not even be considered.

Doc's plan involved cremating millions of animals. Each bat

was to be a living firebomb: when the incendiary was ignited, the bat that carried it would go up in smoke along with the structure it was meant to destroy. Even von Bloeker and myself—confirmed bat lovers, a seasoned biological ecologist and his idealistic pupil—did not raise our voices in protest at the projected slaughter of wildlife.

Why not?

To define the answer one must look at the proposal in the context of the times. To anyone who did not experience those days of hatred and all-out effort, the mass mind-set of Americans during the war must seem incomprehensible. The dedication of humans on both sides of the struggle created a peculiar psychology unknown in times of peace or even of uncommitted war. Hysteria was fed by the press, by radio, by film and official propaganda. Few Americans would have argued in those times about the truth of Doc Adams's statement in his letter to President Roosevelt: "The slimiest most contemptible creature in all the world is the Japanese military gangster."

My mother, sending off a young marine friend to the war, said, "Bring me back a Nip's ears." She was speaking figuratively, of course, but this was a reflection of the widespread hatred of the time. The Japanese had made the surprise dawn attack on Hawaii which temporarily extinguished the U.S. Pacific fleet. Six Japanese aircraft carriers put forth 370 planes that sank four, and severely damaged two more, U.S. battleships at anchor. Hundreds of U.S. sailors and civilians were killed. The sneaky way the Japanese opened the Pacific war did much to characterize the enemy in the minds of Americans, and it bound our otherwise diverse citizenry into a single body with the same strong resolve. The "Japs" were the despised enemy, guilty of the most heinous atrocities. To many Americans of the time the Japanese were a breed apart from the rest of humanity, easily mind-warped due to their strange Asian customs, exalting in the execution of incredible acts of barbarism, torture, and rape, even to the self-immolating horror of kamikaze pilots who deliberately blew themselves to kingdom come and eternal glory by diving their bomb-laden planes into the sides of American warships.

The people of the United States were committed to winning this war they had not asked for. Few held back. Sons and husbands and fathers were dying; hundreds of thousands of young men were fighting under the most awful conditions, and women in uniform served close to the front in many ways. Women toiled at home in the defense factories which ran day and night churning out ships, planes, munitions, and all the other necessities of warfare. No one was untouched.

I doubt that Doc Adams meant it literally when he wrote to the president that the only reason God created bats was so the United States could use them to incinerate Japan in this war. It was only his eccentric way of making a point. Still, it didn't occur to us at the time to question the morality or the ecological consequences of sacrificing a few million bats.

Months later, when the young marine to whom my mother had bid good-bye with her offhand request returned from fighting in the Pacific, he proudly presented her with a small box. Inside, she found a dried human ear. She was repulsed, of course, but the marine's literal reply to her figurative remark was characteristic of the mind of the fighting man in the Pacific in World War II.

During such an extraordinary time it was natural that we would be indifferent to the ethical issue of killing bats as a method of waging war. Adams may have used exaggerated language to attract attention to his idea, but his letter to Roosevelt was illustrative of the collective mind of the country—if killing one or two million bats was an effective way to fight the enemy, using the method was not only prudent but was a moral obligation.

If times have changed, so have I. It's hard to imagine now putting myself into a frame of mind to kill a million anything—birds, bats, or bumblebees. It is just not within the realm of my creed at this time. But then it was, and because of the perceived greater good I was ready for the sacrifice without a second thought.

# 2

# *Secrecy Is Obviously Essential*

THOMAS R. TAYLOR was director of staff of the civilian group, National Defense Research Committee (NDRC), appointed by President Roosevelt to coordinate the scientific community with the military. It was to NDRC that Colonel Donovan directed Adams's proposal.

In the meanwhile, Adams headed for Harvard University with the hope of meeting the reigning bat expert, Glover M. Allen, the author of the best reference book of the day, *BATS*. At the university, Doc discovered that Allen had just died. He was referred instead to a research associate in the Psychoacoustic Laboratory who was working on improving military communications equipment for use in high noise levels. Donald R. Griffin was also interested in bats. After meeting Adams, Griffin discussed Doc's plan with his superior, Professor S. S. Stevens, who authorized him to spend some time investigating the feasibility of the project. Griffin seemed to see the biological validity of Adams's plan and submitted the following memorandum:

MEMO TO:  Mr. Thomas R. Taylor, Director of Staff
              National Research Defense Committee (NDRC)
              The National Inventors Council, Washington
FROM:  Donald R. Griffin
              Special Research Associate
              Harvard University
SUBJECT:  Use of bats as vectors of incendiary bombs.
DATE:  April 16, 1942

      The [Adams] proposal calls for the use of very large numbers of bats, each carrying a small incendiary time bomb. The bats would be released at night from airplanes, preferably at high altitudes and the incendiaries would be timed to ignite after the bats had descended to low altitudes and taken shelter for the day. Since bats often roost in buildings, they could be released over settled areas with a good expectation that a large percentage would be roosting in buildings or other inflammable installations . . . when the incendiary material was ignited.

This "vector" method of incendiary bombing would be most likely to cause severe damage to property and morale if used against Japan where inflammable construction is widespread, and where much of the war industry is scattered into small workshops.

Because of the writer's experience with bats, both in the field and in the laboratory, he was consulted as to the biological aspects of this project. This experience includes the banding and tagging of over 13,000 cave bats to trace their migrations, and the recent experimental demonstration by Dr. Robert Galambos and the writer that bats navigate in the dark by an echo-sounding system. They emit supersonic cries on too high a frequency for the human ear and locate obstacles by hearing the sound deflected back to their ears.*

One's first reaction to this vector method of warfare is likely to be one of horror. Unfortunately however, we are engaged in total war against completely ruthless enemies who have already used poison gas in China and have certainly showed no hesitation to bomb and machine gun civilian populations in the Philippines. . . . Damage would be mainly to property and morale, and hundreds of thousands of fires started in the *interior* of scattered structures should have a devastating effect. The final decision as to if and when we should retaliate with this weapon rests with our military commanders, but it is suicidal folly to leave it unprepared.

Griffin's official document went on to list seven main topics of biological investigation which should be explored to prove or disprove the practicality of the plan then offered:

RECOMMENDATIONS
This proposal seems bizarre and visionary at first glance, but extensive experience with experimental biology convinces the writer that if executed competently it would have every chance

---

*A revolutionary biological finding that demonstrated a device in nature operating on the same principle as radar.

of success. An investigation should be undertaken at once and with all possible speed, accuracy and efficiency to (1) locate and take stock of the available supplies of bats; (2) find by experiment their load-carrying capacity, the best shape for the load and the best method of attachment; (3) learn by simple pressure chamber experiments and observations the maximum altitude and the minimum temperature which the bats can survive and remain in good condition; (4) work out practicable methods of transportation and release; (5) investigate such problems as the necessity for killing the bat at the time of ignition of the incendiary material to prevent its taking flight and reducing the chances of starting a fire. Possibly a small explosive charge would be required for this purpose.

. . . Practical experience with bats and with physiological techniques is indispensable in this sort of investigation. The problem is a difficult one, but it can be solved with reasonable speed if competent men are put on the job. Of course similar investigations must be made by specialists in explosive and incendiary chemistry to design suitable small-sized incendiary bombs. The air transport problem must also be worked out in conjunction with the biological and chemical investigations.

Secrecy is obviously essential; but speed and efficiency are even more so. Perhaps the best procedure would be the immediate establishment of a small research project under the Air Corps or the Office of Scientific Research and Development to investigate this type of warfare. If it is found practicable, the same group could assist in its immediate preparation for active use if and when our commanders give the orders.

It is interesting to read Griffin's comments in a letter to researcher James Chester in 1984. "I would certainly react differently now were the idea presented to me; I would be much more negative about its practicality, to say nothing of ethical issues. But the summer of 1942 was when the Japanese were pushing everything before them and our army and navy were just beginning to put up effective resistance as on Guadalcanal. It is sobering and salutary to read what one said under war-time conditions."

I sat opposite von Bloeker at the museum work table writing up labels for the series of small mammals we had collected on the island fieldtrip. We had heard nothing more from Dr. Adams and his bat plan and thought that, in spite of the validity of the biology, the basic idea was probably too fantastic to go any further. But we did discuss the idea endlessly. As always, v. B. worked with head canted, eyes squinted nearly closed, trying to dodge the smoke from the cigarette hanging from his lip. It puzzled me why he didn't remove it when he wasn't actually puffing and spare his eyes and nose the annoyance.

"As wild as it seems," von Bloeker said, "the idea's got something going for it. Fanciful, yes. Yet the individual elements, crazy as they are, make fundamental sense."

We didn't know it yet, but Griffin's letter to the director of NDRC was already creating the same thinking elsewhere. The prestigious group of scientists made a formal declaration: the recommendation to conduct an in-depth study. Their approval was enough to stir the interest of the U.S. Army Air Forces.

V. B. knew that many of the conclusions that Adams had put forward as hard facts were actually only reasonable speculations based on neither systematic knowledge nor experimental evidence. Doc was not a scientist; he was a dental surgeon with inexhaustible energy and an inventive mind, a visionary who saw the potential in this bat bomb scheme and had the practical knowledge, if not the technical background, to put it together. He also had contacts in high places and the versatility of personality that allowed him to go anywhere and mix with people from any level of society. But many questions in addition to those basic ones posed by Dr. Griffin had to be answered before the true feasibility of Adams's plan could be either proved or disproved.

Von Bloeker squinted through his smoke, printing the small tags that recorded the vital statistics of the recently collected mammal specimens with a precise script worthy of the calligraphy of a medieval monk. To this day, because of his insistence that I emulate his passion for penmanship, my handwriting, while far from the perfection he aspired to, is in the same half-printed, half-written style he demanded on those labels.

V. B. got up and the keys on the clip hanging from his belt jingled. Like an auditor or draftsman, he stuck his pen in the celluloid holder in his shirt pocket. "How much weight can a bat really carry in flight?" he mused. "Can an effective miniature incendiary bomb be produced that a bat can actually carry?"

His mind was not on the labeling, but on Adams's strange plan—and how he, as a bat expert, could make a special contribution to the war effort. V. B. went on, again summarizing the list of problems that would have to be investigated before Adams's idea could be proved.

Was it really possible to treat a living bat like an inanimate machine and induce it to enter into a state of prolonged suspended animation, or could this condition of hibernation only be brought on by natural causes? If one could will a bat to hibernate, could one also induce it to end its torpid state at a given moment so the proposed air raid could be flown at the appropriate time? How did one go about telling a hibernating bat that it was time to wake up and go to work? If in fact the conditions of hibernation and dehibernation could be brought on artificially, exactly what climatic and physiologic situations must prevail to induce the conditions, and for how long a period could the animal maintain this torpid state and come out physically fit?

Was "dehibernation" a word at all? Or were we coining a new expression along with a new process? Had anyone ever before had the occasion to artificially induce a hibernating animal of any kind to come out of its state of lethargy? Not to our knowledge.

Where and how could millions of bats be captured in secrecy, transported, and fitted with their miniature weapons? How far could a bat fly when encumbered with a bomb? Would it really seek out the inflammable nooks and corners and dark, inaccessible places to roost that Doc and Griffin said it would? How did you set the triggers on a million tiny bat bombs so they would all ignite when the bats were hidden in their roosts and not while they were packed aboard their airplane transport en route to the drop site? How did one disperse the bats from the planes—shovel them out like lumps of coal into a furnace?

As so often happens when one has been awaiting a decision from on high, when the signal of approval is finally given, one's static world explodes and everything seems to happen at once. The day the Adams Plan, as our project was now officially called, got the signal "Go!" Doc arrived at the museum with all of his irrepressible energy boiling to get started. One day we were writing labels on mouse skins and the project was only an idea, the next day the National Inventors Council, encouraged by a vague boost from the Air Force, would sponsor some exploratory research and we were suddenly catapulted into a development of utmost urgency.

Doc had some ideas for other individuals to join our team; but most important to me, the date for my induction into the Armed Forces came due.

Then, just when things seemed to be shifting into high gear for a fast drive ahead, the transmission of our war machine made a disheartening clunk and ground into neutral. We hadn't shifted into reverse yet, but the clutch was out and the heavy foot of the Army was poised.

# 3

# *The Suggestion Is Returned as Impractical*

MEMO FOR: The National Inventors Council
Department of Commerce
Washington, D.C.
FROM: The Chemical Warfare Service Liaison
Officer with The National Inventors Council
SUBJECT: N.I.C. Suggestion No. 51162
Dr. Lytle S. Adams—Use of Bats For Incendiary
Purposes
DATE: May 18, 1942

The above identified suggestion has been examined by technical personnel of the Chemical Warfare Service. All correspondence pertaining thereto is returned herewith together with the
following informal comments:

The incendiary action would have to be initiated by white
phosphorous. The latter must be kept from exposure to oxygen
until just before ignition is to occur. Since bats require oxygen for
breathing they would be asphyxiated by any material used to
keep the phosphorous inactive. In addition, the low temperature and pressure at which bombers fly to avoid anti-aircraft fire
would be detrimental to the life of the bats.

The suggestion is returned as impractical.

William G. Wiles
Captain, C.W.S.
Liaison Officer, N.I.C.

1 Incl.
Suggestion No. 51162

The memo from the all-important Chemical Warfare Service,
whose advice would be routinely heeded by the Air Force, seemed
to turn on Doc's faucet of energy rather than shut it off. Now that

[ 15

he had his machine in gear he refused on the basis of this disappointment alone to call everything to a halt. It would take precious little time for the reversal to make its way through channels; but in the meanwhile work could be done. Living under the cloud of wishful thinking, Doc proceeded almost as if nothing had happened, only quickening the pace to offset the inevitable. Doc couldn't face the reality of the System.

Was it possible that a mere Army captain, reacting on the basis of long-established *modus operandi* rather than opening his mind to innovative new technology, could throw up a roadblock and bring a halt to the Adams Plan before it really got rolling? Doc had properly expected the officer who served as a connection between the Chemical Warfare Service and the NDRC branch of the National Inventors Council to be on the lookout for something new, something revolutionary. After all, that's what inventions *were*—something different! Adams properly expected an inquiring, imaginative mind searching for revolutionary ideas that would break through established regimens and forge new ground. Instead, he ran into a brick wall. He had encountered an obstacle in the person of a junior officer whom he considered to be a reactionary who turned down the entire concept just because he couldn't see his way through a few technical hitches. In developing any new process one expected to throw out the old. If the standard white phosphorous method of fueling an incendiary wouldn't work, that didn't make it logical to shelve the whole project. Doc reasoned that this was a new application that needed a new formula, that was all. The appropriate response was simple: if the traditional material wouldn't work, find a new material that *would*!

Henceforth, throughout the continuing development of the Adams Plan, technical hitches that stumped a hidebound Chemical Warfare Service plagued progress. To Adams's way of thinking it wasn't because the problems were unsolvable, but because the officers in that department seemed to be particularly unimaginative.

Doc telephoned his contact, Thomas R. Taylor, at the National Inventors Council and asked him to respond to the Chemical Warfare Service and to the obstructive Captain Wiles. Meanwhile, at this low stage of affairs, with everything up in the air as to the future of the bat project, but with orders assigning me to the Army Air Forces and to detached service to Dr. Lytle S. Adams upon completion of basic training, I went off to Utah for six weeks to learn how to become a soldier. Along with my fellow inductees I was taught how to make a GI bed so tightly that a dime tossed onto its middle bounced an inch high—the test of inspecting officers for a passing grade. We learned how to fire and care for an M-1 rifle, carbine, and machine gun; how to shoot grenades and lob them by hand; how to stick a straw-filled dummy with fixed bayonet and the proper way to garrote an enemy from behind, at the same time jabbing him in the guts with the six-inch-long blade of the government-issue combat knife. We saw the indoctrination film *Kill or Be Killed* not once but several times. It scared us, as it was meant to do. For anyone who had never thought of killing another human being in hand-to-hand combat, it justified the act purely on the basis of survival.

It was while on bivouac somewhere south of the Great Salt Lake where we had been hiked far into the foothills of a high mountain range that I was taught in a most roundabout way the important lifesaving lesson Always Expect the Unexpected. The bizarre experience, which was outside the official curriculum, remains the highlight of my military training.

Our pup-tents were pitched in rows near a stream which had been partially diverted to flow through the latrine area, creating a sort of naturally self-flushing sewer. Walls of canvas for privacy stood on each side of this ditch of running water, appropriately called a straddle-trench. At six A.M., when a line of recruits stood impatiently outside the canvas screen waiting for their turns to step inside and squat head to tail, one foot on each side of the trench to facilitate the evacuation of yesterday's K-rations, a joker upstream floated a huge wad of flaming newspaper down between the canvas walls. Shouts of indignation and pain and the smell of singed hair rent the air as the conflagration sailed past, and not a few that day, myself included, nursed red blisters on our backsides as tender as the ones on our heels.

I didn't know it, but while I was undergoing my trial by fire, Thomas R. Taylor, director of staff at the National Inventors Council, prevailed upon Captain Wiles of Chemical Warfare to keep the file open on Adams's proposal. Again, the papers embracing Doc's "Suggestion No. 51162" were back on the desk of the Army's Chemical Warfare Service and Adams was instructed to "present further information on the type of incendiary material to be used and how it is to be ignited."

The cards had been tossed back into Doc's hand and his next play was a daunting one. Adams had been given one more chance and knew that the wrong card would blow it. He wrote immediately to Taylor in Washington, D.C.

In my original proposal addressed to the President, I suggested Dr. Robert Milliken of the California Institute of Technology as the proper person to direct the chemical research in
connection with this plan. I made the suggestion because I knew
Dr. Milliken had the facilities to make the necessary experiments and because I am not a chemist. . . . However, since this
phase now seems to be the stumbling block I have given it consideration and believe I have the solution . . .

Adams continued with the outline of a method by which he
thought Captain Wiles's main objection could be put to rest. Wiles
had stated that living bats and the incendiary chemical white phosphorous were incompatible. Bats need oxygen to breathe; white
phosphorous bursts into flames when exposed to oxygen. To Doc the
solution seemed straightforward—isolate the incendiary material
from the life-giving oxygen. At the time of ignition, let them get
together. To resolve the apparent incompatibility he proposed a
simple physical barrier.

The incendiary bomb that Doc envisioned was a finger-sized
capsule made of inflammable celluloid perforated with small holes
that would be plugged by coating the capsule with wax, thus keeping oxygen away from the contents. The wax would be mixed with
a solvent to melt at a predetermined temperature, say 70 degrees F.
When the bats were released from their chilled containers and flew
down to roost, the air temperature at ground level would melt the
wax, allowing oxygen to reach the white phosphorous, which would
then burst into flames.

Doc's solution was far from perfect. It left open too many
chances for disastrous malfunctions, but it did demonstrate, at least,
that the issue was not cut and dried, that there could be a solution
to a detail that after only superficial analysis seemed to make the
whole plan unworkable. Later experimentation by qualified chemists produced an incendiary far superior to Doc's groping attempt
made under such threatening circumstances, but there was just
enough merit even in his first primitive idea to keep his baby alive
for the moment.

Taylor responded by requesting a meeting between Adams and
staff of Chemical Warfare at their Aberdeen headquarters. Here
there is a gap in the official correspondence which makes it impossible to completely explain Taylor's apparent enthusiasm for
Adams's idea in the face of such direct opposition from the key military service that would be most directly involved in any development of the incendiary. But evidently Adams had a champion in the

person of an important general. His position or the branch of service with which he was connected is not known, but Taylor seemed impressed enough with what must have been the mysterious general's approval that he used his name as a lever. "You have seen our comments on Dr. Adams' proposal," Taylor wrote to Captain Wiles, "particularly the comments of General W. H. Tschappat, and I think therefore it might be well if this additional step in development could be undertaken."

# 4

# *The Army Air Forces Will Cooperate*

ON JUNE 13, 1942, in response to the urging of the National Inventors Council's Thomas Taylor, Col. W. C. Kabrich, chief of Technical Service of Chemical Warfare, wrote to the commanding general, Army Air Forces.

Kabrich, later to become a brigadier general, would become a key player in the theater of the Adams Plan. His vacillations, as hard as they were to take at the time, were an aspect of the drama that propelled the Adams saga through its comic and bitter ups and downs, ever nudging it a page or two closer toward its eventual place as a story.

Colonel Kabrich's letter to the commander of the Air Force outlined the objectives of the Adams Plan, including a brief overview of the methods of delivering bat-borne incendiaries from aircraft, and ended with this sentence: "It is requested that this office be informed if you see any possible use for such a munition."

Doc's reply to the rejection of his idea by a member of the lower echelon in the CWS had produced positive action at upper levels of command. The answer to Kabrich's letter came back from Air Force Headquarters only twelve days later. When Doc Adams read the correspondence he was walking next to his shoes. The key paragraph said: "Fantastic as the proposed plan appears, there might be a time in the future when it would be desirable to execute such harassing missions . . ."

A list followed detailing seven areas of exploration to determine the plan's practicability. The officer writing on behalf of Hap Arnold, commanding general of the Army Air Forces, ended his communication: "The Army Air Forces will cooperate with the Chemical Warfare Service when experiments reach the stage requiring tests from airplanes."

That evening at the museum office Adams produced a bottle of Old Grand-dad bourbon, the only spirits he would imbibe, modestly but with staunch regularity—two ounces per evening—and the bottle was passed from man to man by members of the bat patrol.

When I returned to Los Angeles as an airman in the 5th Air Force, with official orders to report to Dr. Lytle S. Adams for duty in connection with a secret project, I found our outfit already beginning to form.

Von Bloeker had enlisted in the Army: because of the urgencies of his duties he had been spared the training I had endured and became an instant soldier, a warrior in title and uniform only, I thought with my now-superior education behind me.

While I had been away, Doc Adams, with the deft strokes of a mad theatrical producer, had begun to assemble other members into his diverse and unlikely crew—clever and inept, skilled and maladroit, we became a team of 20-odd, in the broadest sense of the expression. It was as if Doc had searched the casting lists of all that treasury of as yet unwritten war stories, pulled out the most outrageous characters he could find, and enlisted all into his private Army. We were *Catch-22*, *M*A*S*H*, *Sergeant Bilko*, *The Black Sheep Squadron*, *The Caine Mutiny*, *Mister Roberts*, and *Hogan's Heroes*, rolled into one.

Doc had been joined by a young chum from Pennsylvania, the ex-manager of the Jacktown Hotel near Irwin, whose restaurant, we were led to believe, had the finest reputation in the area. Bobby Herold had been classified 4-F, physically unfit for military duty. (Why, I never knew—he seemed fit enough to me and appeared to be one of the most sexually athletic men I ever met—or so he led one to believe.)

Militarily, Bobby would be designated as Doc's adjutant or aide-de-camp. Bobby had a jolly baby face that Doc was used to and liked to have around. In spite of his lack of technical input, Bobby was socially astute, always ready with a humorous quip and with wise insight useful to negotiate a way through the difficult political situations that frequently faced us. Like his mentor, Bobby had an artful way of getting what was needed when the getting seemed impossible.

Soon Bobby was joined by his brother, Eddie, who like myself had just completed basic training and came with special orders and a duffel bag stuffed full of newly issued GI khakis and ODs, as the dress uniform was known. The soldier's cloth was of a color and style totally in keeping with its lackluster name—olive drab. Eddie Herold was the first in our unit to turn over his baggy GI uniforms to a private tailor. In a few days he looked as chic as a Hollywood soldier. The rest of us were not long in following his example but never were to achieve the degree of sartorial splendor reached by Eddie. His body was built in just the right proportions for wearing his clothes well.

Except for the shapes of their bodies, one plump, one thin, Bobby and Eddie Herold could have been twins. Bobby was the elder by three years, yet with his cherubic baby fat he looked to be in his teens rather than early twenties. Bobby paid no attention to his shape; Eddie, however, worked on his regularly with diligent isometrics. This method of body-building was popular at the time, the promotion of one Charles Atlas, champion muscle man whose slogan was printed in every men's magazine beneath the portrait of his perfect body: "I was once a 97 pound weakling." Sitting in a chair, standing against a wall, Eddie strived to attain the body of Atlas. Although he seemed to be relaxed, his muscles constantly twitched and jerked like a dog dreaming—but it was only his isometric exercises.

My former fellow student-assistant and friend at the museum, Fletch, with whom I had dug fossils at the island, had recently heeded the call and enlisted in the Marine Corps. Fresh out of boot camp, he came visiting at the museum in his new dress blues. Resplendent in shiny-billed cap, high-collared jacket with metal emblems, and enough gold buttons to fill a treasure chest, he made the rest of us in our vapid ODs look like bums. Fletch was stationed temporarily at San Diego and brought along a new marine buddy, a clean-cut looking recruit named Ray Williams. At the time, we were using the museum Mammalogy Lab as a base of operations, and that's where Doc met our visiting Marine Corps friends.

Doc asked Williams what he'd done before enlisting. When the young marine said he'd been an apprentice lobster fisherman in Maine, Doc seemed to think that was precisely the background required to fill some undisclosed vacancy in his burgeoning unit. How he arrived at this astounding conclusion we'd never know. He just had an eye for talent, I guess. Doc took an immediate liking to Fletch as well and suggested that he might request they both be transferred to the bat project, a manipulation of power over the military which seemed to us a fantasy far beyond the realm of any mere civilian's talent. But in a few days Fletch and Williams were back, sea bags in tow, with newly cut orders assigning them to Doc. Fletch's qualifications as a scientist were perhaps even less than mine; although he had a few years on me in age, his biology experience consisted solely of digging fossils on museum fieldtrips and he had not yet graduated from wallowing in the earth to my broader range of experience—chiefly as label writer—in various biological departments.

Maybe Doc simply liked the cut of the snappy Marine Corps uniforms, or perhaps he was intrigued with the notion of a multi-service unit, a radical idea at the time. Whatever the rationale, Williams's lobster fishing experience seemed even more shaky as a scientific qualification than mine or Fletch's.

Seven of us, including Adams, sat crowded in the stuffy museum lab inhaling von Bloeker's smoke. The odors of moth crystals from the cases containing collections of small mammal specimens overpowered even the stink of tobacco. And there were other pungent odors, too. Exuding from vents on the metal case where dermestid beetle larvae were at work cleaning the rotten flesh off the skulls of mice, squirrels, and gophers and from cracked seals on bottles of various animals preserved in alcohol or formalin you could almost see the wafting of strong vapors. Then, of course, there were the smells of the animals themselves, for many cases held research collections of the skins of skunks, weasels, badgers, and other members of the family Mustelidae, animals that once possessed scent glands of various magnitudes of pungency, many of which had not completely lost their formerly smelly attributes through the tanning process.

Until now, the museum lab had been adequate as an office, but with an actual live-in staff beginning to assemble under his command, Doc needed larger digs to administer business and house us. With the exception of the meager salaries and small meal allowances paid by the government to his military assignees, all expenses of the project to date were borne by Doc's private bank account—his car, gasoline, hotel bills, phone, and considerable other miscellaneous costs. Except for a small per diem allowance to cover our meals, the military had made no provision for the accommodation of its personnel, an oversight that Doc uncomplainingly corrected by footing the bill.

Two of Doc's sisters lived nearby, and to the sanctuary of their property Doc delivered us. One sister, Judge Ida Mae Adams, the first female municipal court judge in America, lived in a large two-story Victorian house off Adams Boulevard. (Were the names merely coincidental, or did this represent the site of ancestral roots?) Judge Ida Mae, a kindly spinster, presented a picture of Victorianism as valid as her gingerbread home, and the faded blonde wig she wore so constantly was as much a part of her senescent years as the beveled glass, Tiffany lamps, and chintz curtains in her musty sitting room. Her hair, with its tobacco-yellow stains around the ears, was as obviously unnatural as those wigs worn by British barristers.

Fletch, hurrying down the hall of the judge's house one evening from the kitchen where he'd been sent to fetch a pitcher of milk for our late coffee, met Ida Mae by surprise in slippers and robe, head uncovered, between bedroom and bath. This unnerving experience caused Fletch a near fatal attack of face flushing, an affliction brought on by any occasion of intense embarrassment or emotional discomfort—a telltale burden, by the way, which made it virtually impossible for Fletch to tell a fib effectively. This weakness, over which he had no control, did not in the slightest, however, prevent his frequent, nearly pathological, proclivity to try.

The occasion for Fletch's consternation this night was that he had stumbled onto the explanation for Judge Ida Mae's yellow-blonde hairpiece. It was not worn in Anglophile mimicry, to denote her place on the bench. Fletch, almost speechless, could only stammer a nearly inarticulate explanation for his chameleonlike change from the usual pink to vivid red: "The Judge—I saw her. I saw her without the wig. She's bald as a cantaloupe!"

Adjoining Judge Ida Mae's garden stood the Adams School, another turn-of-the-century structure which was not actually a school so much as a boarding home for Down's syndrome children and young adults. On the grounds of the school a small ivy-covered guest cottage became the Los Angeles headquarters and barracks for the staff of the Adams Plan. Our immediate neighbors were engagingly cheerful and friendly, but the atmosphere was depressing. Yet for a secret project could anyone dream up a more perfect cover? Ours was the ultimate "safe house."

From our digs on Adams Boulevard we often sallied forth for dinner and evening's entertainment. The closest place to offer it all in one happy package was the Rodeo Inn, on Figueroa Street. Here a honky-tonk band provided nightly entertainment and young women dressed like cowboy-showgirls served the tables. Appropriately, some of us took to affecting western garb—long-heeled boots, Levi's, silver buckles with engraved bucking horses, and tailored shirts with pearl snap buttons. Our deviation from regulation uniform was part of the idiosyncrasy of our unit, a chauvinistic display of individuality, not disrespect for our places in the military, of which we all were immensely proud.

It could be wrongly believed from the following superficial glance at the leisure-time activities of the members of Doc Adams's best that our researches hereafter took place more or less exclusively at the Rodeo Inn or other places of such ilk. Our official duties, however, were diligently pursued with all the respect due the importance of the war effort, to which we all were seriously committed. Our off-hours recreations were merely the natural result of youthful urges and are set forth herein only as supplemental observations in addition to our other, more serious, activities.

V. B. called us together to review again the all- important letter from the office of the Air Force commanding general with its seven research problems to be solved.

> TO:   Chief, Chemical Warfare Service.
>
> In order to determine the practicality [of the bat bomb project], it is suggested that experiments be conducted with live bats and the proposed incendiary capsule.
>
> Any experiments conducted along this line should, among others, answer the following questions:
>
> 1. How long a period can bats be kept in the hibernation state while being transported?
> 2. Can incendiary capsules be attached prior to transportation of bats by air and will these incendiaries remain inactive until after bats are released from the plane?
> 3. Will incendiaries ignite prematurely in the air after bats are released and before they come to roost?
> 4. What percentage of incendiaries will ignite spontaneously upon the bats coming to roost?
> 5. How effective will such a small amount of incendiary munitions be?
> 6. At what altitude and distance will they have to be released in order to insure reaching the objective?
> 7. What assurance is there that their homing instincts over a strange locality will not lead them to roost in woods and buildings outside the cities thereby missing the objective?

Then, for the second time, von Bloeker read us the winning words:

> Although not desirous of sponsoring such experiments, the Army Air Forces will cooperate with the Chemical Warfare Ser-

vice when experiments reach the stage requiring tests from airplanes.

For the Commanding General, A.A.F.
H. A. Craig, Colonel, G.S.C.
Asst. Chief of Air Staff, Plans

"I've got to give credit to Colonel Craig," v. B. said after reading the letter. "Considering that he probably isn't a biologist his depth of thinking shows a lot of insight. But he didn't even get a good start on all the answers we've got to find. And it's only natural that four out of seven questions from the Air Force should concern the bomb side of the study. That's the soldier's as opposed to the biologist's mind at work. We can expect to get short shrift from the military for that reason from now on." He added with resignation, "Never mind. They need us. They just don't know it. Our side of the study concerns only questions one, six, and seven. But not necessarily in that order. And there are many more problems than those. For starters we'll work out all the questions, then we'll list them in order of priority, divide up the work load, and begin ticking them off."

# 5

# *Flamethrower*

IN ANTICIPATION of the need for bats to help with our initial studies, I set out to check on the status of a few small colonies around Los Angeles. The distinctive musty smell and piles of brown pellets on the belfry floor of the old church in Pasadena told me that I was following a good lead. My flashlight probed the eaves and cracks under the shingles but revealed nothing of interest. Bats had been there recently, but the roost seemed at the moment to be deserted. Then I saw gray fur wedged deep in a crack between two-by-fours. I squeezed my fingers into the gap, seized a fold of skin, and pulled.

Powerful jaws grabbed the web between my fingers and sharp teeth began chomping. Before I could adjust my hold and grip the bat by the shoulders and around the neck where he could not continue to gnaw, my hand looked like minced meat.

I realized immediately that this was not the small free-tailed bat I was expecting. I was looking into the horrible face of a specimen of the largest flying mammal in North America—a mastiff bat.

Its misshapen face—the sooty color of lead, with a devil-like nose and fearsome dentition—might have been dreamed up in a nightmare and sketched by Gustave Doré. Next to its teeth, the mastiff's monstrous ears were its most striking feature. Wrapped along the whole side of its face and joined together across the brow, they were convoluted with folds of bare flesh and odd veins of skin designed to receive with perfect accuracy the bounce-back of radar emissions when in flight. The mastiff's weight was ten times that of a free-tail, and his wingspread was 21–23 inches as compared with only 11–13 for the commoner species. If we could use these giants, I thought, we could almost move into the operation without developing a special bomb. I could imagine strapping the standard incendiary currently in use onto a mastiff's chest and watching him fly away with it. This, of course, was exaggeration, and the use of mastiffs in our project was made impossible by their rarity. Nevertheless, I placed the mastiff in a collecting sack and took him back to our base at the Adams School.

I had never kept a bat as a pet before. In fact, I'd never heard of anyone who had, but since I was in the bat business now, I felt it was appropriate that I should get to know one of the order's most spectacular kinds. I built a living environment for my mastiff by screening the open side of a reinforced wooden apple crate and adding a door. To make his home comfortably dark during the day, I covered it with a black drape. On the first night, as on every evening thenceforth, I let him out to explore my room.

The space was crowded for such a large flying mammal. Clearly he would prefer grander spaces to exercise his wings. He managed to flap up without crashing and lock his toenails into the old-fashioned cornice between wall and ceiling. There he hung, staring down at me expectantly. I offered him a cricket and was surprised that he took it readily from my fingertips. He munched it, softening the shell with the rapid chewing movements already painfully familiar to me, swallowed, and looked down as if asking for more. I gave him another, and another, and quickly realized that keeping him in vittles was destined hereafter to be my eternal chore. With this in mind, I decided to set up a mealworm reproductive colony for the times when it would be impractical to spend hours crawling around the garden on hands and knees searching for crickets. Mealworms are the succulent larvae of a prolific beetle, greatly esteemed by keepers of insect-eating birds, reptiles, and other exotic pets.

As I handed the mastiff his fifth cricket, there was a knock at my door. I opened it a crack and peered out. Fletch slouched in the hall. "What's going on?" he said suspiciously, as if he thought I might have smuggled a woman into my bedroom. "Who's in there?" He tried to look past me into the darkened room.

"Just me and my bat," I said.

"Sure," he said with a coy wink.

"Come on in and see for yourself. Be quick about it! Don't let him out."

Fletch grinned when face to face with my mastiff. He had never seen a bat so large. "Man!" he said appreciatively. "Just think what Doc could do with a plane-load of those puppies. Where'd you get him from? Africa?"

"Pasadena," I said. "Ain't he just a dilly?"

We spent the next two hours watching the mastiff. When I held a pie tin filled with water up to the bat, he lapped greedily.

During this time in the Pacific war, a particularly horrible weapon was being used by infantry soldiers to flush enemy holdouts from caves. Flame from a backpack canister was shot into dugouts through a handheld hose and nozzle, creating a deadly spurt of fire. It was called a flamethrower.

In appreciation of my bat's imagined potential for making war of the most horrible kind, I named him after this devil's weapon.

By mixing ground-up crickets into pellets and gradually adding bits of beef, I trained Flamethrower to eat red meat. But in those days of war, even hamburger was not easy to come by and could only be purchased after presenting hard-to-get rationing stamps. Then I discovered that Flamethrower preferred the more accessible lean horse meat offered in butcher shops for human consumption and turned up his already snooty nose at fatty hamburger.

As Flamethrower became used to me, his fierce antagonism waned. In a few weeks he became tame and I often carried him around, hung up inside the sleeve of my jacket, where he seemed happy to snooze. He no longer tried to make raw steak out of my fingers when I picked him up, but his captivity was not to be taken for granted. I knew that if I let him loose unrestrained, he would fly away.

Doc was delighted with my pet. Never one to avoid a dramatic gesture, he asked if I could come up with a trick or two that Flamethrower might do to add some zest to his presentations for bigwig visitors. I said I'd try to think of something.

Flamethrower became Doc's favorite object to break the ice for skeptical colonels or generals at the briefings he found himself ever more frequently called upon to present. My bat's grotesque mien and ample size immediately caught everyone's attention. Whenever an inspecting officer came to call, Doc asked me to break out Flamethrower and put him through his paces. Then it became necessary to change the venue from ordinary conference rooms to larger meeting places. Flamethrower needed space to stretch his wings. His conformation was a B-17 compared with the free-tail's P-38, a giant bomber as opposed to a maneuverable fighter plane. It became my chore to fly my bat around airplane hangars or gymnasiums for the entertainment of generals. I never made it all the way to Washington with my show, but it was the hit of the day in Riverside. The occasion was secret, of course; thus it was not only for Flamethrower's security that the meeting was held behind the guarded doors of an unoccupied mess hall. Adams directed the ranking general, majors, and captains to seats in the front row, the better to observe the show. When the cynical brass had assembled to hear Doc's discourse, he called for me. I entered, shook my bat out of my sleeve, and showed him around.

I would have liked to have had a rehearsal, a fly-through to accustom the star to his surroundings. But as it was, the room and its furnishings were strange to the bat. I released Flamethrower and he flapped a few fast laps around the room bearing my latest update to the show—a model soldier sitting astride his back, aiming a bazooka and looking surprisingly lifelike. The model held his seat with the aid of a tiny harness of rubber bands, but the illusion was perfect. It lacked only a bit of smoke and fire to rate an Oscar in any movie's special effects.

While the common belief that bats can't see in the daylight is false, the bright tube lights in the ceiling didn't help his vision. With the tiny man astride his back, Flamethrower circled the room again and again. He began to get tired; on the ninth circuit, unable to find a high cornice where he could pause and wanting to land and take stock, Flamethrower chose a perch on the only angular structure near the ceiling, a fluorescent fixture. When he fluttered to the light, grabbing at a glass tube, his wrist hooks failed to catch, and he slipped off. There is no doubt that the model soldier was an encumbrance, at least a contributing factor, perhaps even the cause, of his crash. It created a loss of balance, the added weight didn't help, and, although Flamethrower made a valiant attempt to recover, he failed. He came down fluttering, flapping wildly, trying to stay airborne against the forces of gravity and balance, heading for an emergency landing on the highest platform in the room—directly atop the general's head.

Amid a hail of slapping hands and oaths the officers responded predictably militarily: when confronted with attack—counterattack. The captain on the general's left leaped to his feet and began to hit his superior on the head with a rolled-up newspaper. Such instinctive behavior might make heroes on the battlefield, but it didn't enhance the propriety of either officer, and it was definitely a threat to my pet. That I said something disrespectful was only my reaction to what I perceived as a deadly threat to Flamethrower. But I was never convinced that my exact words were as Doc later reported. I don't believe I really shouted the expletive for which my boss chastised me: "Leave him the fuck alone!"

If in the heat of passion I expressed such disrespect for a superior officer, evidently nobody but my boss heard me—at least I wasn't called up for disciplinary action. But the day didn't earn me any medals, either.

While the captain swatted the general with his newspaper, the less valiant major on his right scrambled to escape what he perceived as a frontal attack and opted for retreat. He fell over his chair and hit his chin on the floor.

Flamethrower, of course, was flustered. Thus he could be excused for reverting to his predomesticated habits. When I grabbed him off the general's pate, Flamethrower sunk his teeth into my hand in the way so familiar to me. Blood immediately spurted onto the general's chest and he shrieked: "My God! The fucker bit me!"

While holding Flamethrower at arm's length with one hand, at the same time trying to wipe the blood off the general's tie with the other, I mumbled apologies and tried to convince him that it was my blood, not his.

At length the officers regrouped, had a chuckle, and took their seats again. Doc's presentation was rather anticlimactic after such a dramatic prelude. I put on a Band-Aid, and Flamethrower was rewarded for his performance with a handful of juicy mealworms.


The people at NDRC, in the meanwhile, seemed to be dragging their heels. Doc sent off several memos suggesting chemists to head up the branch of the Adams Plan that would develop the miniature incendiary. His missives were dispatched, but nothing concrete came back. And in the biological department we were hit with another frustrating delay.

Von Bloeker, with his sharp Germanic features, impressive attention to detail, and pugnacious nature, was perfectly typecast as our military commander. In obeying the genes of his Prussian ancestors, v. B. was a warrior by nature. Had he applied his bellicosity to the sport or profession of prizefighter, he would qualify as a flyweight—or perhaps bantam, as in bantam cock. But a flyweight soldier can pull a trigger as fast and accurately as a heavyweight, a fact of life v. B. would contentiously spout to anyone who dared to knock the chip off his shoulder.

V. B. didn't cotton to his role as warrior in command of troops who had been to soldier's school and knew more about soldiering than he did. He envied our training and yearned to be like us. He loved to shoot and his marksmanship in museum field collecting was notorious, but he'd never had his itchy finger on a machine gun; thus his education was incomplete. When v. B. heeded the call to arms he truly heard the bugle call, and he didn't want short shrift on all that macho stuff that went with it.

By simply avoiding the issue von Bloeker could easily have escaped the grueling hardships of basic training, but he felt cheated out of a vital aspect of the military experience and played his hand to correct the situation. Surreptitiously, he solicited higher command, ambiguously calling to the attention of the base personnel officer the oddball soldier who had never been to boot camp; he sent anonymous memos and agitated headquarters. V. B. dared not fan the fire openly or Doc Adams would have chewed him out ungraciously. Doc, after all, had gone to considerable trouble to get him excused from the arduous and time-consuming military training which our civilian leader, in v. B.'s case, so rightly considered to be unnecessary.

Finally, to von Bloeker's delight, proper military procedure caught up with him. Despite Doc's pleas to the establishment that his top researcher couldn't be spared for six weeks, and notwithstanding all that Bobby could do to turn around SOP, von Bloeker got his irrevocable orders to report for a crash course in soldiering.

He took to the training like a terrier. When he won the top Sharpshooter grade in marksmanship he wore the silver medal proudly on his breast ever after. But aside from the manly arts of soldiering, certain basic martial maxims did not deeply penetrate von Bloeker's psyche. Through obstinacy, rugged individualism, or a blank area in his otherwise prodigious brain, he did not absorb the concept of "established channels" of authority. I'm sure he knew what red tape meant and respected its place in tradition—but the process took too long. And we were in a hurry. His method of administration was more direct than militarily circuitous. Although like the rest of us his Air Force rating was only private, he assumed his position of leadership and made decisions independent of any higher authority like a born supreme commander.

Perhaps v. B. took his cue from Doc, who had a complete disregard for the military system. Or maybe von Bloeker felt his cleverness in getting his own way and winning the coveted assignment to boot camp was as far as he wanted to push his luck and hereafter he'd better play Doc's game by the Adams Rules. Doc's aloofness to things military was not contempt for martial matters; it was rather an attitude that requests for approvals from on high took unnecessary time and energy and were therefore a wasteful enterprise. Although he cultivated and enjoyed the company of generals, Doc either didn't understand, or didn't want to understand, their ways of doing things. His method of cutting red tape was to approach it with a sharp scissors of disregard. If you didn't recognize the System, if you simply denied an established protocol was in place and refused to follow the rules, the rules disappeared. If there were no maxims then it was simple to follow one's own standards or change them to fit any given circumstances. And to Doc, especially as regards the war-winning Adams Plan, the end justified the means.

All of us in Doc's Army were officially designated in the real Armed Forces as privates. Adams felt that this was an intolerable slight and that his troops should carry rank. Recognizing the unimpressive standing of our military credentials and the lack of prestige of a staff of mere privates, yearning for a general or at least a colonel or two in his band, but until the moment of his inspiration restrained by the conventions of military promotion, Doc now threw caution to the wind. He would assign his own ratings to his deserving private corps.

Dissuaded by the well-known retribution imposed by real officers for those frauds discovered impersonating one of their kind, von Bloeker refused to accept his Adams-bestowed commission as captain, the lowest rank Doc felt his commander deserved.

When v. B. explained his position to Adams, Doc said, "Well, surely noncom ratings are not so zealously protected by the officer establishment." With that, he presented v. B. with staff sergeant's stripes and ordered him to sew them on his jacket.

Seeing the justice, if not the total legality, von Bloeker complied.

Now, evidently for the first time, Doc began to take notice of the variety of stripes some soldiers wore on their sleeves. On a visit to March Field Army Air Base, where his troops drew their official orders, Doc chatted up a soldier whose shoulders were weighted impressively with more chevrons than he'd ever seen before.

When Doc returned to the Adams School headquarters, he came with tidings that von Bloeker's rank had just been upgraded to master technical sergeant, the same as the man with the heavy sleeves and the highest noncom's rank in the Armed Services.

In this way, through the concept of wishful thinking fulfilled, instead of Private von Bloeker, our military boss became J. C. von Bloeker, Jr., Master Tech. Sgt. (Acting), with six stripes on his sleeves, three above and three below with a diamond in the middle, the most chevrons one could acquire in the U.S. Army Air Forces. At least Doc hadn't invented his own new grade and filled a whole sleeve from shoulder to elbow with stripes of his own design. The

"(Acting)" designation was v. B.'s inspiration, a loophole he figured might get him off the hook if he was ever called to task. At least it would give him some place to go in the way of defense.

It was this laissez-faire attitude toward military rigidity that inspired this first of Doc's extraordinarily bold and effective anti-establishment military coups. And Doc, of course, wasn't satisfied with just one noncom on his force. He wanted *all of us* to be impressively bedecked. Von Bloeker's successful promotion was only the beginning. Following my superior's directive I happily stitched three buck sergeant's stripes onto my shirts and jacket. There was, of course, no official or nonofficial visual symbol which one could apply to shoulders designating the stripes as militarily unsanctioned, no parenthesis containing the key word "(Acting)," so we merely ignored the conditional designation that should be, but was not, a part of our sleeves. All military members of the Adams Plan were assigned new ratings, all suffixed with the magic word, and our prestige thus was upgraded a mote, even though our pay remained the same. Surprisingly, it was many months before we were challenged by our legitimate peers in the real world. But when we were, it was a disaster.

# 6

# No Questions Will Be Tolerated

ON THE DAY I CAUGHT FLAMETHROWER, Dr. Donald Griffin, the Harvard bat expert, caught a sampling of bats at Carlsbad at Adams's urging. In his motel room, he tested the weight-carrying ability of one bat three hours after capture, and the next day took about 300 more back to Cambridge for hibernation and further weight-carrying tests. After keeping them for four days at 5 to 10 degrees Centigrade, he tested about ten of the Harvard bats for weight-carrying ability. Griffin's data based on these tests produced a startling detail, one that nearly stopped things where they were: they couldn't carry the payload we had anticipated. Griffin suggested as the weight of the prospective as-yet-undeveloped incendiary, a bomb of three to five grams, less than one-sixth of an ounce.

Frederick L. Hovde, executive assistant to the chairman of NDRC, reacted to this news with predictable dismay. "The fact that 'carriers' can only carry a weight of three to five grams seems to militate seriously against their use, since incendiaries of that weight are not likely to be very effective."

No one, not even Doc at his most optimistic, could argue with that statement. But the figures didn't make sense to von Bloeker, who returned from basic training at about the time these results came in. "Free-tailed bats," he said, "weigh in at ten to eleven grams. That's more than twice the weight of Griffin's proposed payload. And we know that although mother free-tails don't carry their young, some species fly with twins or even triplets." He scratched his head, wondering at the dilemma. Could a free-tail's weight-carrying ability differ that markedly from a red bat's capability to fly with three young hanging from her chest? Nobody doubted the method or accuracy of Griffin's research—still, something had to be wrong with the data.

Years later, with the belated urge to look into the researches that had brought fame in the bat world (if not fortune in the real world) to our Harvard associate, I pulled a reference book from one of the two sets of encyclopedias, both published in England, from a library shelf. I thought I would probably find only generalized characteristics of the flying mammals and not the specifics I was looking for, but I had a look anyway.

In the first set of books with well-worn covers, I found but a single reference under the BAT heading: "A BAT may be described as a flat piece of wood with a handle, which is used for striking a ball. Bats are used in several games, the most notable being cricket. Wicker bats are used for beating carpets."

So much for *Harmsworth's Encyclopedia*. I next removed *AUK* to *BUF* of *The New Universal Library*. After learning that "a BAT is a portion of a brick of full section but less than a full length," I read on to find that "in brick walling it is sometimes necessary to use a half-bat and a three-quarter bat. A bat should be cut with a bolster and hammer, though many bricklayers cut it by striking with the edge of a sharp trowel."

All fascinating information, and I had definitely learned something new, if not what I was seeking. I knew that no encyclopedia near the years of our bat work would include the main point of interest contained in the next paragraph—the information was too new.

The data under BAT, *Mammal* summarized very well the essentials of bat lore. I read that bats are the only mammals capable of true powered flight (the wings of gliderlike flying squirrels and their kind are useless to achieve altitude or sustained flight) and that the several thousand species of bats found throughout the world are divided into two groups, the smaller insectivorous bats and the larger fruit bats or flying foxes. I read that the fingers of a bat's hand are enormously elongated to serve as struts supporting the flying membrane of the wing and that the unfurred membrane also includes the legs and frequently also the tail. "Most species are nocturnal and many are able to find their way among obstacles in the dark by a system of echo-location in which a series of ultrasonic squeaks are emitted in rapid succession so that the echoes returned from nearby objects give the animal its bearings."

Here, at last, was what I was searching for. I recalled that

Dr. Donald Griffin, who had so enthusiastically endorsed Adams's idea, had been the one who discovered the echo-location ability of bats. Since this was an attribute evidently unique to their kind, I searched out his paper on the subject.*

Along the way to this information, I discovered that the first experimental study of the bat's ability to find its way in the dark had been made by an Italian naturalist named Spallanzani, in the eighteenth century. He had observed that bats nearly invariably avoided obstacles in flight and even dodged a shoe or hat flung their way when flitting around in his dark bedroom. He knew that, contrary to the old saying "blind as a bat," the mammals could see very well, but he felt that an extra sense accounted for the fact that they could "see" even in the absolute darkness of deep caves where no known eyesight would work. So useless were eyes in the total darkness of caverns that many cave-dwelling fish and salamanders had through evolution lost their eyes completely. Spallanzani blinded a few bats and observed that they were still able to fly without bumping into obstacles, but he was unable to guess how they accomplished this amazing feat. The Italian was evidently the first to explore this unique attribute that Griffin and his collaborator, using modern technology, were able to reveal.

They first repeated Spallanzani's experiments by blindfolding bats with wax patches over their eyes and confirmed that eyesight played no part in avoiding unexpected obstacles in flight. The bats dodged around small objects suspended with threads as if they could see without eyesight. The next experiment included covering their ears in addition to the blindfolds. Now the bats seemed reluctant to fly at all. When they were induced to take wing, they blundered about and repeatedly flew into obstacles.

With one ear covered they flew with only moderate success and often ran into objects, but their performance was better than when both ears had been blocked. Then Griffin and Galambos uncovered both ears and covered the noses and mouths of the bats. Again, the bats blundered around in flight, running into obstacles indiscriminately.

By using high-frequency sound receivers, the investigators learned that the bats emit a continuous succession of supersonic squeaks as they fly; the echoes from the squeaks bounce back from objects ahead and are received by the bat's finely adapted ears, giving the animal perfect bearings on the direction and distance of obsta-

---

*Donald R. Griffin and Robert Galambos, "Obstacle Avoidance by Flying Bats," *Anatomical Record* 78(1940):95.

cles ahead. The discovery explains the highly developed external ears of many bats and also explains the leaf-shaped protuberances on the noses of some species and the curiously fleshy knobs or grotesque folds of facial skin, all of which play roles in transmitting or receiving the sounds, which are far too high in pitch for the human ear to hear. I had used this knowledge to excuse Flamethrower's ugliness.

The principle is the same as the one employed by electronic radar. It was even discovered that, similar to its electronic counterpart, the bat's radar momentarily shuts off during transmission so the echo does not become confused during receiving time with the sound of the next transmission, the result of a muscle contraction while squeaking that simultaneously puts the ear out of action. When the squeaking muscle relaxes the bat can hear again—all at the rate of approximately thirty cycles of squeak and listen per second.

Doc's next recruits were another pair of brothers from Pennsylvania. It's odd. You just can't remember much about some guys that you used to know. Others, fifty years later, you can see as clearly as yesterday. Frank Benish's most memorable aspect is that I don't remember much about him. I suppose even that says something about his character, but not a lot. I know he was a big, well-built young man of about twenty-eight, with a nose that looked as if it had been smashed into his face by somebody bigger's fist and the swelling never went down. He loved the sax playing of Coleman Hawkins— the Mighty Hawk, Benish called him. Benish was from the coal mining district of Pennsylvania, and his pet expression whenever he saw a pretty woman was "There's a real beetle. You know what a beetle is? It's got a hard back and a soft belly." Never before or since have I heard female pulchritude described in just that way.

He had another oft-spoken saying: "He don't know sic 'em from come here," which sounds like a hillbilly expression to me, and that's probably what Benish was. When I think about him, I can put more of Frank Benish together than I thought. But he's still pretty much a blank. His brother Mark I don't remember at all except that he was younger.

Perhaps even more than the rest of us, von Bloeker took our security classification very seriously. I think he had a tendency toward paranoia, but perhaps he was just naturally careful—or suspicious. Or maybe he merely relished the drama. While we still occupied the museum office he rigged his desk with booby traps to thwart the unauthorized prying of any night watchmen, janitorial staff, or legitimate spies. He set several large rat traps scrounged from the field collecting kit in closed desk drawers to deal with prying fingers, and each evening when he left the office certain cabinet doors were marked with tiny wedges of paper slid in a crack where they would fall out and become telltales if the door was moved. He sealed some cases with inconspicuous slivers of transparent tape so he would know if there was a stray mole burrowing around in the Mammalogy Lab.

One morning he found a desk drawer ajar, rat trap sprung. He gloated at his cleverness and stalked the halls that evening when the night shift came on duty, searching for the offender. In the Department of Herpetology, among the shelved bottles of pickled snakes and lizards, he found the enemy—a ruddy-faced woman with bucket and mop and the evidence he sought: right hand sporting a fresh splint and bandage. Von Bloeker raged at her, accused her of spying, and made formal charges to the museum director's office, but the lady denied complicity with unbreakable resolve and claimed she'd caught her hand in a bus door on the way home. In the face of only circumstantial evidence, our commander was unable to make his accusation stick; but thereafter, although the traps remained and were never set off again, the drawers were kept empty of everything except paper clips, pencils, rubber bands, and tobacco crumbs.

Although Williams, Fletch, the Benishes, and myself outfitted ourselves appropriately in western garb for evening's festivities at the Rodeo Inn, two of our crew invariably stayed military—Eddie Herold because he discovered that there was a devoted class of patriotic young women who disdained urban cowboys in favor of soldiers dressed in snappily altered military regalia. A whole new industry had sprung up with the induction of thousands of men into the military, and any soldier, sailor, or marine could sharpen up his image by the purchase of material accoutrements just slightly jazzier than the corresponding items issued by the government. Belt buckles with more shine, web belts with a different weave, GI shirts of other cloth, peaked caps with altered cut, shoes that weighed one pound rather than three pounds and had a correspondingly snappier look—everything issued could be purchased in slightly modified form, but not customized so much as to make it nonregulation. If it was bought it was better, of course, even if, as was usually the case, it was actually worse.

Von Bloeker was the other one of our crew who was never out of regulation uniform. In contrast to Fletch and myself, who reveled in the tradition-breaking freedom our special orders allowed and attired ourselves in Levi's and cowboy boots, v. B. always wore his GI issues. But his style was more conservative than the flamboyant Eddie's. Von Bloeker adopted the Ivy League military dress. There was, of course, no Brooks Brothers of regimentals, and v. B. wouldn't have patronized it had there been. He knew that the government cloth was best: it had quality—it was only lacking in fit. His were the first issued shirts in our outfit to be tailored from the baggy-chested, slope-shouldered models of GI issue into tight-fitting items with three sharp vertical creases ironed into the back. Even Eddie ran second place in the smart shirts race—v. B. would never reveal his tailor. But although von Bloeker's shirts were chic, he never looked good in them. They were cut too tight, for one thing, so they had no slack across the middle, and between the buttons on the front there was always a gap or two showing thin lips of white undershirt or pink skin. And the sleeves were always too long, with cuffs that came clear down to the knuckles. Von Bloeker's arms were short in proportion to his torso; maybe the tailor couldn't believe his own measurements. In any case, the extravagant sleeves gave v. B. a slightly sluggish look, hardly anthropoid but nearly so, an odd contrast with his cocky character. In their location so close to his hands the cuff-edges were prone to abrasion and seemed to become frayed before they were a week old.

As if to break his own rule to stay within the confines of government issue, von Bloeker was the first soldier in our outfit to affect the nonregulation blouse (as GI jackets were called) known as the Eisenhower model, which Eisenhower might well have stolen from Field Marshal Montgomery—although to suggest such a notion at the time would have put one in danger of being stood up before a firing squad, so fierce was the antagonism between the two generals. The jacket had no skirt and was cut-off with a built-in cloth belt at the waist. This, along with the heavy mass of stripes of master technical sergeant, made v. B. cut a fine military figure—even if the sleeves of his shirt did scratch his knuckles.

He wore the silver Sharpshooter medal earned in basic training as if it was a Congressional Medal of Honor. That, the stripes, and the gaudy patch of the 5th Air Force—gold wings on a blue field—gave him all the confidence and bearing of a real top sarge.

One evening around closing time in the Rodeo Inn, several men carrying nightsticks and wearing MP armbands sauntered in. They surveyed the few uniformed clientele, checked their liberty passes for validity, nodded their heads approvingly, and approached our table—four young men of draft age who looked healthy enough to be in a uniform of the Armed Services rather than cowboy's garb. We had no draft cards, the ID of young civilians, those having been surrendered at the time of induction. Our declarations that we were assigned to a secret project and that we didn't need passes from a base because we were stationed in a house just up the street a block away (although there was no recognized military establishment within miles) apparently lacked the ring of truth. The military police took us to be either draft dodgers or service personnel who were AWOL and unceremoniously herded us into their paddy wagon and hauled us off to the stockade, all the way across the city to Fort McArthur.

Doc got us sprung the next day, but this humiliating incident became the catalyst for von Bloeker's most stunning bid for anti-establishment literary laurels. He composed a brief but effective letter of introduction which we were authorized to show whenever the occasion warranted.

CONFIDENTIAL

To Whom It May Concern:

The bearer of this letter, Sgt. Jack C. Couffer (Acting), is engaged in a military project of a highly secret nature under the direction of General Hap Arnold, Commander of the United States Army Air Forces. Sgt. Couffer's method of travel, attire, and the location of his activities are not to be challenged. As this project is of a strictly confidential nature, unnecessary questions are to be avoided, and undue curiosity or any discussion of this matter with unauthorized persons will not be tolerated by the United States Government. However, any cooperative assistance that can be afforded will be greatly appreciated.

Jack C. von Bloeker, Jr.
Master Tech. Sgt. (Acting)
U.S. Army Air Forces
(Special Aide to Dr. Lytle S. Adams)

The letter bore the standard official impression of secret U.S. documents, a rubber stamp that specified the dire consequences if confidentiality was breached. Each of us in Adams's Army was issued such a document. It never failed to produce the desired effect, although it was occasionally used under circumstances far more bizarre than intended. By virtue of its broad wording and apparent verisimilitude we became perhaps the most unaccountable "free agents" in the entire U.S. Armed Forces.

NDRC assigned Dr. Louis F. Fieser, a distinguished chemist from Harvard with a background in incendiaries and time-control devices, to work with us and develop the bomb aspects. When we read his qualifications we were impressed. Our prestige, which Doc had found so lacking in military grandeur, rose considerably under the institutional credentials of our new chemist.

Fieser had done his research for the doctorate under Professor James B. Conant, chairman of the National Defense Research Committee, and H. M. Chadwell, chief of Division 19 of NDRC, had been a former roommate of Fieser's at Harvard Graduate School, so our chemist came well connected with the organization that would be supervising our study.

Fieser was currently at work on several other projects for the Chemical Warfare Service. One was the development of the Permanente-filled 500-pound bomb, with production of this new weapon to reach 30,000 per month in November 1943. He was also researching a cast-iron 500-pound bomb designed for penetrating concrete pillboxes, and he had under development a messenger pouch destroyer with a time-delay explosive charge that allowed the messenger time to escape if forced to abandon his satchel. In a breakdown of his activities (letter to Earl Stevenson and Chadwell, October 25, 1943) Fieser said:

> Plans for over-water attacks call for transporting by air as many as two to three fully equipped Divisions, and a sure method of guiding the paratroops and gliders is urgently needed. In Tunisia guidance by underground-operated radio failed and our troops were dropped in the midst of a German Division and annihilated. In the Sicilian campaign gliders released without proper control landed in the sea.
>
> One possibility is to drop by day, from low-flying mosquito-type planes, flares timed to go off at zero hour the following night. An area as much as five square miles may be marked out, with designation of specific concentration points for five or six different service units.

Fieser was working on the time-delay signal flares for this type of operation. It was the parallel between the time-delay requirements of the bat bomb and the small time-delay for the messenger pouch and for the flares that suggested to NDRC that Fieser could combine efforts and assist us.

Militarily, those of us who were members of the Army Air Forces were attached to March Field Air Force Base at Riverside, California. Officially we were on "detached service" assigned to Doc Adams. We drew our pay of $65 per month and a small meal allowance from the base paymaster. At the beginning, before Bobby Herold got things sorted out so our checks were mailed, it took each of us a personal monthly visit to Riverside to collect our pay and sign the required requisition for meal vouchers for the next month.

It was during one of these improvident occasions that I had another humiliating brush with military law. The parking lot at March Field was an immense plain of flat gravel, acres of ranks of parked cars surrounded by a barbed wire-topped chain-link fence. After the long drive from Los Angeles in Doc's borrowed Buick, my first impulse after parking was to relieve my aching bladder. I got out, glanced around, determined that no one was within eyeshot, and unbuttoned my fly. Relief came quickly against my wheel. Then, only halfway through washing the dust off the tire, a shout erupted from close by: "Halt!"

I froze, trickle arrested.

"Hold it right there, soldier!"

I was, of course, in military rather than cowboy uniform. I looked around, buttoning up.

The commanding voice sounded again: "I said, Hold it, soldier! Don't move!" A sentry in a steel helmet holding a rifle aimed at my chest stepped into view. My fingers froze on a button halfway into its buttonhole. Now the sentry's voice soared higher over the silent rows of parked cars: "Officer of the Guard!"

I heard running footsteps crunch on the gravel.

Red-faced, a second lieutenant trotted up, gold bars reflecting the Riverside sun, and sharply returned the sentry's salute. "What's the trouble, sentry?"

The rifle still aimed steadily at my heart.

"I caught this here soldier pissing in the parking lot, *sir!*"

"Urinating in the parking lot?" Gold bars was incredulous.

"Yes, *sir!*"

I had no idea of the magnitude of my crime, but to judge by the demeanor of these two, I figured I'd be lucky to get off with a General Court Martial and another, more extended, trip to the Fort McArthur stockade.

The lieutenant said, "What have you got to say for yourself, soldier?"

I kept my mouth shut, choosing instead of speaking to exercise my status as a member of a top secret operation. It didn't seem to be the kind of situation that v. B. had in mind when he'd composed his letter of introduction, but . . . I pulled it out, unfolded it grandly, and, without a word, handed it to the officer.

He read it, slowly shook his head, read it again, and handed it back.

"Next time," he said, "see if you can hold it for the latrine." Then to the sentry: "Dismissed!"

We exchanged polite salutes and went our separate ways.

# 7

## *They Can Fly!*

LOUIS F. FIESER, the chemist from Harvard who had been appointed by the National Defense Research Committee to develop the bat bomb, brought along an associate, William Young, from the University of California, for our first meeting at the Adams School headquarters.

Von Bloeker got the session underway by telling the chemists as much as was known about the applicable characteristics of bats. The chemists were most interested in the animal's carrying ability.

V. B. shrugged. He knew this was coming and, in view of Griffin's recent unsettling data, wished he could temporarily avoid the issue. But he couldn't, so he edged into the delicate subject slantwise. "Female red bats carry their young in flight until they're nearly grown, that's at least a third of their own weight. And sometimes they have twins and triplets. Quadruplets are not unknown. In that case, they carry more than their own weight in flight."

"So how much does a bat weigh?"

"There's a lot of variety over the world in different species. There's a tropical bat, the flying fox, that'll go two or three pounds." V. B. knew he was hedging and eventually he'd have to face things as they were. He took a breath and looked at Fieser eye to eye. "But the one we're probably stuck with, because it's the species available in large quantities and it hibernates, is the Mexican free-tail. It weighs . . . what? Maybe ten, eleven grams."

"Grams?" Fieser said with surprise. "Or ounces?"

"Grams, I'm afraid," v. B. confirmed.

"Jesus!"

I wondered if I could melt the ice by breaking out giant Flamethrower, but decided against this inane offering. Fieser didn't seem to be the type who would take kindly to comic relief.

"And there's a further complication." Von Bloeker stood up so he would have his feet on solid ground when he made this next announcement. "Some confusion about this factor. We don't really know yet, you see. A colleague, Dr. Griffin, has recently conducted some flight tests and came up with an estimate of three to five grams total payload. But in view of what I've just told you, I don't buy it. Has to be something wrong."

"That's what . . . ?" Fieser stared with dismay at his partner. "Less than a sixth of an ounce! Forget it, chaps!"

"We're shortly going to make our own definitive flight tests," v. B. said. "For the moment, let's assume that there was a fundamental error in the Griffin data. Say ten grams is the payload. What then?"

"Christ almighty! The smallest standard incendiary, the M-52, weighs two point two *pounds*!"

"Well, what we're doing is not *standard*," Doc said.

"So I see."

"That probably puts napalm out of the picture," Young said. "So we're talking white phosphorous."

"And the difference?" v. B. asked.

Fieser answered: "Of the incendiary chemicals, white phosphorous burns the hottest. We're working with a new incendiary material, gelled gasoline or kerosene—napalm, I've named it—that has a lot of useful characteristics, but the flame is cooler. With napalm you need more mass."

"And it's easier to get phosphorous cooking," Young said. Then, putting the conference back into scientific jargon, he added, "thermologically speaking."

"If we can ignite an effective conflagration with, say, ten grams of white phosphorous—and we *can* if your bats will really place the device in the optimum position—we still won't know until we work out the bugs what the combined weight will be for the container that holds the chemical, plus the igniter, which will have to be fitted with some sort of accurate time-delay device, and a safety to keep it from going off prematurely."

"I thought a wax-coated capsule that would melt by air temperature at ground level, obviating the igniter," Doc said.

"I read your suggestion," Fieser said shaking his head. "N. G., too hairy."

"Cellulose for the capsule, I'd think," said Young, getting in between before Fieser's abrupt dismissal of Adams's suggestion could go any further. "Highly combustible, resistant to solvents, and light in weight. The weight factor per BTU a definite plus."

As Doc and von Bloeker and the two chemists talked, I studied these newcomers to our exclusive club. Fieser was the more interesting of the two. He projected a strong aura of self-esteem. There could never be a question as to which of the two chemists was senior—although their age appeared to be about the same, early forties. Fieser was definitely the boss, Young his junior collaborator.

At my age of youthful unworldliness—or perhaps because of a lack of guile which I thought of as incredible perception at the time—I had somehow come up with a most original method of character assessment. It makes no sense at all, except that on about one occasion in ten it has been known to be accurate, thus giving the observation sporadic confirmation—all I needed to make it profound. Although my unscientific method of personal psychic assassination is far from unfailing, and is usually more wrong than right, even to this day, in spite of all evidence to the contrary, I cannot shake an inkling of mistrust of any man who wears his watch lower on his arm than the customary above-the-wrist position. A watch installed on that part of the anatomy between wrist joint and upper hand quickly arouses my suspicion.

Prejudices are silly, akin to superstition, yet most of us have one or two. Mine is that the low-on-the-arm manner of watch-wearing bespeaks a strong, self-conscious vanity, an affliction that I cannot abide.

Fieser wore his watch in this way.

It is only natural that my original impression of the chemist is now colored by time, by retrospection, and by later events I could not have known on the day of our first meeting. It is now difficult to separate my "pre" from my "post" views. One opinion of Fieser, however, definitely has come to me long after the first day of our acquaintance.

As I flip through the pages of Fieser's published autobiography, written years after this first meeting, I discover a revealing trait that in its own curious way supports my watch-low-on-wrist theory with almost scientific certainty.

The two photographs of himself that Fieser chose to illustrate the chapter on the bat project in his book are totally different in setup, yet amusingly similar in one respect. Both are dramatic angles meant to appear to be off-the-cuff snapshots, but they are instead quite obviously self-consciously posed. Both pictures were taken from low angles with strong crosslight, the photographer's device to portray a heroic image. Fieser's was not a face to depict in this kind of stylized photography; these are glamor pictures of an unglamorous face.

The single photo in the book of Fieser's associate, Bill Young (later vice-chancellor of UCLA), was also shot from the same dramatic low angle, obviously again self-consciously posed, so I wonder at my own harsh assessment of Fieser's motives in photo selection. All the pictures appear to have been exposed by the same shutter, possibly from the same photo session. Maybe Fieser didn't have a lot to choose from to illustrate this chapter in his life, so let us not judge him too harshly—yet.

When I returned from my daydreams to the conference at hand, Fieser was saying: "Well, before we set out to design a bat bomb, you're going to have to tell us a hell of a lot more about bats."

Von Bloeker nodded and turned to us. "Our first job, boys, is to make some accurate weight and size-carrying tests."


We knew we would eventually use the species called the Mexican free-tailed bat. We had no choice. We would prefer Flamethrower's kind for their weight-carrying potential, but mastiffs were too rare. Free-tails were the only species that fit all requirements—availability in vast numbers and hibernation, a necessity if we were to use them as living machines. The species was widely distributed in the Southwest, with concentrations in New Mexico and Texas. Because their diet consisted solely of flying insects, several bat-housing structures on tall stilts had been built in San Antonio for mosquito control. In the decades since our research, when little beyond folklore was known about the species, it has been estimated that in one year the 50 to 100 million free-tailed bats believed to summer in Texas consume between 6,600 and 13,000 tons of moths, mosquitoes, and other winged night-flying insects.

In 1942 the largest bat colony in the world was thought to be at Carlsbad Caverns in New Mexico, where the evening exodus was a popular tourist attraction. Like other local bat caves, people called Carlsbad a "smoke hole" because the emerging bat clouds resembled black fumes boiling against the evening sky. With a special permit from the National Park Service, we collected a hundred bats from Carlsbad. Doc and Bobby made arrangements with the Navy to use one of the huge airship hangars at Moffett Field, originally built to shelter the dirigibles *Macon* and *Akron*. An Air Force B-25 bomber flew our whole crew with our box full of bats, camouflaged to look like an ordinary carton of documents. A label (*Bookkeeping—A to F—L. S. Adams*) was stenciled on top, but the air holes would be a dead giveaway to anyone who noticed. Still, we thought the disguise sufficiently clever. In addition to the bats, we also carried a box full of equipment, balance scales, and an assortment of weights and devices to attach the weights to the bats.

We landed close to the giant dirigible hangars at Sunnyvale, California, and Doc and Bobby presented our credentials. One hangar had been completely vacated for our use. When we entered the huge empty hulk—a high structure of ribs and metal skin shaped like a gigantic whale—and the jaws rumbled closed, shutting out the sunlight, it was as if we had been swallowed alive. Open light-bulbs hung from a ribcage of catwalks high above. Our figures seemed tiny on the vast plain of the concrete floor, and our voices echoed oddly in this immensity of space. The importance of this experiment on which so much depended created a mood of profound solemnity. We all felt it. There was no levity—we were all business.

Outside, a squad of military police patrolled to keep away prying eyes as we proceeded into our first work with the expectant anticipation of discovery. Fletch, Williams, and myself, with the boxed bats, weighing equipment, and notepad, climbed the tall flights of steel stairs, footsteps echoing off the rungs. Stooping under the roof beams, we crept out to the middle of the narrow catwalk that hung in space close to the ceiling. Far below, Doc, von Bloeker, Eddie, and Bobby awaited the releases.

I reached into the dark box full of warm, squirming bats, felt around, and grabbed one. It squeaked and struggled in protest at being held, and its small sharp teeth punctured the skin in the web between my fingers. Two fresh rows of bloody droplets appeared, painful little wounds. I tried to avoid more bites by holding the bat with thumb and forefingers, scissoring its head from behind. But those moments between grabbing a bat out of the box and adjusting it to a safe holding position always allowed for a few more abrasions. Gloves were impractical: the bats were small and delicate, and gloves interfered with one's tactile senses, so we merely endured the bites and allowed our fingers gradually to take on the look of fresh minced meat.

With the minute stainless steel clips sometimes used instead of needle and gut to close wounds following surgical procedures, we attached a weight of double the payload Griffin had suggested. An eight-gram weight was clipped to the loose fold of skin pinched up from the first bat's chest. The sharp-toothed clip, a couple of millimeters in length, was Doc's idea of an attachment device that most closely resembled the natural clinging of a baby bat locking with its sharp teeth onto its mother's chest. Indeed, the little stainless jaws grabbed a mouthful of hair and skin in precisely the same way. The clip was pinched into place with small medical forceps. It took two sets of hands to do the job—one to hold the bat, the other to apply the clip with its attached weight. In retrospect, because of the apparent validity of Doc's original concept, we stuck with this method of attachment long after we should have abandoned it in favor of the more practical adhesive method later used.

When the weighted dummy bomb was secured, I held the animal out on my open palm and allowed it to launch itself into space.

At first it was impossible for the men on the floor so far below to see the little bat. Then, as it spread its wings, backlight from the naked bulbs shining through the translucent wing membranes created an eerie glow, making the animal's flight pattern easy to follow.

The first six releases—six bats, each carrying eight grams, launched one at a time—flew almost as if unencumbered. They flapped erratically here and there, and we spent the next hour crawling around inside the ribcage of the whale with butterfly nets swooping up weight-laden bats from landing places.

What did this mean in reference to Griffin's test? His bats had been able to carry only two to five grams. Already we'd doubled the payload and we hadn't approached their limit yet. Von Bloeker speculated that Griffin's bats, by the time he got them to Harvard where he conducted the tests, had lost too much condition to perform. Or perhaps it was because the tests were made when the bats were in breeding condition, a factor that might change their metabolism and affect weight-carrying abilities. This was the explanation eventually accepted, however unscientifically grounded, and the one that went into official reports. Studies made after the war, conducted by researchers not under the pressure of urgent wartime need, suggest different reasons. The test of one freshly caught bat in the motel room was not statistically significant. Free-tailed bats can quickly orient themselves to an environment, and in a small room with little area for flight, a bat might refuse to even attempt to fly. It's not the same as dropping from a height. But what about the ones Griffin dropped from the roof of a five-story building in Cambridge?

Free-tailed bats occupy sex-exclusive roosts during the birthing season—a cave may be inhabited by all females or all males. If the specimens Griffin collected from Carlsbad were females, they would have been lactating heavily during the mid-summer season, when he took them. The weight of their mammary glands, in combination with the physical and psychological stresses of rearing young, could well play a role in their weight-carrying ability. Or perhaps the difference could be attributed to the less-than-ideal conditions of transport to which Griffin's bats had been subjected. In his report of the tests to Frederick L. Hovde of NDRC, Griffin pointed out that due to insufficient refrigeration during transit, the bats had been kept active, without food, for forty-eight hours.

The bats that we tested several weeks later, with different results, were in peak condition. The young bats had been separated from their mothers for some time and all were physiologically prepared for the long migration to Mexico on which they would soon be embarking. It had been a quirk of luck, not scientific genius, that accounted for our different results. But in 1942 no one knew the bats undertook this annual journey; if Griffin had made his tests a few weeks later, as we did, when the bats were in prime shape, his results would have shown a significant difference.

We increased the weights in increments of half a gram, observing the flight reactions to the greater weights until we found that a bat carrying twenty-five grams was unable to support the load. It spun down on collapsed wings and dropped unhurt into von Bloeker's hand-held hoop net.

From that first simple but important experiment we determined that a free-tailed bat in prime condition was able to fly and maintain controlled maneuvers while carrying a payload of from fifteen to eighteen grams. We still had to find out the possible weakening effects of forced hibernation, handling, or extended time in captivity, and we expected other, as yet unknown, factors to play roles in the bats' weight-carrying capabilities. But, for the moment, the Sunnyvale tests told us that a bomb weighing between fifteen and eighteen grams should be designed, and we passed the word to our chemist associates, Fieser and Young.

# 8

# *Chemical Warfare Concludes*

ON JULY 1, 1942, another setback struck. In spite of the approving letter from Colonel Kabrich of Chemical Warfare to the commanding general of the Army Air Forces and the positive response he had received in reply, Kabrich now took a sudden reverse turn and wrote a surprisingly negative message to Adams. What had turned him around? It was a blow that seemed impossible to explain.

Doc's old nemesis, Captain Wiles of Chemical Warfare, no doubt happy to hear his superior whistle a different tune, was quick to communicate the turnaround to the National Inventors Council. In his official notification, he quoted the most pertinent parts of the colonel's letter to Adams verbatim: "Your proposal has been carefully considered by the Chemical Warfare Service and the Army Air Forces. As a result of this study there are many questions which remain unanswered and which would vitally affect the proposal. Some of these questions are as follows . . ." Again the familiar seven problems which already topped Doc's agenda for research were listed. In addition, several of Captain Wiles's original objections were stated again, criticisms that Doc thought had already been answered to everyone's satisfaction. Wiles's letter to the Inventors Council, again quoting his superior's language, ended with this disheartening summation:

> The Chemical Warfare Service concludes that your idea does not warrant the expenditure of the time and material to completely develop the same and to answer the above questions. Other and more satisfactory means of accomplishing the same objective are available at the present time. It is desired to express the appreciation of this service for your interest in the National War Effort and the obviously large expenditure of time that you have devoted to this subject.

No new development, so far as Doc knew, had been injected into the picture that might explain Colonel Kabrich's switch of attitude. Indeed the Air Force letter which had given the green light to the project and which Kabrich now quoted to support his negative position revealed a most highly selective reading. By editing out the positive remarks of the Air Force, and by choosing the single paragraph that seemed to show disinterest when read out of context, Kabrich made it seem as if the Air Force had refused cooperation—clearly a deliberate misrepresentation. It seemed to Doc that Kabrich either had completely misread the communication from the Air Force or had intentionally chosen to ignore the positive aspects of the response. Yet neither explanation seemed entirely likely. Coming as it did out of the blue, it seemed far more credible to Doc that the obstructive Captain Wiles had somehow gotten the colonel's ear.

In addition to the seven familiar questions, Kabrich now added four "basic faults" to the list. To Adams, these so-called defects confirmed that Wiles's hand was stirring the stew. The colonel was repeating the captain's original objections verbatim. The letter was so far out of left field that Doc wondered if Wiles could have taken the bold step of calling the plays and writing his own opinion under his supervisor's signature.

Adams wrote a reply to Kabrich, answering each of the seven points and detailing the steps being taken to resolve the questions. As for the four "basic faults," he wrote:

> The basic faults as listed in your letter, some of which were substantially answered in my presentation to the President and in my letter to Colonel Morrell of your Service, dated June 12, 1942, I will attempt to clarify. . . .
>
> Ques. l. A bat is able to carry only about one-half ounce of material and this minute quantity would probably not ignite the surrounding structure.
> Ans. l. A bat is able to carry in flight not a half ounce but one full ounce or more of incendiary material . . . a bat could deliver greater quantities to [remote] points . . . whereas ordinary distribution would not reach such . . . locations where fires would not be readily detected and extinguished.
>
> Ques. 2. There is no assurance that a sufficient number of bats would roost in the places where a fire could be started . . . or that they would stay in position when the incendiary material ignited.
> Ans. 2. The exceedingly large number of incendiary bats that can

be carried in a single airplane provides a great margin for failures and still leaves a sufficient number that would start fires to insure the success of the venture. As to the bats staying at the roosting place after combustion takes place, this would be no problem, as the first burst of flame would sever the connection releasing the bat, but the *incendiary material would stay put.*

Ques. 3. The special care, including feeding of bats during their transport before release.
Ans. 3. There is absolutely no care or feeding problem except refrigeration. Bats would be in a hibernated state until ready for release on their destructive mission.

Ques. 4. The very definite fire hazard to personnel and the airplane if the bats were not released at the proper time.
Ans. 4. There is not the slightest fire hazard to personnel in an airplane. The method of packaging, storing in the plane, and the release of bats is a positive insurance against any danger whatever. At least it can be said that there is less danger in this operation than in the transportation of other types of incendiaries, bombs and ammunition usually carried in military airplanes.

> Please permit me to show you or the Air Force the containers and explain to you fully how they are stowed and used . . . I am sure that I can satisfy you as to the practicality.
>
> Yours very sincerely,
> Dr. Lytle S. Adams

It seemed strange that Kabrich had possessed such a good understanding of the project when he wrote his original query to the Air Force and now his comprehension of the details seemed to have deteriorated so far. Again, Doc wondered if Captain Wiles had taken the initiative and written the text under the colonel's signature.

With the satisfaction that he had done all he could for the moment, and confident that his reasoned reply would be met with a reasoned response, seemingly unfazed, as if all was now resolved, Doc plunged ahead on his own—with us in tow—into what he thought of as the most challenging aspect of the plan—sorting out the problems with the bats.

Meanwhile, we in the biological unit were unaware of the depth of the conflict Doc faced with his other team. Probably Adams confided in his young alter-ego, Bobby Herold. If he did, they both kept the confidence and we in the bat team faced the next biological question without knowledge of the delicate balance on which our work teetered. Our next objective was to find the best source of bats to carry out our experiments and perhaps to supply the millions needed for eventual operational use.

Today's authorities on bats—and there are a few—may find it strange that we should have found it necessary to undertake an extensive survey to locate the optimum bat populations of the United States. Nowadays one can pick up any of half a dozen research publications reporting on what it took us three months of dangerous exploration to find out—that two limestone caverns in south-central Texas, Ney Cave and Bracken Cave, are home to the largest concentrations of bats in the world.

When we were conducting our researches, the bat colony at Carlsbad Caverns was well known. We even conveniently captured a few bats there for our first tests. With an estimated 8,700,000 bats, Carlsbad was believed to be host to the largest bat colony in the United States, if not the world. But Carlsbad Caverns was a national park where the spectacular evening bat flight was an important tourist attraction. To utilize this population would not only deplete a major recreational resource, it would open our secret work to widespread surveillance.

We packed the roof-rack and trunk of Doc's black 1941 Buick sedan with collecting gear and a meager lot of cave exploration equipment—a coil of 1/2 inch Manila rope, flashlights, and Coleman gasoline lanterns—and headed east. With Bobby Herold's promise to keep Flamethrower's fire stoked, I left my pet with an ample supply of mealworms.

Outside Los Angeles, we paused at a roadside fruit stand among the groves of Cucamonga and bought a couple of crates of large navel oranges. We didn't know it yet, but these oranges would be our main source of nourishment until they were gone, for this was to be a nonstop trek. Doc loved oranges and he thought a human could exist on a diet of citrus with very little additional caloric supplement. He also thought that bats could live without *anything* to eat while hibernating (and this aspect of physiology, contrary to our own demanding bodies, we would eventually prove to be true). Despite his eternal spryness, Doc always gave the impression that he was at least a hundred years old, and it's a well-known fact that elderly people don't need so much nourishment. But we were not Doc and we were not bats; our young stomachs growled with displeasure.

The Buick was a large automobile, but with three in front and three in back we were as squashed as the oranges stuffed in their crates behind. We took turns sleeping and driving, leaving a trail of orange peels as we went, pausing only at gas stations to fill up and pass over gas stamps from the rationing books Doc had been allocated.

Doc always rode shotgun, as it were, in the front right window seat. From there, when the occasion called for it, he leaped forth to put into practice what he called the Art of Confusion. We didn't drive through the vast spaces of the West on our vital mission at moderate speed; there was too much to do, too little time. While cruising at well above the limit in whatever state we happened to be crossing, when the inevitable red light began to flash in the rear-view mirror and our car was pulled to the shoulder, Doc stepped out, unwound the briefcase rope, and threw himself into his skill at discombobulation. Flashing dog-eared papers stamped with the magic word "Secret," talking about three different subjects at the same time, dropping the names of local heroes, politicians, officials, or business leaders like shaking ripe fruit out of a tree (he carried in his mind a seemingly inexhaustible inventory of highly placed or well-known people from across the breadth of the country), pulling out whichever honorary mayor's certificate or casually bestowed complimentary sheriff's badge happened to be most appropriate to the place, allowing no nonsense about speed limits or delay, he bewildered police officers from California to Texas and back. More than once a pit-stop made obligatory by our excessive speed ended up with siren and red light running in high-velocity escort to the next state line. At the very least, we were sent on our way with a smile, a handshake, and a "Godspeed."

This game of confounding the provincials may have been only practice for Adams, polishing his skills on the rustics to pay off against the big-time operators of Washington. Certainly our leader's motive was not only to impress his already humbled staff, although he obviously took a lot of satisfaction from our appreciation.

Fletch tried hard to emulate Doc and made a concerted effort to learn the basics of the Art of Confusion. Although he hardly acquired Doc's range—Fletch started out with the handicap of immaturity and without Doc's distinctive looks—still, he did better than expected considering his youth and his apprentice status. As time went on, Doc sometimes permitted his pupil to make the first approach, remaining unobtrusively in the car until Fletch blew it or we were able to proceed without further delay. Only if his student's persuasive power seemed to be wilting under the inflexibility of a stern-faced officer did the master step out and take over. Faced with a daunting loss of advantage—the surprise attack already used up—and with standard cards played, he had to use his aces. Such a case required a range of virtuosity from hard-boiled to subtle: Doc depended upon intuition to size up the opposition and, before the situation deteriorated so far that face-saving would bring the case to a stone wall, quickly brought his gifts to bear.

Even on those occasions when Fletch alone had been able to convince the Man to let us proceed unticketed, Doc happily contributed a fine-point or two to his proud student and to those of us in his captive seminar and advised on how technique might be improved upon the next time.

In Arizona, we headed south toward the Mexican border, where Doc had heard there were bat caves in the mountains. We found ourselves following a vague rough track through the desert where a few preceding wheels had left double ruts. With his experience on field collecting trips, von Bloeker took over the driving. He gunned expertly through sandy washes, crept over boulders, noisily dragging bottom through both, leaving behind a few odd, unnecessary pieces of automobile on high centers, and Doc's Buick began its evolution from city car to country wreck. Given today's rage for 4x4s tearing up the boondocks, cross-country jocks don't realize how far a skilled bush driver can go with an old, low-slung conventional car. The track we were on was used occasionally by U.S. Border Patrol officers, smugglers, prospectors, and aliens risking the danger of the long hike across the hottest spot this side of Hades. It was an ancient way, having first been used by Indians and then by exploring Jesuits. In those times it had been called El Camino del Diablo, the Road of the Devil. We passed graves here and there, some alone, some in groups of two or three, simple piles of boulders. A few bore crude monuments, weather-worn words chipped in a stone; where wooden markers had once stood there was only dust.

At Tinajas Altas, our destination, we found a stone mountain rising like a steep island out of the flat desert, bare brown granite blocks and boulders stained with watercolor washes of dark iron-colored smears. Along a precipitously sloping depression of slick rock a chain of natural catchments held mossy pools of rainwater wriggling with tadpoles and water-striders, and the area abounded with life. The moisture was a magnet for flocks of quail and doves, coyotes, and mountain sheep. So far as we knew, the pools were the only water in hundreds of square miles, a welcome beacon to a flotilla of lost craft.

While climbing around in the cliffs, I poked my head into an overhanging rock shelter. It was a foot deep in the dusty droppings of wild mountain sheep, but there were no bats. Then toward the back I saw an unnatural-looking hump that could have been, but wasn't, a rounded boulder. It didn't seem to match its neighboring rocks—too smooth. I dug down into the dry dung around it with my hands and realized that it was the bottom of an upside-down olla, a prehistoric ceramic of considerable beauty. I wanted to keep it, but there was no way. It was the size of a large beachball. So I pushed back the packing of pellets that had protected it for a hundred years and hoped my pot would stay there forever, my secret treasure.

We spent the night in a lonely cabin built by the Border Patrol to give shelter to those exhausted travelers who might otherwise lie under piles of dry stones. Inside the unlocked door were a few cans of food on a shelf, a barrel of sweet water for times when the catchments were dry, spring beds with rough mattresses, and a sign on the wall: "Welcome. Take what you need; leave what you can spare. Courtesy of U.S. Border Patrol."

At dusk tiny *Pipistrellus*, canyon bats that live in rock cracks and so had ample housing in this huge boulder pile, flitted around the cabin and over the palo verde and mesquite, dodging through the hot twilight chasing insects, but there was no sign of the great bat flight we were searching for.

That night, lying on the squeaky springs in the cabin, the last thing I saw before I dozed was the notice on the wall. Was it really what it seemed to be? At last a place of real men of the West, idealists with compassion for travelers, with undemanding hospitality, with a code that depended upon the generosity of others so that every passerby became a host.

Or was it as Eddie, ever the cynic, put it: "It's easier for the Border Patrol pigs to stock a way-station with food and water than to dig graves in the heat of El Camino del Diablo."

We headed east; somewhere south of Ajo in a dead cave of dusty stalactites, we discovered a bat species, *Leptonycteris*, that we had never seen before. It turned out that it had been reported once previously in the United States, in 1934. Still, the find was of great interest to v. B. and myself, but of no help to the project because the species was rare and did not fit our requirements. The bat had a long muzzle and a matching tongue and fed like a nocturnal hummingbird on the nectar of those cactus flowers whose petals opened only after dark.

We drove on across Arizona and straight through New Mexico in one night, pausing only to tank up with gas and fill our thermos bottles with coffee. It was a tough journey of magic discovery for me. Roaring through the night and day with my friends in Doc's huge automobile, our goal an important mission, was an adolescent adventure of the most romantic kind.

A few miles east of the famed country courthouse-cum-general store of the "hanging judge," Roy Bean, in west Texas, we all sat staring at the odometer of Doc's Buick as it turned over from the numbers 999,999 to 000,000. Fletcher was driving at this noteworthy time, and Doc ordered him to pull off onto the highway shoulder for a rare pause. Adams pulled a new bottle of his hard-to-get Old Grand-dad bourbon out of his suitcase and everyone had a snort. After toasts to the success of our mission and to the continuing trustworthiness of the faithful, seemingly dauntless Buick, we piled back in and headed on.

Our next destination was the limestone country in the general vicinity of San Antonio, Texas, where—rumor had it—huge colonies of bats might be found.

Somewhere along the way, we paused long enough for Doc to place a telephone call back to Los Angeles and his adjutant, Bobby Herold. He returned to the car with a face like a sad basset hound. The rejection from the Chemical Warfare Service of a week ago had been followed by a further turndown. First the Army had passed, now Rear Admiral J. A. Furer, coordinator of research and development for the Navy, had written. His letter was directed to the chairman of NDRC; from the condescending opening, anything that followed just couldn't be good. You can be pretty sure that any letter which begins "My Dear Mr. Anybody" is going to be a putdown, and this one definitely followed the pattern.

> My Dear Mr. Stevenson,
>      . . . It is noted that the bat can presumably carry a maximum load of something in the order of one ounce. If one ounce incendiaries were effective, we would be using one ounce bombs instead of bombs weighing two pounds upward . . .

Furer went on to point out that while no absolute minimum weight for an incendiary had ever been established, "since obviously one could start a conflagration with a single paper match," the two pounds in current use was still considered the necessary minimum to be effective. "Therefore, since the order of magnitude between the incendiary carried by the bat and that carried by the minimum effective bomb is in the ratio of more than 1 to 30, it is not considered worthwhile to conduct any experiments with bats."

Now, to forestall a complete shutdown of the project as a result of the disappointing reactions from both Chemical Warfare and the Navy, Doc sent an urgent appeal to his contact with the National Inventors Council of the Department of Commerce, Mr. Thomas R. Taylor, director of staff, requesting a face-to-face meeting with Chemical Warfare Service officers.

On June 4, a couple of weeks after the obstructive Captain Wiles in Chemical Warfare had repeated his superior's fork-tongued words rejecting Doc's plan *in toto*, Taylor responded to Adams's latest request with a letter to Colonel Kabrich asking him to keep options open for the moment and to meet with Doc personally and hear out his proposal.

Eight days later, Adams took a temporary leave of absence from the quest for bats to fly to Chemical Warfare headquarters at Aberdeen, Maryland. He opened his remarks to a council of CWS officers chaired by Colonel J. C. Morrell. In an uncharacteristically long and lackluster summary Doc provided little new information and merely presented a general overview of the original idea. It was old hash, and the colonels swallowed it with little enthusiasm.

But the meeting warmed up a bit when Adams told the assembled officers that a new type of incendiary now being considered by Fieser and Young was entirely automatic as to desired delay in combustion, being controlled by mechanical means. Now at last Doc felt a spark of inspiration and brought some life to the party. He couldn't resist the opportunity for a dig at his main detractor. It was dangerous, since he was playing on Wiles's home field, but Doc said that one of the captain's main objections was (and here he read directly from the captain's demeaning memo) that "the low temperature and pressure at which bombers fly to avoid anti-aircraft fire would be detrimental to the life of the bats."

"Hogwash!" Doc exclaimed as he thumped the table. "Captain Wiles's objection is an *advantage* rather than a disadvantage. Bats lend themselves perfectly to low temperatures, which will be desirable in keeping incendiaries of the type we propose cold enough to ensure safety. Dr. Campbell says, and I quote: [Doc opened a book by Dr. Charles A. R. Campbell, another bat authority of the time] 'A temperature of 25 degrees below zero does not seem to disturb bats at all, for they are found in Vermont in caves where temperature falls that low in winter months.'"*

Doc can be excused for accepting the apparently authoritative statement at face value, but it was not true. Hibernating bats sub-

---

*Charles A. R. Campbell, *Bats, Mosquitoes and Dollars.*

jected to this temperature would surely die. As to the possible effects of high altitudes, Adams let that issue slide and no one present called him on the omission. Doc was happy enough to bypass the point. He knew that atmospheric pressure and the effects of diminished oxygen were questions yet to be explored.

Doc's inventive if sometimes devious mind had been operating on a principle he fully employed on this as well as other occasions: "Sometimes a seemingly insurmountable obstacle, if turned around and looked at from a completely different angle, can be changed into a positive advantage." It was an inspired way of thinking that had a lot in common with the Art of Confusion—but now Adams wasn't practicing on country bumpkins.

"I heard the damnedest thing while I was in D.C.," Doc said when he got back from Washington. "Some general I met regarding appropriations confused our secret project with another secret project that's apparently going on somewhere. It's the silliest nonsense you ever heard of. And evidently this project has got the backing of the president and they're blowing millions of dollars on it."

Von Bloeker looked up through his smoke and frowned.

"This general practically threw me out of his office, he was so enraged at the waste of time and money. 'Don't tell me you're the one promoting that crazy notion of making bombs out of atoms?'"

"I had a hell of a time convincing him that I had nothing to do with that kind of fraud," Doc continued.

"What are atoms?" Frank Benish asked.

"The smallest particles of matter. You know, everything's made out of cells. You break down cells and you've got something even smaller—atoms—something like that."

"And they think they can make bombs out of them?" Benish shook his head. "Man, they don't know sic 'em from come here."

"Can you imagine such an idea?" Doc said. "*They're* throwing away millions, and *I* can't get a staff car and driver!"

"Where's all this happening?" v. B. asked.

Doc shrugged. "As soon as he found out I had nothing to do with it he clammed up. But he first got the idea I was involved when I said we had some work to do in New Mexico."

"Unbelievable!" v. B. said.

"Yeah! We got a sure thing like the bat bomb going, something that could really win the war, and they're jerking off with tiny little atoms. It makes me want to cry."

Our search for great bat caves was haphazard, executed like a detective story by following up rumors and clues. Somehow we ended up in the Texas cowtown of Del Rio, an area where bat caves were rumored to exist. We had no introductions or specific knowledge of where to go. Doc began his research by interviewing anyone who'd talk to him—gas station attendants, bartenders, store clerks, and the always-suspicious ranchers and cowpokes to whom he introduced himself on the street.

We tried to follow his lead—Fletch, von Bloeker, Eddie, Williams, and me. We hardly projected the aura of secrecy that our mission aspired to, but were instead as conspicuous as six Friesian milk cows in a field of red Texas longhorns—and were observed by the locals with equal suspicion. Doc dove into the situation with his usual aplomb and unflappable verve.

First reactions to us, as obvious outsiders from the North, were much the same as they would be to something slimy that had crawled out from under a rock. One felt like a small helpless creature being ground into the soil with the heel of a cowboy boot. But even the close-mouthed suspicion of taciturn Texas ranchers eventually melted under the warmth of Doc's winning personality. It was hard to insult this little old man in the wrinkled suit and soup-spotted bow tie, his invariable costume. The weathered men in Levi's and boots looked out from under their Stetsons and found this jovial little person with pig eyes harmless—gradually Doc began to stuff his pockets with torn-off bits of paper napkins, newspaper margins, and other odd scraps with jotted notes about bat caves.

All the caves or clues to caves mentioned by range riders were on huge private ranches closed off to the casual explorations of a Buick-load of strange, close-mouthed city slickers. Doc couldn't reveal the true nature of our mission, so how could the single-minded cattlemen regard us other than with suspicion?

One cave, however, emerged in the lore of the land as the one with most widespread recognition—even though no one we talked to had actually been there. This cavern, the legendary Devil's Sinkhole, seemed to have an aura of almost magnetic power. Inevitably, it seemed, our inquiries pulled us toward this horror of a cave.

Since the advent of modern speleology or spelunking, as cave exploration is now called, as both science and sport, a lot has been learned—some, unfortunately, the hard way—about exploring underground. In 1942 we had never heard the words for it, much less the methods of caving safety practiced today, nor did we have the equipment. Hard hats, wet suits, abrasion-resistant ropes of strong artificial fibers—the modern hardware of rock climbing—were all unknown, uninvented, or, we naively thought, unnecessary. The few adventurous incursions made into the nether world that preceded us had been fraught with danger and dire mishaps, but we knew nothing of that. We were bat people, not cavers. Unfortunately, bats live in caves.

We bumped along in the Buick, scraping bottom on the high centers between two ruts. We followed a dilapidated pickup over a stony track, crossing a level plain with dark clumps of scrub oak blotching the bright yellow-green grassland—hardly cave country, or so we thought. After a long way and additional bruises to the Buick's already ruptured underbelly, a torn muffler, and gouges on the fenders where sharp mesquite crowded the lanes, our guiding pickup rocked to a stop. We stood on a featureless boulder-strewn plain without landmarks, looking around, wondering what the trouble was. Had our guide run out of gas or broken a spring? The land was flat as far as the eye could see, with no barrancas or cliff faces where a typical cavern might show its mouth, no clue that we might be in a cave area. The man climbed out of his pickup on legs that had spent the best part of seventy years straddling a horse and waddled painfully toward a fallen-down ring of cedar posts and rusty barbed wire.

"To keep the stock from fallin' in," he said. "Got to mend it one day." He stopped at the wire and nodded into the circle. "Be careful. You git in any trouble, it's yer party. Don't holler fer me." He turned and waddled back toward his truck, shaking his head. It was obvious that he thought his boss had made a grave mistake in telling him to bring us here. "Nope, don't holler fer me," he mumbled again as he slammed the pickup door. "You git in any trouble . . ." He banged the door a couple more times trying to get it to stay closed. "Whatever happens, just don't holler fer me."

As the pickup crawled away, bumping over boulders like it had square wheels, we crawled through the wire, slipped gingerly down a slope, and there it was, yawning mysteriously at our toes. We peered down with strange feelings of apprehension and excitement: a black pit, sheer, fifty feet across, dangerously undercut around its circular mouth.

We had been told that once, a long time ago, guano had been pulled from the sinkhole. To get the miners in and the sacks out a small hole had been cut through the overhang some twenty feet back from the edge. Weather-checked ends of wooden two-by-fours held by rusty windings of barbed wire stuck up from this shaft. We lay on our bellies, heads over the edge, peering down into the blackness. Our flashlights barely touched the dark immensity. A ladder of splintery rungs nailed to the two-by-four rails hung in space, falling away in diminishing perspective. It curved in to land against an outcropping, clung to the rock for a few yards, then disappeared completely in darkness.

Williams dropped a stone and we watched it fall in the flashlight's beam. It grew faint, disappeared, then many seconds later we heard a thud from the blackness as it hit bottom. "Two hundred feet," Doc said as if he had mentally calculated the falling time and knew exactly what he was talking about. I doubted his technology; in fact, he was dead-on.

The cavern had been formed in typical sinkhole fashion. As seepage gradually eroded away an underground pocket of soluble limestone, expanding a chamber over many centuries, a subsurface stream carried away the mineral-laden solution. The slow wearing away of underground stone gradually ate into the overbearing until the ever-thinning ceiling could no longer support the weight of rock above and the whole mass crashed down into the underlying chamber. Somewhere below there probably was or had been a lateral connection, the course of the underground river, possibly with an inlet or outlet miles away, or the whole system could have been sealed beneath the surface, solubles carried away through a porous geology, and this black mouth where we lay with our feelings of awe and hollow stomachs the only door open to the topside world.

Our guide from the ranch had said that no sacks had been pulled from the pit in the past ten or fifteen years and so far as he knew no one had been down the ladder since then. The guano mining had proved dangerous: after only a few dozen sacks had been removed, nearly at the cost of two lives, the operation had been abandoned.

The prospect of entering this black pit, our first large wild cavern, was frightening. No one was quick to volunteer. With a hand on a two-by-four I tested the only means of descent. The rickety ladder swung ponderously on the wires, a pendulum into blackness, creaking and rotten.

Williams looked at me ominously. "Whatever happens . . ."

"I know . . ." I interrupted.

Then everyone spoke together: "Just don't holler fer me."

The nails holding the weather-checked rungs were rusty and backing out. Only the hope of discovering the huge colony of bats rumored to live down there held the slightest appeal. No one, with the exception of the ever-adventurous Fletch, was lured in the slightest by the excitement of the prospective descent. I for one was glad to hear Fletch say, "Well, I'll go first."

While Eddie and Williams scavenged more barbed wire from the tangle of fencing, wrapped it around the projecting two-by-fours, and clinched the ends around an anchor rock, von Bloeker drove the Buick up to within twenty feet of the entrance hole and looped our rope through the bumper.

Fletch tied the end around his chest as a safety line, stuck a flashlight in his back pocket, and put a foot on the first wooden rung. He carefully shifted his full weight onto the step then bounced a couple of times on the rickety ladder. It creaked, but held. Solemnly Fletch nodded and put both feet on the ladder. He took a cautious step, trying the next rung; it held, and he started down.

V. B. and Eddie Herold held the rope, slowly paying it out from the bight around the bumper, keeping it taut as it crept away following Fletch over the edge.

I hadn't volunteered and no one had said it yet, but I suspected that I had been elected by unanimous unspoken vote to be the next to descend. This exploration called for a team of two. An adventurer—Fletch—and a mammalogist—me. With this highly unsettling hunch gnawing at my mind and innards I watched Fletch's progress into blackness with ever more sickening fascination.

His comments as he descended came up hollow-sounding with echoes. "Not bad . . . solid enough so far . . . a bit wobbly here. Swings a bit."

I kept my flashlight pointed down, aimed to illuminate the ladder, trying to help him see where to put his feet and where to grab with his hands.

"Don't get seasick," he called. "Whoever's next. It's got a motion like going over waves." I was sure he thought he was being funny.

Then after about sixty steps Fletch reached a point where the flashlight beam no longer helped him. Faint daylight still sifted down and we could barely see him in the twilight of the cave. He had not yet entered the absolute Stygian blackness of the netherworld. "Careful here," he called. "Ladder's soaking wet, covered with moss . . . damned slippery, too. Hell, there's *ferns* growing out of it. Ferns and mushrooms." He had reached the point where the final reach of light permitted a last growth of primitive plant life.

Fletch switched on his own flashlight, which he kept sticking up out of his pocket so both hands were free to grab rungs. The beam illuminated the steps above but his feet had to find the ones below by feel, not a happy situation when one expected at every step a gap in the rungs or the ladder itself to be broken off.

The flashlight glow became a small dancing star as he slowly went down, and his voice grew fainter, echoing oddly. Then the point of light stopped its descent, swerving out of our sight as he removed it from his pocket, and the beam jerked around erratically.

"What's going on?" Doc mumbled.

"What's happening?" Williams shouted into the hole.

"Shhh!" Doc said. "Our questions can't help. Whatever's happening, he'll work it out. Us yelling at him is only distracting. If he wants anything, he'll tell us."

The silence from below was nearly unbearable. Then the sharp sounds of splintering wood echoed alarmingly in the cave. Was the ladder coming apart?

In spite of his orders, Doc shouted: "What's happening?"

More snapping of wood, crackling, thuds—no voice.

We were horrified. Our worst imaginings were becoming reality.

Then Fletch's voice, still calm, no hint of the expected panic: "Careful here . . . damned tree got stuck in the ladder. Must have fell in . . . all tangled up in the rungs." We heard more breaking of branches, the sound of hammering with a large limb as he struggled to clear away the obstacle, then the sound of many branches breaking all at once as the dislodged tree sailed down and crashed against rocks at the bottom.

"Okay . . . got rid of that."

More agony of silence, again the light winking up into our eyes, then: "Ugh! Damn! There's a rung or two rotted out here . . . Gone . . . Almost took a free-fall. Next time, let's have a parachute." Silence. We waited—incredibly long, then: "Okay, got by that. Next guy—gotta let yourself down on the side rails . . . hook your ankles over the two-by-fours on each side and slide." I was listening to Fletch very closely. "It's slippery as hell—be careful." I looked at Doc. He looked at me, nodded, said nothing, and I knew my gut-wrenching suspicion had been correct.

More grunts from below, the bobbing light, on and off, a few muffled curses, then: "Okay. I'm at the bottom." Another long silence until he spoke again. "I mean the bottom of the ladder. It's busted off." We could see the pinpoint of his light playing around on rocks below him. "About an eight foot drop to the floor."

"What are you going to do?" I yelled, defying the rules, hopeful that he would take my next question as a suggestion. "Come back up?"

"Got this far . . . " The voice came muffled, the first time he had answered a question directly. "Slack off on the line so I can jump."

"He says slack off a bit," Doc said to the line tenders at the car. "He's going to jump."

"How much?"

"Eight feet, he says. Then he's on the bottom."

Von Bloeker and Eddie paid out line. Suddenly the rope sprang taut. Immediately Fletch's pained voice: "Damn! More! More rope! I'm hung!"

"More line!" Doc yelled. "Let it go!" And the tenders paid out. Then all went slack.

"You all right?" Doc yelled into the hole.

"Guess so. Damned near jerked my arms off, though. Glad it wasn't around my neck. Okay, haul it back up."


My descent started out much as a repeat of Fletch's pioneering way. What had appeared to a nonparticipant looking down from above to be only a slight swinging of the suspended ladder became, when one was doing the swinging, a frighteningly pendulous movement which made one cling to each soggy rung that came to hand with now-enhanced strength. Only thirty-four steps down—I was counting each one—my arms ached, and I paused, breathing heavily, realizing that I was overly tense and gripping far more desperately than was actually required, wearing myself out unnecessarily. I talked myself into relaxing and took some deep breaths, trying to slow down the pounding of my heart. I started down again. Moments later, I became aware that I was tense again, shoulder and arm muscles quivering, fingers hooked around the rungs like claws, as a drowning man clutches a life ring.

To hell with it, I thought, and went with the tension, allowing it to take control and hanging on with all my strength, exhausting as it was.

I came to a point where the ladder lay against an anchoring projection from the wall, arresting the swinging movement, allowing me a few steps on solid footing and the chance to even out my breathing and heartbeat. The feeling of security in those few steps with something solid underfoot was a relief as great as the comfort of lying down on a soft bed when one is immensely weary.

Then the ladder fell off into space again, zigzagging, so that what had been top was now bottom and I had to crawl around the ladder's edge to keep going. Again, I dangled in the void, swaying in the darkness with the impetus of each step. The swinging took on a rhythm like the high rigging of a ship rolling with the swells on a black night at sea. It seemed safer to go with the flow rather than to interrupt the rhythm, and I paced my steps to stay with the motion. My descent took on a dreamy cadence, lulling me into a false sense of security.

Fletch's light came closer as I went down, hypnotically drifting up toward me out of the darkness. His light seemed detached from the bottom, as if floating up on an invisible string. Then an echoing voice startled me. "Careful. Next step's the big one. You're at the broken rungs."

I groped into the darkness below with a foot—nothing, only empty space. I swung my leg sideways, back and forth, feeling for something. The side of my foot hit a rail, and a shaky cold sweat came over me as if my blood had been suddenly injected with a syringeful of fear.

"That's the worst place," Fletch called. "Better be damned careful."

His advice was superfluous. I was more than careful. The demon of terror sent shivers fluttering through my gripping claws. I clung to the ladder with one arm wrapped like a knotted rope around a rung, took my flashlight in the other hand, and studied the void through which I must pass. "A couple of rungs missing . . . " A typical Fletcher exaggeration. Instead of two rungs, a stepless gap of eight or ten feet lay between me and the next rotten-looking foothold. I imagined what had happened. A large boulder had crashed down from above, wiping out the row of steps in one swipe. Broken slat-ends, jutting nail heads, and splintered one-by-twos made the gap more formidable than a smooth slide between steps would have been. Unfortunately, the parallel side rails appeared to be sound; otherwise, if they had also been shattered by the rock, we could have given up the descent at this point, having done our best, and climbed back to the real world without guilt. But the rails appeared to be solid—and Fletch had made it. So with the goading of face-saving—a most dangerous motive—summoning all the false courage I could muster, I had to try it, too.

"You git in any trouble," Fletch called. "Just don't holler fer me."

I ignored him, stuck my flashlight back in my pocket, hooked my ankles around the two-by-fours, grabbed a rail in each hand, and lowered myself into the gap. With no reassuring pressure of cross-rungs across my tummy, my body hung like a sway-backed horse in the empty space. Straining mightily, I dropped down in increments of only a few inches at a time. A continuous slide was made impossible by the many sharp projections. Splinters of wood stuck into my flesh; iron nails tore at my shirt, trousers, and skin. A nail grabbed me—I felt it as a hot rip of flesh and imagined the chunk it was tearing out of my inner thigh. Wherever my body touched the rails and their projecting daggers it grew hot from what I pictured as hundreds of cuts and gouges. The swaying ladder twisted and the torque threw me off-center. Now I clung off-balance with more of me hanging onto the right rail than the left. A broken-off rung-end grabbed my leg and I didn't have the strength to lift myself up to get over it. I slid on down and felt with regret the loss of that vital piece of myself that I'd barely had use for in the past, but had great plans for in the future.

At last my feet felt a rung again and I rested, heart hammering in my chest, afraid to take out my light and inspect all the damage that my hurting body told me had been done.

"Come on," Fletch said. "You're almost down now. Only one small obstacle yet to go."

"What the hell is that?" I croaked wearily.

"No big deal. Just the drop off at the end."

I took a deep breath and again started stepping down. More swinging, more of my heart doing funny things.

"Okay," Fletch said. "Only three more steps, then you're on the last rung. I hope they give you more slack than they did me."

"They will," I said, feet groping wildly for the bottom step. Empty space told me that I was already standing on it. I clung to the rope at my chest with one hand, fished around for my light, and pointed it down onto the rocks, looking for a landing place.

Fletch aimed his light on the spot where he had cleared away some space between boulders and kicked aside the bones of deer and sheep that had fallen in. "Right here," he said. "I'll grab you when you land."

"Damn!" I said. "It's a hell of a lot more than eight feet."

"No, honest. It just looks further."

"Well, how the hell are we going to get back up?"

"With the rope. They can pull us. Piece of cake."

"Are you kidding? It's not that easy." I stalled, uncommitted. "Besides, I weigh more than you do."

"Come on," Fletch said. "Get it over with." Then he yelled to the surface, preempting me. "He's going to jump! Slack off!"

I felt the line go loose—and I jumped.

As soon as I got my breath back and was able to stagger to my feet, I played the flashlight on the parts of my body that hurt the most and found the damage not so severe as I had imagined. I was scratched and would have to dig out a few splinters, but nothing was missing or beyond repair. Even the part of me from which I feared I had been forever separated seemed to be surprisingly intact and if I was lucky, would be able to perform its primary function in a week or so. At the moment, it served its secondary duty with satisfactory, if painful, relief.

We found ourselves on the apex of a steep cone-shaped peak, covered with a rubble of boulders and bones, all overlaid with a carpet of small brown pellets. We worked our way down toward the floor of the circular grotto, slipping on the slope and climbing over huge chunks of stone. I dropped off a ledge—and landed squarely in the middle of a dead skunk. Years later, reading an early account of cave exploration, I came across the report of a similar incident. I guess nothing in life, even an experience seemingly as unique as jumping into the middle of a dead skunk, is ever unprecedented or truly new. The writing had an old-fashioned charm and brought back poignant memories of my first descent into a major cavern: "I spun around at the end of the rope until I was glad to land even upon a skunk whose defunct body was in perfect harmony with his malodorous life. . . . What it left to be desired in the way of odor was more than supplied by the bats."

Like the bottom of a flat-rimmed soup plate turned upside down, a more or less level area lay between the foot of the cone and the walls of the dome. We scuffed through guano around the perimeter searching the walls and overhangs for bats. Fifty here, a hundred there—where were the millions? Countless small holes and honeycombed rock pockmarked the high concave walls of the dome, reaching up beyond the range of our lights. Millions of bats could be packed into those niches. If they were, we could not see them. It was not the season for hibernation—maybe they had migrated away to another roost. We searched completely around the bottom circumference of the huge room, expecting to find the lateral branches which might hold the millions. We saw none, only the place where a river tunnel might once have been, now sealed off by fallen debris.

"I guess they knew we were coming," Fletch said. We consoled ourselves with the realization that even if the bats were here in their millions it would be next to impossible to conduct the researches we had to do in this horrible place.

Feeling let down, we struggled back up the slope to the rope below the ladder.

"You go first," Fletch said when we reached the summit and stared up at the ladder, its broken-off end out of reach. He shouted up toward the ragged circle of daylight far above: "You're going to have to pull us up aways on the rope."

"Come again?"

"The rope . . . pull us up so we can reach the ladder. About ten or twelve feet."

"Ah-ha!" I thought. "Lying bastard! So he *knows* it's more than eight feet."

Fletch wound the rope around my chest, beneath my armpits, and tied a bowline. "Hang onto the rope until you can catch the third or fourth rung—so you can get a foot on a step, then you'll be home free."

He shouted up toward the light and the circle of silhouetted heads staring down. "Take a strain!"

I looked up. In the small dot of light where the precious ladder reached the world, I could see the heads disappear as they moved back; only a single small dark dot remained. That would be Doc peering down—the others would now be standing back from the edge gripping the rope, ready to begin a game of tug-of-war with my inert body. The rope grew taut as they pulled, the strain coming in jerks as they hauled together by count. It cut into my armpits and I grasped the knot, waiting to feel my feet leave the ground. The rope pulled harder, pinching into the flesh, and my spine stretched toward the surface. But I didn't rise.

On top, von Bloeker, Eddie Herold, and Williams strained at the rope. From where it bent over the edge of the abyss, the line went once around the Buick's bumper, then back to the men. Doc hurried from the edge of the pit and grabbed the tail end, adding his weight to the effort. With a purchase of only two to one, and that around the hard edge of the bumper rather than through a pulley as it should have been, four men couldn't lift me. A proper block and tackle with a roller at the edge and a mechanical advantage of three or four to one would have done it, but we didn't have the equipment.

The rope went slack again and a head appeared in the hole. "It's no use," v. B. shouted. "We can't lift you."

I glared at Fletch in the darkness. At the moment I felt more anger in our frustration than fear. "Only eight feet! Jump! They'll pull us with the rope! A piece of cake! Damn you, Fletcher!" I thought of our guide's prophetic words: "If you git in any trouble . . . " If Fletch repeated them again I'd punch him.

It was already late in the afternoon and a small flight of bats, disturbed by the flashlights and shouting, began to mill, circling in the huge dome above us, getting ready for the evening exodus.

"So what now?" I asked, slipping out of the rope loop.

Fletch didn't answer. We sat for a few minutes, thoughts to ourselves, becoming more scared as all the possibilities ran through our minds. Then a voice echoed down: "We'll try to pull you up with the car."

"Obviously," Fletch muttered. "I wondered how long it would take them to figure that out."

Faintly we heard the car start, the hole in its exhaust exaggerating the sounds of maneuvering, hoping they were doing everything right up there. I knew v. B. would have taken charge and I trusted his experience at improvising in the bush.

A voice sounded. I thought it was his but, if it was, it had been made indistinguishable by the echoes. "Okay. Tell us when you're ready. We'll pull up ten feet, then stop."

I slipped back into the loop, grasped the knot. My muscles that I thought were too tired to function seemed to find strength again. My heart began its familiar tattoo. "Okay," I said. "I guess I'm ready."

I looked up. Again I could see the small dark dots that would be the heads of Doc, Williams, and Eddie, peering down, seeing nothing but blackness. Von Bloeker would be inside the car, slipping the clutch to ease the jerk on the line.

Fletch yelled: "Ready! Pull!"

Slowly the rope grew taut. It settled into my armpits, my torso stretched, and my feet left the ground. Not bad, I thought. It's working. Then the unexpected.

Using outcroppings for support, the ladder did not come down in one continuous linear fall, but in three long zigzags. The rope, on the other hand, stretched down in a long straight line, and I, like a plumb-bob on its end, caused it to want to hang in a naturally perpendicular fall. At the moment my feet left the ground I swung away from the spot below the ladder and soared out into space away from the peak. The pulling from above stopped and I dangled. I would have been ten feet above the apex of the cone had I still been over its center; now I hung, spinning and swinging, twenty feet from the rungs and thirty or forty feet above the sloping ground.

I was stuck, dangling like a dead spider on a thread. "Damn! What next?" I couldn't go up or down.

Fletch scrambled down the slope, reached the spot below me, and grabbed the trailing rope end. "Hang on. I'll swing you in to the ladder."

He shouted up toward the dot of light. "Hold it there. We've got a problem."

"What's the matter?" someone yelled from above.

Fletch ignored the query. Suddenly my swinging was jerked to a stop by Fletch's tug on the tail of the rope and I began to spin more rapidly. Fletch scrambled back up the slope, stumbling in the darkness, dragging the end of rope with him. Then he reached the summit and began to haul me in. He got as much as he could on the rope and let go, paying out. I sailed giddily away into the darkness in a giant arc; at the end of the arc I started back, and Fletch quickly took up the slack, pulling me closer. Pull and pay out, pull and pay out; the arcs grew longer, like swinging a child from the limb of a tree in an old tire.

I tried to aim my flashlight, but the swinging and spinning made it nearly impossible. I glimpsed the ladder, coming closer, sailing away, coming closer, going away.

I got some control over myself. I had to aim my light on the ladder to see where to grab.

Fletch was grunting with effort. "Get your light on it," he yelled. "I can't use mine. Need both hands."

"I know. I'm trying! Damn! Can't you stop the spinning? I'm getting dizzy."

"Grab it! Grab it! Damn! You almost had it."

"I didn't see it."

"Next time. Get your light on it. Come on! Now! Quickly! Behind you!"

I tried to twist my body against the spin so I'd be lined up and facing the ladder as I swung toward it. My light found the ladder and I reached the far end of the arc, but as I reversed direction and started back the spin took it away. I couldn't twist my body far enough and again lost the target. Too much was happening all at once, too many movements countering each other. Again I glimpsed the ladder in my light, coming fast; I grabbed at it, missed, and swung away again.

"I can't keep this up much longer," Fletch yelled. "Another couple of swings and I've had it."

My arms didn't work as they should with the rope binding under my armpits. I grabbed the knot and with a huge effort pulled myself up a few inches. Now sailing away, I saw the ladder again over my shoulder. The arc ended and I started back, picking up speed; I tried to twist to meet it, got halfway around, lost it, found it again, grabbed. My fingers clutched wood. Then my weight ripped it away with a hot flash of pain and I knew that my fingernails were bloody. Again I sailed far out over the sickening height, spun, losing orientation, felt the pendulum of myself pause at the outside end of the arc and start back.

"Only once more," Fletch yelled. "I'm pooped out."

Panic came over me, the horrible feeling that we'd never escape, that I'd pass out hanging from the end of the rope. The spinning would stop one day, but by then I'd be as lifeless as a hanging sack of guano. Then there was the ladder again, coming at me fast, a bright series of angles caught in my light and rushing at me out of the darkness. I crashed into it, banging hard into the wood with my shoulder. I grabbed desperately, caught it, hung on. But I couldn't hold myself against all the momentum with only one hand. I was losing it again. I dropped the flashlight, grabbed blindly for the ladder with the other hand, got it.

The ladder creaked and shuddered with the shock of collision and sudden strain. I clung, feeling it sway ominously, wondering when the whole structure would collapse and come tumbling down on top of us.

Pedaling, groping blindly, my toes found a rung and hooked it. I pulled myself in and lay against the steps, panting, clinging like a crab on a wave-battered piling.

Gradually the ladder settled and hung, swaying slightly, alive, like a breathing snake.

"Okay," Fletch yelled aloft, restoring a little calm. "He's got it. It's okay." To me, he said: "For a minute I thought we'd bought the farm. If the ladder'd broke . . . Well . . . Don't forget to drop the rope back."

"But there's nobody to swing you in to the ladder."

"Yeah. I know." Fletch said. "We'll have to work that out. I'll tie myself into the rope. When everything's set, I'll run off the peak and start myself swinging. The car's gotta pull me up at the same time. I'm swinging while it's pulling, okay?"

"Got it," I said lamely. "I hope it'll work."

"It'll work," Fletch said. "Pull higher next time—twenty feet."

"Twenty feet," I repeated, starting to climb. "Good luck." I was sorry for the last. It sounded somehow ominous.

I thought I'd never reach the top of that rotten swaying ladder out of hell. It seemed to have no end, as if it stretched on up into the blackness toward the infinity of distant stars. It swung and creaked as rungs strained by the only action in years broke and I expected the whole decayed contraption to fall apart with every step. I pulled myself up on the side rails through the awesome gap between broken-off steps—a crowbar couldn't have pried me loose from the splintery two-by-fours. But going up it was easier to push my body away as I passed over the sharp projections. I climbed and climbed and my arms ached and then orange daylight magically flared into my eyes, and I just kept going, mechanically, in a daze; step, pull, step, pull, until I felt the hands of my friends grabbing me and helping to drag me over the edge into the world of sunsets and starlight and I collapsed on the ground. I only knew I was hurting and trembling and worthless for anything requiring strength or muscle power, but we had to get Fletch out and I couldn't do what I felt like doing—crawl off and lie down on the rocks and close my eyes.

I told them about Fletch's plan for escape, and we measured off twenty feet on the ground and placed a pile of stones to mark where the front wheels should stop. Again von Bloeker drove; there was little the rest of us could do now other than lie on our bellies staring down into the black hole, playing our flashlights down, seeing nothing but a whirlpool of circling bats and the occasional wink of Fletch's light and relaying his shouted "Stop!" and "Pull!" instructions to v. B.

We tried his plan, but he didn't swing in arcs wide enough to bring him in to the ladder. We could see his light spinning and swinging through the wings of a few thousand swirling bats and I knew the helplessness he was feeling. He missed the ladder, his swinging grew less, and he shouted for the car to lower him again.

After an agonizingly long silence which we didn't want to break with useless questions, he called again: "Ready here. Pull!"

This time, he swung himself so far out that when he came back with dizzying momentum and hit the ladder the impact dazed him and the whole ladder creaked clear up to the barbed wire anchors at the top. We watched the stub ends creak and groan and threaten to tear loose. Then the movement settled and at last Fletcher's voice echoed out of the depths. "Okay. I'm on the ladder. Just take out the slack as I come."

When at last we grabbed his shirt and pulled him over the lip of the pit and he made an attempt at a toothy grin, we all sat down on boulders and had a swig of Doc's medicine.

The Old Grand-dad made a hot sensation going down, and my bone-aching body at last relaxed. I lay back, hands behind my head, the cold sweat of fright adding to the evening chill now being driven away by the warm rush of bourbon in my blood, looking up at the stars now winking in the night sky and realizing how very bright darkness is on the surface of the earth. Even on a moonless night one can see shapes in the darkness, so very different from the absolute blackness of underground.

Fletch had his breath back and his spirits up and with an air of convincing sincerity said, "Yep, that was good fun."

Now I *knew* he was crazy.

Adams's meeting at Chemical Warfare headquarters resulted in no official response. We seemed to be at an impasse. Doc had written his reply to Colonel Kabrich's reneging letter on July 8, before we had left on our search for bats. No answer from Kabrich is to be found in the declassified materials in the National Archives, but on the copy of Adams's letter is a one-word notation "File," dated "7-21-42," and initialed "R. W. H." The next correspondence on file is a brief handwritten note, undated, also under the same mysterious initials: "I talked with Dr. Adams and am not certain he doesn't have something. A few hundred thousand bats so equipped if released at many places from a sub along our Pacific coast might very well cause so many forest fires that an almost total loss of timber would occur."

The Japanese weren't considering using bat bombs, of that we can now be sure, but by odd coincidence they would later use another method nearly as ingenious to achieve the same result. By sending unmanned incendiary balloons borne by the prevailing winds from Japan eastward across the Pacific they aimed to incinerate our Pacific Northwest forests. Although several balloons made the long crossing on their own and fires were ignited, the effectiveness of the effort was practically nil. The first of them sailed across the Pacific in November 1944. Thus it was not this as yet unknown threat that caused the mysterious R. W. H. to consider the firemaking capabilities of vector bats a reality. His note continued: "I sent him [Adams] to sell the AC [Air Corps?] since we have no military requirement for his offering. He will probably get Ewell and Stevenson [of the National Inventors Council] to go with him."

R. W. H. remains to this day an anonymous friend, but a friend who must have carried considerable clout. His interest—as impractical as the idea of releasing bats from a submarine might be and in spite of his reaction being based on the unlikely possibility that the enemy might be the first to use the weapon against us (there are no large colonies of bats in Japan from which to draw vectors)—kept the project alive until more answers could be found.

When Doc put together all of the slips of paper gleaned from interviews containing notes about the bat caves of Texas, he found one name frequently repeated. Again and again, we heard reference to this redoubtable specialist. Repeatedly, we were told: "Talk to the bat-shit man." This singular individual was Emil Rugh of Bandera, Texas.

# 9

## The Bat-Shit Man

TO SUPPLY HIS BUSINESS with bat guano, which he packed as fertilizer, Emil Rugh held leases on most if not all of the large bat caves in Texas. "He knows more about bat caves than any man alive" was the chorus of every song we heard about bats. When we'd heard this report enough times to believe it might be true, we made a beeline for Bandera.

Adams found Rugh at his old two-story clapboard paint-peeling house on the outskirts of Bandera. While Doc disappeared into the door with his rope-bound briefcase under his arm, the rest of us had a look at the town. Like most Texas cowtowns, it was spread out along less than a quarter of a mile of Main Street. The Medina River ran parallel, slow and clear under wild pecan and cypress trees, but Bandera's dominant feature was a tall metal water tank on spindly legs that reared over the village like a black widow spider ready to pounce. The usual gas stations, drugstore, general store, feed barn, a couple of bars, and a combination bar and restaurant—the OST Cafe—were the anchors for the community. The large windows of the OST Cafe (which stood for Old Spanish Trail) fronted the street. We had a look inside. A mirror-backed bar with a brass foot rail and no stools stood at one end and a dozen tables and chairs occupied the rest of the spacious, nearly empty sunlit room. It looked cheery and we took a table and sat down to order lunch.

We couldn't know it then, but the OST Cafe was to become our Texas headquarters. It would be message center, entertainment bureau, hospitality house, mess hall, office, and part-time home.

Squinting through smoke from the cigarette stuck in his lips, von Bloeker had his nose in a menu trying to decide between Top Sirloin or T-bone, when suddenly he grabbed at his side as if he'd been touched with an electric cattle prod, leaped up from his chair, and came face to face with the pickpocket he'd felt probing his back pocket.

A very large black and tan goat with a dark beard and an enormous set of curving horns wasn't surprised or intimidated in the slightest by v. B.'s sudden reaction. He seemed to be used to such human behavior. He stood nose up, limpid brown eyes staring appealingly through their oval pupils at the soldier. The goat held his ground; v. B. held his. It was what they call in Texas a Mexican standoff.

Then a pretty waitress sauntered over to take our orders. She seemed hardly to notice the uninvited intruder. "Beat it, Billy," she said with a cursory glance in the goat's direction.

When the beast failed to respond and demandingly shoved his muzzle again into v. B.'s pocket, she said: "Got your cigarettes in that pocket, do you? He sniffs 'em out just like a coon dog goin' for possum. Better give him one if you want any peace."

Von Bloeker pulled a cigarette from a pack and handed it to Billy; the town mascot, happily munching, strolled on to the adjoining table to intimidate the next contributor to his habit.

The waitress paused over her order pad and checked out our odd amalgamation of dress, part cowboy, part ordinary civilian, and part military. "You boys *all* AWOL?" she asked. "Or just *him*?" She nodded toward Eddie, who—except for v. B., always in full uniform—wore the most military components.

"Just me," Eddie said. "These guys are MPs, come to take me in. See? Takes four to one, I'm so dangerous."

"I'm Connie," the girl said, "and I'll help you escape. We haven't seen a soldier here since the start of the war. And I love 'em dangerous."

"Then I'm your man. Beat it, you guys, Connie here and me have got some serious military maneuvers to conduct."

And that's the way it was. We had stumbled into a soldier's dream. Bandera was the center of Texas's dude ranch country, and half a dozen cozy spreads surrounded the community like the spokes of a hayride wagon wheel around its hub. Young women from all over the country, wealthy and poor, beautiful and plain, but mostly wealthy and beautiful, came to winter or summer among the lovely hills, to pick pecans, ride ponies, drink from the lemonade springs where the bluebird sings, and otherwise make the best of bad times. Bandera wasn't the Big Rock Candy Mountain—but it was the closest thing in the real world to it. The good life wasn't flaunted, as perhaps it had been before the war, and most of the young cowpokes had hung up their spurs for the duration and were away in uniform, but the women of Bandera tried to make the best of empty saddles. The present ratio of young men to young women in Bandera County was something on the order of one to ten.

Doc, sparkle-eyed and smiling, came in with his new friend Rugh beside him.

Connie beamed. "Hey! He's cute! Is he with you?"

"That's the boss," Eddie said. "Doc Adams. And watch out. He's twice as dangerous as I am."

Connie bounced over to the newcomers and gave Rugh an off-hand nod. "Hiya, Emil." She smiled charmingly at Doc and took his arm, hugging it. "Welcome to Bandera."

Doc was beaming. I had never seen him so smitten. Was it Connie, the discovery of Rugh, or what Emil had told him?

"Boys," he said. "I believe we've found paradise."


Emil Rugh, Doc told us after introductions, was the newest enlistee into the Adams Plan. Typically, Doc had made an immediate assessment of the grizzled guano miner, approved of what he saw, produced his impressive folder of papers marked "Secret," and convinced the ruddy-faced Texan that he should enlist as our cave technical advisor. Not being one to shirk his duty to his country, Emil accepted. Another of Doc's intuitive first glance appraisals proved to be on the mark.

Having been completely briefed by Adams, Rugh told us that two caves competed with each other for being the best to meet our requirements. He chuckled when he heard about our adventure at the Devil's Sinkhole, but a wistful look crossed his face, the consequence of a flashback to some time past. "It's to give you the heebie-jeebies, that place," he muttered. "Dreadful perilous."

Then he told us that the caverns he had in mind were not like "the Devil's Own."

"You can trot yerself into these caves astandin' up on yer own two feet. Just like walkin' into a railway tunnel."

Rugh wouldn't commit as to which one had the most bats—in fact the advantage might change from one to the other week by week, he said, depending on migrations. But he allowed that at one time or another either one could hold the title for housing the most bats of any Texas cavern.

Emil didn't know it—no one did at the time—but that meant that his caves sheltered the largest concentrations of bats in the world.

"How many are there?" von Bloeker asked eagerly.

Rugh shrugged. "Wouldn't know. Never counted 'em." He winked at me. "But we've time aplenty to skedaddle on out there fer tonight's sally. You can count 'em yerself."

The white caliche road to Ney Cave wound through thickets of dark scrub oak crouched against bright green meadows—cattle country. A turquoise sky was flecked with hundreds of identical-sized white puffs of prairie clouds. We passed limestone ledges colored with orange and yellow lichen and clear slow-moving streams where turtles plopped off rocks at our approach—a young naturalist's delight. We pushed through several Texas bump-gates, structures remarkable to me. As the youngest, I was used to getting out and opening and closing the damnable ever-sagging primitive gates. These gates, with their simple automatic mechanism of cables attached to each end and to the top of a tall central pivot pole, one merely approached with the car and shoved with the front bumper without disembarking; all by itself, the gap swung wide and then magically swung closed after one had driven through. With half a dozen wondrous bump-gates behind us, we arrived at the ranch of Ben Gerdes, a cluster of barns and buildings surrounded by giant pecan trees. A little further on stood the ledge of limestone where Rugh said we'd find the cave.

The clouds were turning pink when we climbed up a trail well-worn by fifty years of guano miners and stood before the mouth. The entrance hole was about a hundred feet wide and thirty feet high, in no way impressive, only a dark mouth in the side of a bushy hill.

Rugh looked at the sky. "It'll be a half hour yet till the bats begin to hum."

It was late summer and hot with moisture-laden air. Masses of cumulus had built up in the afternoon, rumbling in the distance above a horizon of rolling hills. Humidity pressed down from the puff-flecked sky. A creek lay still in pools below the cavern, and frogs were starting to pipe. It was that time of day when briefly, just before sunset, the songs of frogs and cicadas blended into a wild cacophony of shrill screeches and deep croaks. From the hillside above the silent cave a wild turkey gobbled. Soon it would be taking its perch for the night.

The orifice of the cave stood black and open. Rugh sat on a boulder and we followed his example, speaking in hushed, expectant voices. Nothing moved at the dark mouth of the cave. A red-tailed hawk soared purposefully along the hillside and landed on a dead snag. It shuffled its feathers, seemed to doze, waiting, as we were. Shafts of sunlight searched through purple clouds; the clouds changed to deep rose and dark gray. Flashes of far-away lightning lit their rims. Still, the cavern mouth lay gaping, black and silent.

Then from somewhere indefinable we heard a sound, barely audible at first, an awareness only. It persisted, became a whisper, then grew to a murmur, a rustling like wind approaching through dry leaves. The sound came from beneath the earth, swelling, mysterious, the flutter of many restless wings, the awakening of the bats. The bats, as Rugh had said, had begun to "hum."

From the blackness of the open mouth a winged thing quickly flitted out and darted back. Another phantom flickered out and retreated. They were the advance guard, individualists whirling away from the mob that churned within the cave, darting away as if to test the outside air, reluctant to leave the dank subterranean labyrinths. Like a wisp of smoke hurrying from a kindled fire, a tendril of fluttering bats swept out and curled back. It was quiet again. The humming stopped. The colony had returned to the depths. Then a seething cloud swarmed out into the evening air, boiled at the threshold, and swept in again as if sucked back by a massive inhaled breath. Once more the black mouth gaped empty.

Several times the vanguard hovered at the point of emergence, like a delicately balanced cup teetering to spill. Waves churned out, boiled back in, unsettled, surges fuming at the mouth of a sea cave. At each false start the sound rose in a crescendo of fluttering wings and high-pitched voices.

Then suddenly, all at once, like a gush of primordial lava erupting from a fissure in the earth, the bats poured forth. The sound became intense as millions of leathery wings beat the air. They flowed from the cave in a compact stream, a heavy snake crawling from a hole and slithering across the sky. A mile away the stream broke into seething clusters; the clusters swarmed away to dissolve further as each bat broke off to seek its repast of flying insects.

The red-tailed hawk went to work. It launched from its perch, flapping easily toward the column. The mass veered away slightly as the large bird entered and went through, the swirl opening ahead and closing behind, so it seemed as if the red-tail was surrounded by a clear, impermeable capsule. In the midst of the bats, the hawk merely opened its talons, reaching out of its invisible corona into the mass, and pulled in the first bat it contacted. It couldn't miss. The hawk flapped over to perch again and picked at its prey. Presently the red-tail was joined by a couple of falcons; later, as darkness fell, two great horned owls took over.

For three hours the bats continued without pause to emerge

from the cave. It was an endless river of bats, a huge artesian spring gushing from the earth, its source unseen and apparently inexhaustible. It made an interesting basis for comparison, I thought. It has always been difficult for me to grasp an appreciation of numbers. I can barely understand the *value* of a million dollars in the things it will buy, but how does one comprehend the *volume* of a million actual dollar bills? How big a pile is ten million? Twenty million?

It is a stream of bats, each leathery wing a one dollar bill, carried by a whirlwind, swirling from a vault; a stream twenty feet in diameter, a fast-moving river of worn, fluttering banknotes that flows without slackening for three continuous hours.

"Count 'em," Emil said to von Bloeker, and he laughed as if it was the biggest joke he'd ever heard.

Three hours passed. The bat flight was tapering off and came now only in sporadic waves. I had wondered why Doc brought a newspaper tucked under his arm. Now he proceeded to fold it into a triangular hat.

"I want to see what it's like in there," Doc said.

While v. B. and Williams pumped up Coleman pressure lanterns, Doc began to strip off his clothes. We looked at him in amazement. Had he finally gone completely 'round the bend? Carefully he folded his suit coat, trousers, shirt, and undershorts and hung them from a bush. Then, stark naked, he stepped back into his shoes, picked up a glowing lantern, and wearing the triangular newspaper hat like Washington crossing the Delaware strode toward the cave.

"I've got to fly to D.C. tomorrow," he said, "and that's my only suit. I'm not going to an audience of generals with my pockets full of bat shit."

The fact that he'd been wearing the same suit since we'd left California two weeks ago didn't faze him. He always seemed able to produce a clean shirt; with his bow tie, which seemed to be fixed permanently around his neck, he invariably looked dapper even in his wrinkled trousers and jacket.

Inside, bats hung in writhing clusters like bunches of animated grapes. The ceiling and walls were covered with small gray bodies. They clung to one another in a canopy three or four inches deep. "Those are the babies," Rugh said. "They stay behind. And when their mommies come back, somehow they find 'em again."

We clambered down a gentle slope and the inner chambers were nearly deserted now. Only a few stray bats swirled through our lights. Then we noticed the crawling vermin that occupied the floor, the tiny biting things that swarmed felt but unseen over the deep carpet of ammonia-laden guano and surged up onto our skin and into our clothes. The various external parasites of the bats swarmed over our bodies, biting and making our skin itch. Streblid flies and cimicid bugs, closely related to bedbugs, mites, and fleas, burrowed into our skin, crawled through our hair, and invaded our persons with a blush of tiny life that couldn't be turned off with a bath or simply forgotten after a shower. The small creatures became a part of us, and even after they were gone our skin itched and we had the feeling of things crawling.

Dermestid beetles walked through the guano, their larvae consuming the dead bats that through natural mortality dropped to the floor by the hundreds every day. Our feet sank to the ankles as we walked. Beneath us, Rugh said, the ancient deposits of guano were fifty feet deep.

Doc saw what he wanted to see, a truth he evidently felt was necessary for his report of personal researches, and we climbed back out.

Then we all ran down to the creek that sparkled clean in the moonlight, ripped off our clothes, and rubbed away the minute biting, crawling things, laughing at our own distress, at Doc's foresight in stripping *before* he went in the cave, and at the knowledge that we had accomplished the second phase of research. Yes, in this cave alone there were enough bats to bomb several cities—and still have a few million bats left over.

# 10

## *Ozro*

DOC AND HIS TEAM of bat hunters were forging ahead. But meanwhile the Adams Plan still lacked a committed sponsor in the Armed Forces. On July 10, six months after Doc's original proposal, Earl Stevenson of the NDRC, in spite of Admiral J. A. Furer's previous sarcastic putdown of the bat incendiary idea, again wrote to the coordinator of research and development for the Navy Department: "This idea was first presented to the President of the United States last January and has since been brought to the attention of various individuals and organizations, without, however, being finally disposed of in one way or another."

Stevenson's letter went on to describe the objectives of the project again. Then he put forward a most surprising idea, which had not been seriously considered before. As much as Doc deplored the lack of imaginative new thinking in regard to his baby up until now, Stevenson's revolutionary proposal, remarkable for its incredible lack of understanding of the basic principles of Doc's plan, would confound Adams.

> Dr. Conant [Stevenson's boss] in assigning this problem
> to my Section, requested me to determine in the first instance
> whether there would be any conceivable tactical interest in this
> idea. Conceivably bats could be released either from submarines
> or planes, and my purpose in addressing this letter to your office
> is primarily in connection with the first of these alternatives.

Stevenson's letter went on to describe the problems yet to be researched and concluded with the upbeat remark: "The NDRC is prepared to go into this matter in whatever detail may be desired."

The suggestion to release bats from submarines was a blind

alley that any biologist familiar with bats would have squelched forthwith. The idea did not take into account one of the most important principles on which Adams had based his concept—to release bats from planes, thus dispersing them widely over inflammable cities where they would have only one way to go—down.

There were three things very obviously wrong with the new notion initiated by Stevenson: bats released from the ocean's surface would lack the maneuverability and range they would have if launched from the air; they would not have the benefit of gradual descent and progressive warming, which would allow time to recover from a cold lethargic condition; and, if released from the sea, the bats would have a choice of any direction in which to fly. There was every reason to believe that under these circumstances, with the strangeness of a large expanse of water beneath them, they would have no way to orient themselves toward land. According to the law of averages, half would fly straight to sea, others would parallel the coast, and only a small percentage would head directly for shore.

Admiral Furer had no basis on which to evaluate the biological aspects of the suggestion, so his reply to Stevenson did not touch on these valid objections. Instead, the admiral rejected the plan on a basis that would enrage Adams. Furer's was the familiar old reactionary point of view that the method couldn't work because the incendiary bombs currently in use weighed two pounds, far too heavy for a half-ounce bat to carry. This, of course, was the problem being attended to at this very moment by Adams's chemists, Fieser and Young—the development of a powerful incendiary that would weigh about the same as a bat.

Still, in his partly misguided efforts to get some decisions, Stevenson did not confine his communications to the Navy Department. This had been a shot in the dark. Nor did Adams let the moss grow.

Doc saw his project, which he sincerely felt could turn the tide of the war, slipping away. With a barrage of letters, telephone calls, and personal visits, Adams put on the pressure. In response to Stevenson's and Doc's flurry of activity, correspondence on the long-languishing project began flying between different agencies.

F. L. Hovde, Stevenson's executive assistant, wrote to their boss, James Conant:

> During the past two weeks Dr. Adams has telephoned me periodically to report his activities in the promotion of his scheme

and to ask whether or not NDRC is proposing to take any action. I can't give you complete chapter and verse on Dr. Adams' activities, but he has reported verbally the following:

1. He has obtained a source of private capital to provide aircraft and civilian pilots, provided the Air Corps will allow such a venture.

This referred to a commitment from Jack Frey, president of TWA, that assured Doc his support. The idea was even more revolutionary and crazy in its way than the bat concept itself and didn't have a hope of going anywhere. The military would never allow civilian planes with civilian pilots to conduct an air raid over enemy territory.

Hovde's letter continued:

2. He has secured the tentative service of several well known civilian flyers who would be willing to form a unit, to set up headquarters in India, preferably Bombay where supplies of dry ice are available [a further reference to the scheme hatched up with Jack Frey's cooperation].

The next paragraph was surprising: it implied the Doc had found a way around his two detractors in the Chemical Warfare Service, Wiles and Kabrich (who was about to become a general).

3. Dr. Adams reports that Colonel R. W. Hufferd in the Office of the Chief of Chemical Warfare Service is interested in his proposal.

4. Dr. Adams saw Colonel W. G. Brown in the Office of the Chief of the Army Air Forces. Colonel Brown indicated that he thought Adams' proposal had more than the proposal to drop small incendiaries by means of small balloons. I believe Dr. Adams also saw Colonel Harvey Holland [also soon to become a general], who, I believe, has been interested in the balloon incendiary proposal.

5. Dr. Adams has gone ahead and designed a case in which bats with their incendiaries could be carried and dropped. Adams has prepared a cardboard model, the blueprints of which I enclose with this memorandum.

6. Dr. Griffin of Harvard University, who is the bat expert on the zoological side, together with Dr. Adams, is planning to leave for New Mexico to make preliminary studies at Dr. Adams'

expense. They are asking the National Park Service for permission to collect bats for their experiments.

Griffin, with his coveted connections at NDRC, prominent affiliations at Harvard, and a publishing background more important than von Bloeker's, was kept on the string by Doc as an authority of more distinction than his hard-working, more actively participating field biologist. Griffin's and Adams's plan to take bats from Carlsbad Caverns was obviously dropped in light of our recent discovery in Texas. There is no record of what the experiments might have been or if they were ever carried out.

Hovde continued:

> I would be greatly pleased if you and Dr. Stevenson would let this office have a definite opinion as soon as possible as to whether or not NDRC ought to interest itself in this project and go ahead with the promotion and prosecution of the experimental work. Perhaps you and Dr. Stevenson would be willing to see your Air Corps contacts and ask them whether or not they definitely wish NDRC to go ahead with this project and whether or not the Air Corps is really interested in Adams' proposal.

Conant replied to Hovde's letter with a scribbled memo that seemed to spell disaster for the Adams Plan. "Unless the Army Air Corps shows more interest, I think we shall have to tell our friends that we are out!"

Now the pressure was truly on, and Doc was frantic. Another scribbled missive was entered into the files of NDRC—unsigned and unaddressed:

> Adams called to say the following:
> 1. Col. Harvey Holland, Chief of Personnel, Army Air Force, wants to go ahead—to drop his connection with incendiary problem.
> 2. Jack Frey, Pres. T.W.A., has 14 stratoliner pilots ready to carry bats.
> 3. Holland will take Adams to Col. O. A. Anson of Air Staff.

Without knowing the context, the first statement is loaded with ambiguity. Was Holland referring to the bat incendiary or to the balloon incendiary, the other project on his agenda? Did it mean that the Air Force wanted to move ahead with the Adams Plan or drop it? Paragraph three seemed to indicate Holland's readiness to assist Adams, a step forward.

At last the issue was resolved when Brig. Gen. H. M. Mc-Clelland, director of technical services for the Army, wrote a perceptively brief communication to the NDRC. It was a short memo, but the gist was all *go*. "Before deciding as to whether or not any use is to be made of this method of scattering incendiaries, I believe it is desirable to verify some of the claims Dr. Adams has made."

General McClelland suggested a series of static tests with the prototype small incendiaries now on the verge of production by Fieser and Young. For this purpose the tiny newly designed bombs would be placed by hand in various areas where bats could be imagined to roost and the resultant fire-starts would be tabulated. Curiously, it seemed to be taken for granted that all of Doc's claims for the performance of the bats were valid; at this point, only the effectiveness of the new incendiary was to be verified. McClelland's letter continued:

> If it appears that a large number of fires in highly inflammable structures can be started in this way we can then go to the next step of dropping "carriers" from aircraft.
> I don't know if it is appropriate for me to suggest that these initial tests be carried out by NDRC. If it is, I request that such tests be made.

With the director of the Army's Technical Services behind him, Doc now had the military wherewithal to charge ahead. It had been seven months since his letter to the president, and Adams was impatient.

"We're going to get caught with our pants down," von Bloeker said. "Fieser's way ahead of us in the development of a bomb. If his tests pan out like he says they will, the Air Force is going to be on our backs to see some stats on our bats. And we're going to be sitting there with egg on our faces."

"What are you talking about?" Doc said. "We've got bats coming out of our ears."

"Yeah, now we know where to find them, but we don't know beans about their hibernating habits. We've got to run a series of tests. That's next on our agenda. But I'm a field man, an old-time naturalist, not an experimental biologist. We need the help of a different kind of guy, a slide rule boy. I don't know one end of a slide rule from the other, and all you can say about this bunch of jokers you've picked up that you call your 'team' is that they try hard, and they're loyal."

"Just one minute . . . !" Doc was getting red. He wasn't used to such outbursts from his head field biologist. "We've got a fine bunch of men here. I won't have you talking them down."

But v. B. was feeling the pressure and wasn't about to back off. "Oh, I'm sure they're all great at what they do, but we just don't happen to need any more lobster fishermen, coal miners, kids just out of high school, and hotel clerks! What we *do need* is a guy who can tell us just what makes a bat tick!"

The anger that v. B. was getting off his chest was due to the frustration he felt about how to arrive at the scientific answers he knew we must have—how to induce a bat to enter into artificial hibernation and what conditions were required to keep its dormant body in a state of suspended animation, then bring it out at the snap of the bombardier's fingers as an active, vigorous bomb carrier. He knew that to answer these questions we needed a highly qualified physiologist to orchestrate the studies, and he saw no move on Doc's part toward getting such a person—or even acknowledging the need.

We had the practical expertise to do the legwork; even our inexperienced team of nonscientists, with a little help and guidance, could carry out the nuts and bolts gathering of information and amassing of facts, but the supervision of a trained mind was necessary to tell us what data to collect and then draw conclusions from our statistics and put it all into perspective.

To v. B.'s surprise, Doc cooled off and nodded as if he'd been the one to think of it. "Right! Find us a physiologist, then," he said, and charged off to see how his chemists were faring.


Louis Fieser had been busy. A few weeks after von Bloeker's appeal for help, the chemist presented Doc with a tiny new incendiary device which fit all the specifications imposed by the weight-carrying limitations of a bat. We had determined in the dirigible hangar that a bat weighing 10–11 grams (roughly 1/2 ounce) could carry a load of from 15 to 18 grams, or nearly half-again its own weight. Fieser handed Adams an inflammable celluloid case filled with the new incendiary material—napalm ( jellied gasoline)—that along with its igniter weighed only 17.5 grams.

The chemists had switched from white phosphorous to napalm as the inflammable constituent because it was far safer to handle and they found its combustible qualities adequate. Fieser had been leader of the team that invented napalm; in describing the compound, he wrote: "To [a gel] made from aluminum *nap*hthenate and aluminum *palm*itate, I gave the name Napalm." Napalm was not yet in general use by the Air Force; it was first dropped in jettisonable fuel tanks from fighter aircraft in the Pacific on October 22, 1944. But once ignited, a small amount of the material burned with an intense flame; as it heated the gelled gasoline ran down into cracks and hard-to-get-at places, where it was very effective.

Time-controlled ignition was accomplished in Fieser's first bomb with a small chemical igniter (picture the head of a match) placed at one end of a tube containing a compressed copper-plated spring with an attached firing pin. The spring was held back in cocked position by a thin steel wire. The device was activated by injecting a solution of copper chloride which ate away the steel holding wire but wouldn't touch the copper-coated spring. With a 30 percent solution the chemical eroded through the wire, setting off the igniting device in twenty minutes. By changing the strength of the steel-eating chemical the time of ignition could be adjusted to precise intervals of up to several hours.

"This simple chemically activated time-control device will get us through the initial testing phase," Fieser told Doc. "But it'll never do for an actual operation, far too half-baked for that. Difficult to arm and apply a safety mechanism. We'll probably eventually need something fully mechanical. But to produce that, with all the functions it will have to perform in the size required, will take more development time."

Doc nodded. "You've made a big step forward," he said. "We'll make a note to Chemical Warfare of the stopgap nature of the time-control so we don't get challenged by its shortcomings. In the meanwhile let's get a good idea about where we're headed with its replacement. That'll be their first question."

Fieser agreed.

A short time later, in a letter describing his progress with the bat bomb to NDRC, Fieser got off the track and let his own imagination run as wild as Doc's:

> One new idea on which I would be glad to have you get the opinions of our saboteur friends is to design a modified H-2 Unit [his nomenclature for the new bat bomb] having a clasp for its easy attachment to the tail of a rat. I understand that rat catching is a rather common art to many Europeans, and the idea, of course, is that this would provide a means of sending incendiaries into well policed factory and dock areas.

While Doc was attending to the development of the incendiary and its accessories, von Bloeker and I took a ride with Emil Rugh in his old pickup. The cab smelled like the depths of a bat cave. Guano from many trips had leaked from sacks into every nook and corner. Inside the glove compartment an inch of pellets was mixed with maps, old Kleenexes, rusty pliers, a dirty coffee cup, ancient receipts, a half-full flask of Southern Comfort, a box of .30–.30s, and a stained spoon. It looked like the inside of a pack rat's nest. An old set of coveralls hung from the deer rifle rack behind the seat. Holes in the pockets dribbled little brown turds that resembled dirty grains of rice, and the pungent dust of crushed guano sifted down with every bump, swirled through the air vent, and clouded the cab. Windows wide, we drove southeast from Bandera through the outskirts of San Antonio, east toward New Braunfels, then circled north through the settlements and neat ranches of generations of Texans of German ancestry.

Eventually we arrived at the hill country ranch where we were headed and Bracken Cave, a slightly more imposing hole than its sister, Ney. Emil told us that he'd been digging out around twenty tons of guano per year from this cave and hadn't yet dented the main supply. In places, ancient compacted deposits lay in unknown depths; he merely skimmed off the top strata of yearly accumulation.

The cavern was approximately the same overall size as Ney. Unlike the complex series of interconnecting vaults and passageways of the great caverns such as Carlsbad, Bracken and Ney both were simple corridors about 1,000 feet long, widening into chambers 30 to 50 feet high and 40 to 100 feet wide. Rugh's predecessor in guano extraction had chipped a vertical shaft through the limestone from near the cave's end 120 feet up to the surface, the most convenient way to hoist out sacks of fertilizer.

The first thing that v. B. and I noticed was the colony of predators that hung around the cave's mouth, depending on the bats as a food supply. In addition to a complement of raptorial birds similar to those we had seen at Ney, there were half a dozen raccoons and at least one family of hog-nosed skunks, a species that interested me greatly. With their pure white backs and black underbellies they were most striking animals; these undisturbed and therefore tame individuals that lived in grottos near the cave's mouth seemed disinclined to discharge their scents and could be approached and observed from close range. Beautiful ring-tailed cats lived in the rocks. They were more secretive, however, and we saw them only rarely and always in lights at night. Other interesting residents were the rattlesnakes that on sunny days lay out on warm ledges around the cave's wide mouth. We left them alone and avoided the areas of their dens. Other species of snakes, some of colorful beauty, also lived between boulders around the sink into which the cave's mouth opened.

Here at Bracken there seemed to be even more bats than we had seen at Ney. Again, the evening exodus took over three hours of continuous outpouring to empty the cave.

On our way back to Bandera, Rugh took us to another guano mining location—Frio Cave. Here in a small colony separate from the huge masses of free-tailed bats that rivaled the other caves in their millions v. B. discovered a rare species of bat never before reported from the United States, called *Mormoops*. It was quite large as North American bats go and like so many of its kind had an incredibly ugly face. Fold upon fold of furry skin overlapped between eye and blunt nose, giving it a monsterlike visage. It was even uglier than Flamethrower, I thought. Again, like the rare bat we had discovered in Arizona, *Mormoops* was of no interest to us as Adams Plan investigators, but of great fascination to us as students of bats in general. Later v. B. would write up these discoveries in the literature of mammalogical science.

A crumbling stone structure stood near the mouth of Frio Cave, the remains of the kiln where bat guano had been leached and dried to make saltpeter, a constituent of gunpowder, during the Civil War—bats had long ago made their contribution to human combat.

Shortly after we visited Bracken Cave and decided it would be as good as Ney for the collection of as many bats as would be needed, v. B. returned to Los Angeles to get on with the urgent necessity of finding a physiologist.

Through his connections with the Allan Hancock Foundation at USC, across Exposition Boulevard from the museum, von Bloeker was introduced to Ozro B. Wiswell, who had just earned his doctorate in physiology with a thesis involving research very much parallel to that required by our study. Wiswell seemed to be just the right man for our inquiry. He was interested in the scientific challenge offered by von Bloeker, but as a fresh new doctoral graduate in experimental physiology, about to be drafted into the Armed Services, he had his sights set on a career in a medical application of his education. The human problems connected with flight particularly intrigued him, and there was a place for his interest in the Air Force. Besides, he had legitimate expectations of entering the service as a commissioned officer; his classmates were being enlisted as lieutenants, even captains, and it was only natural for him to expect the same.

V. B. explained the dilemma to Adams, and Doc requested his adjutant, Bobby Herold, to arrange a private audience with the reluctant Wiswell.

Doc much preferred to have the members of his team join by their own choice. He didn't want to have to go to the higher echelons of military command and get people assigned against their wishes, though no one doubted that he could make it happen. It would make for an unhappy crew, and Doc didn't want that.

For the occasion of Wiswell's interview, true to his wily promoter's heart, Doc took extraordinary care to create an aura of patriotic grandeur. To Doc, the end justified the means, and the goal he envisioned was nearly holy. If we needed Wiswell, he'd resort to any duplicity to get him. With his letters from the top echelons of government requesting cooperation, Doc had no trouble arranging for the temporary use of an office at nearby Santa Ana Army Air Base. There behind a door freshly marked with a discreet placard "Secret" and guarded by an impressively starched representative of the military—Fletch in his finest Marine Corps blues—Doctor Adams sat behind a desk with an unfurled American flag draped behind him and received Doctor Wiswell.

Exactly what transpired behind the secret door was known only to the two who participated. In spite of his most clever efforts to eavesdrop, Fletch was unable to overhear a single word. But when Wiswell emerged two hours later, he did so with shoulders back in patriotic pride—and the promised military rating of Ozro B. Wiswell, Master Sergeant (Acting).

I was proud of von Bloeker's and Doc's choice for the position of unit physiologist. Wiswell had a warm personality with a wry sense of humor. He obviously had the credentials for the scientific work required, but the aspect of the man that pleased me most was that he *looked* even more like a scientist than the snooty Fieser. He was small, on the portly side, and the heavy horn-rimmed glasses with thick lenses he wore seemed like a caricature of professional studiousness. The top of Wiswell's head was as smooth as an egg and nearly as white, and in a perfect circle around it a fringe of hair looked as carefully trimmed as a friar's tonsure. He spoke with impressive technical jargon and uncondescendingly included even the most lowly of us in this erudite patter, just as if we were his scientific equals.

Wiswell never said "bat shit," for example.

The first time Eddie Herold heard Wiswell say "defecation" in reference to that physiological medium so familiar to us all, he asked, "What's he talking about?"

"Shit," I said, as proud of my own knowledge as of the superior scholarship of our lettered new member. "He's talking about bat shit."

Eddie, being less impressed with the scientific world than I, retorted, "Well, why in hell doesn't he say so?"

One day, shortly after Wiswell joined us, as I lounged in the sitting room-cum-reception of our barrack-office at the Adams School bungalow, I saw through the window a vision striding up the drive—a young woman of incredible beauty was coming our way. My first impression was that she must be lost and seeking directions, then I realized that she doubtless represented a new conquest of the irrepressible Eddie. Unlike Eddie's usual visitors, however, who gave the impression that he'd picked them up off the street or draped over a bar stool after midnight (as, of course, he had), this one radiated a distinct impression of style.

Sure enough, she came directly to our door and rapped lightly. I let her in and hurriedly removed a stack of newspapers and magazines from a chair so she could sit. "Just a moment," I said. "I'll call him."

I couldn't believe Eddie's good taste and fortune. I was utterly smitten by this girl in her cultured wardrobe of skirt and sweater conservatively draped on a great figure. And her face—her hair— well, it was almost too much for my young blood.

"Eddie," I shouted through a draft of pleasant smells. "Someone beautiful to see you."

I knew he had been out to the wee hours and was still asleep and probably hung-over. "Damn!" We heard him grumble from the sleeping quarters. "Who is it?"

The vision of loveliness looked surprised. "Is Ozro here?" she asked.

"Ozro . . . ?" I mumbled in numb stupor.

"Yes. Ozro Wiswell."

"Oh, *Ozro*!" I had known the professor only by his surname.

"I'm Viola Wiswell, his wife," the vision said.

My jaw dropped. His wife? *Our* Wiswell? The one in thick glasses with the friar's haircut? My esteem and respect for the little physiologist leaped almost to reverence. And to think, he looked like a monk!

# 11

## *Osaka Bay*

AT ABOUT THIS TIME, Doc pitched up with a several-month-old copy of *Harper's Magazine* under his arm. He was bubbling with excitement. "This is it!" he said, striking the folded magazine emphatically with the back of his hand. "The most important article ever published!" He looked at us seriously, oblivious to his penchant for hyperbole. "I was sitting in a barber's chair leafing through magazines and there it was—a blueprint of what we must do. It's almost mystical, I tell you. A virtual *mandate* from above, as if this piece has been written expressly with my plan in mind. And to think! It slipped past me until now."

The article that so much engaged his attention did, indeed, seem to be everything he said it was.* It proposed an incendiary air raid on the industrial cities that lay in a crescent around the edges of Osaka Bay.

"Within this area," Adams read from the article with boyish enthusiasm, "are located about one half of Japan's heavy industries, including ship-building and the manufacture of motors, engines, and railway equipment, as well as a major portion of her chemical, electrical, textile, and machine-tool industries."

The article said that the area had undergone a huge increase of workers in the war industries and the present population of Osaka, Kobe, Kyoto, and their suburbs was around seven million, of which three-fourths of the workers lived and worked in paper-and-plyboard houses packed together almost wall to wall.

"Congestion [in Osaka]," the writers said, "approaches the unbelievable. Its three and a half million people, five hundred thousand buildings, seven thousand factories—not counting innumerable

---

*Charles L. McNichols and Clayton D. Carus, "One Way to Cripple Japan: The Inflammable Cities of Osaka Bay," *Harper's*, June 1942, pp. 29–36.

home industries—are crowded on the mud-flat delta of the Yodo River."

By statistical model, the writers calculated that combustible coverage in the 25-square-mile area of central Osaka was 80 percent, as opposed to 15 percent for the modern cities of Tokyo or London.

The authors described a typical Japanese house in the district, the home of Toya Miyaki, which had been visited just prior to the outbreak of war. The picture they drew was of a structure built almost entirely of combustible fish-oil-soaked paper, fiber mats, bamboo, and timber. "The only objects of household furnishing not a hundred percent combustible were a few dishes, the medieval brazier, and the equally primitive bath heater. The big family tub was made of wood."

In such a congested neighborhood, "crowded with buildings from the bank of one canal to the next, with only shoulder-width runways between, the chance of the bomb starting an immediate fire is just about as good as if it fell into a full waste-paper basket." Because of the extreme danger of fire, they said, "Osaka has a large and experienced fire department. It also has a wind that blows almost continuously, varying in direction with the seasons." The city was studded with hundred-foot-tall observation towers that stood above the expanse of roofs all over the city. A fire would be spotted immediately, and primitive man-drawn pumpers, hose carts, and chemical wagons would race the wind to keep a single two-pound bomb from burning several acres.

Adams read on with uncontained excitement: "If two fires started in that district they would have to split their force and attack the second, with a diminished chance of success.

"When an American asked an Osaka fireman what his company would do if it had three simultaneous fires on its hands, he said, 'I don't know. They only teach us to deal with two fires.'"

The authors contemplated an air raid by a single B-17 or B-25 bomber carrying a conventional load of 2000 two-pound thermite-magnesium incendiary bombs (they did not know about bat bombs, of course). They calculated that such a raid would cause the Osaka fire department 1,200 immediate problems—and because of the differences in structures each problem would be three times more serious than a fire in London.

"Listen to this," Doc chortled: "In 1910 a woman [in Osaka] knocked over a cooking brazier and eleven thousand homes were destroyed despite the fact that it was raining."

The authors figured that five planes over Osaka would do the job, only one plane over Kyoto, and Kobe could be covered by two planes. The industrial plants that were not destroyed could not function without their homeless workers, and "the feeding and sheltering of a couple of million destitute workers—and there would be nearer four million if Kyoto and Kobe could be burnt at the same time—would place Japan in an appalling dilemma. Her only reserves are those she has built up to supply her invasion armies."

The authors made the point that loss of life would be less than that already being caused in Europe and the Pacific by demolition and fragmentation bombs. "In Osaka the canals can be a refuge from fire and the tidal flow is sufficient to keep the water from becoming unbearable. In some of the slum sections of Kobe and Kyoto where there are no canals the suffering that an incendiary attack would cause is terrible to contemplate.

"But the fact remains that this is the cheapest possible way to cripple Japan. It would shorten the war by months or even years and reduce American and Allied losses by tens of thousands."

Tears were streaming from Doc's eyes when he finished reading the article to us. "If fourteen thousand conventional incendiaries could do even half of what these men believe, can you imagine what a million bat bombs would do? We've got to get cracking," he said, wiping his eyes with unabashed emotion. "Because every day we lose, Americans are losing their lives."

# 12

## *Muroc*

ON MAY 3, 1943, W. C. Kabrich—Doc's off-again, on-again contact at the Chemical Warfare Service, now a general—following up on General McClelland's order to test the bat bomb, wrote a special order giving the Adams Plan his blessing: "It is requested that the National Defense Research Committee cooperate with the Chemical Warfare Service in promptly carrying forward the development of a very small incendiary for a highly secret project."

The request brought immediate response from officials at NDRC, who, on the basis of Kabrich's former lack of interest, had recently written several memoranda rejecting the Adams Plan as impractical. Now they found it embarrassing to carry on with appropriations and experimental work contrary to their own recommendations. Kabrich got them off the hook by suggesting that a great deal of confusion had come about because the highly secret nature of the project had made interagency communications difficult. The right hand, in other words, didn't know what the left hand was doing.

This satisfied the officials at NDRC, who dove into the work by placing Fieser's researches directly under their umbrella, complete with funding in excess of the modest amount the chemist had requested. Meanwhile, Adams was still supporting the bat unit from his private bank account, an increasingly serious problem which he was soon to try to resolve.

The Adams Plan had become an urgent reality, bona fide U.S. government–sponsored research, but along with this felicitous change in status, a more ominous drift also began to occur. We in the bat unit didn't notice. Perhaps Doc did—if so, he kept it to himself for the moment. But he must have begun to feel uneasy, the first vibrations of an undercurrent that would eventually become a tidal wave of adversity.

The ultimate authorities from whom authorizations, procurement, priorities for materials, and general oversight came were, of course, military men, with training, expertise, and general orientation of the same mettle. It was to be expected that their understanding of the chemical warfare problem was far more complete and sympathetic than their concept of the problems faced by the bat unit. Nor was it unnatural that, due to this propensity and because Fieser had in progress several important incendiary projects other than the bat bomb, their comprehension and support leaned more toward the chemist's work.

Complicating the situation was the fact that Fieser's personality sought the limelight. Doc's selfless efforts were honest—to get an important job done as quickly as possible. He believed passionately in the concept of the bat bomb, which he thought could quickly end the war. He wasn't particularly interested in notoriety and had no future stake in incendiaries or bombs of any kind. He wasn't a career bomb maker. To Fieser, accomplishment was also vitally important, but the spotlight that went with it was his driving force.

And so a tide was slowly building, evident only now in retrospect when one studies the mass of correspondence that originated from Fieser's hand. Of the many memos flying back and forth between departments, by far the majority referred to the incendiary aspects of the project, few to the biological problems. With a steady barrage of paper, Fieser kept his interests in the fore. It is difficult to imagine how he completed his researches—which he did very well—and at the same time devoted the hours he must have spent at composing long and comprehensive memos, loaded with winning military jargon and injected with a subtle but obvious slant toward self-promotion. Adams was seldom sent copies of these communications as he should have been, a devious tactic at best, and when he discovered that memos had been dispatched to which he should have been privy, as he inevitably did, his suspicions of hanky-panky must surely have been aroused.

Doc's more flamboyant methods of operation, on the other hand, although undeniably more colorful, were perhaps naive and simply not as effective in the unfamiliar climate of the military.

Fieser, as we would eventually discover, was seeking control. Now that the Adams Plan had become an important project with the personal interest of the director of Technical Services for the

Army and the cooperation of NDRC and CWS, Fieser began maneuvering to take over the whole operation—and because of the natural propensities of the military to go with the *bomb* side of this two-pronged research, he had the obvious advantage.

The upcoming Muroc test, therefore, would be Fieser's show.

As final refinements in the development of the incendiary capsule (identified as the H-2) came near, the date of May 15, 1943, about a month ahead, was set for testing at Muroc Dry Lake in the California desert, a present-day NASA space shuttle landing site. The area was chosen because of its vast smooth expanse of nearly white clay on which a small dark object like a bat or a small puff of black smoke from an incendiary capsule could be seen at considerable distance.

The original concept as requested by General McClelland had been to determine the effectiveness of the incendiary alone and, if the bomb proved itself, later to conduct a second test to determine the total effectiveness of the incendiary with bat vectors. But this directive had been modified to include the whole show at the first go. Items to be tested and evaluated were:

A. Operation of parachute cartons.
B. Ability or carrier to fly with bomb attached.
C. Fire-starting ability of the incendiary.
D. Functioning of safety and firing mechanism of the incendiary.
E. Dispersion of the carriers.

A four-page list of the materials required at the site on test day was sent by Chemical Warfare to all concerned. It enumerated everything from a B-25 bomber and an observation plane, ground transportation, radio communications, flashlights, incendiaries, and bats, to pencils, notebooks, and all the other incidental paraphernalia that would be needed. A refrigerated bat-carrying truck, to be built quickly at Wright Field, Dayton, Ohio, to Doc's design, would be dispatched upon completion to California. The entire bat crew was ordered to be present on test day, along with Fieser and his crew.

The only problem with this schedule was that the date had been set entirely on the basis of Fieser's work. When he declared that the H-2 incendiary would be ready for testing on May 15, no one thought of consulting the bat crew. Our readiness was taken for granted. After all, you had to design and manufacture an incendiary. Bats already existed in their ultimate form: all one had to do was catch them and use them—or so it seemed to the military minds who were running the show.

The biological unit, however, was far from ready. McClelland's last-minute change of orders, from a test of the bomb first and the bats later, threw a monkey wrench into our schedule. In order to meet this deadline, we would have to jury-rig everything. Nothing would be pretested. Wiswell had only begun his work by writing up a schedule of investigations and experiments to be done. No work had even started on accumulating the data from which he could draw some conclusions.

In the meanwhile, Doc had a long list of other imperative distractions to deal with. Now that Fieser and the incendiary researches were adequately funded, Doc sought the same for the bat unit. He was still paying for most of what we did out of his pocket, and his bank account was running low. Washington gave him the runaround and shuffled him from department to department. In spite of the fact that Chemical Warfare was the agency responsible for the whole project, officials there didn't feel that the bat side of the operation fell under their jurisdiction. NDRC, which had undertaken Fieser's financing, didn't come up with money for the bat branch, the other fork of the two-pronged project. On this fund-raising effort to Washington, Doc decided that my previously successful presentation of Flamethrower with the bazooka-man on his back was too flippant for the military brass and left us behind. I didn't know how lucky I was to miss seeing Doc during this depressing time in the capital. Eventually our leader was trotted off to talk to someone in the photographic section of the Signal Corps. The thinking was that they might be able to pay Adams as a technical advisor if a training film could be budgeted on the Adams Plan. Obviously someone was scratching the bottom of the barrel to justify spending on bat research. The training film idea was delicate because of the conflict between filming and secrecy—but the whole scheme was only a subterfuge anyway.

For the lack of a better offer, Doc accepted a fee of fifty dollars per day plus a small per diem allowance. It was hardly enough to dent his expenses in keeping the bat unit afloat. But with the press of more urgent affairs and the hope that something else would come along to ease the burden in the future, Doc took what he could get.

Money wasn't his motive anyway, and he felt that he could make do somehow as he had until then. He could waste no more time scrounging around in Washington; more important things were his immediate priority.

One of them may have been his feeling about what was going

on with his chief chemist. On April 20, Adams wrote again to President Roosevelt. The content of Doc's letter is not known, only the reply.

The president's secretary, the Honorable M. H. McIntyre, forwarded Doc's letter to Colonel Donovan, the officer who had responded to Adams's original letter to the president. In what could have been a facetious reference—a typed notation on McIntyre's memo, probably an acknowledgment of receipt by Donovan—the following notation appears:

> Letter from Lytle S. Adams, Penn Glyn, Irwin, Pa. 4/20/43, to the President, in further reference to his letter of 1/12/42 to the President, suggesting use of bats for frightening, demoralizing and exciting the prejudices of the people of the Japanese Empire. Encloses various papers and photographs regarding the plan.

Doc's colorful choice of words again successfully—if possibly with a snicker—attracted special attention to his correspondence.

William J. Donovan, to whom the president's original memo that had put all of this into motion had been addressed ("This man is *not* a nut") was now director of the Office of Strategic Services (OSS, the present-day CIA). He replied to the president's secretary with a letter which, without Adams's correspondence to fill in the blanks, only allows one to read between the lines. After a summary of the steps already taken in the development of the Adams Plan and the progress made, Donovan said: "I am informed that Mr. Adams' idea has been thoroughly checked, and so far appears to have met all tests. The single test remaining is the important typical full flight test. Preparations for this are now underway."

Donovan's letter continues with more analysis, then concludes with this provocative paragraph: "Because Mr. Adams in effect asks for Presidential intervention, I respectfully suggest, if you have not already done so, that you thank Mr. Adams for his letter and say that its contents are receiving consideration."

In other words, in response to whatever it was that Doc had asked for, Donovan was saying, "Stall him—brush him off!" Just what was this presidential intervention that Doc hoped for but failed to get? Did it have to do with Fieser, who Doc surely felt was a threat? That we cannot know. Scattered throughout the file of declassified materials in the National Archives are pages with the exasperating heading: "ACCESS RESTRICTED. The item identified below has been withdrawn from this file. Authority of C.I.A."

Doc's letter to the president is among these items.

But Doc had one more mission he hoped to accomplish in the capital. Now, with all the urgent problems pressing and an important test deadline to be met, Adams took off on a screwy tangent that might cast doubts on the president's favorable analysis of his mentality. Although the various Washington departments had failed to come up with adequate funding for Adams, he was provided with a courtesy military staff car and driver to shuttle him around on his fruitless quest through the city. The driver was named Patricio Batista, and he and Doc enjoyed an immediate rapport. Patsy cottoned on to Doc's style straight off, and wherever Doc had an appointment, his driver parked in the most prominent empty space—usually signposted "No Parking at Any Time"—hustled around to open Doc's door, and preceded the little man into the building, opening doors and hurrying ahead as combination guide and major-domo, projecting an image to anyone who saw them coming that royalty had arrived. Doc liked Patsy's style, and this appreciation contributed to the new relationship, but it was a certain facet of his driver's prior life in the private sector that intrigued Doc even more.

On their rides through the city, Patsy entertained Doc by recounting his experiences as driver-cum-enforcer in the employ of Chicago's most famous gangster, "Scarface" Al Capone. Who knows why Doc felt a man of Patsy's background would make a valuable asset for the bat unit? Surely Adams didn't feel he needed protection, and things hadn't gotten so bad with Fieser that he wanted him rubbed out. Patsy's strongarm methods might have worked in Chicago, but they wouldn't help to collect debts owed to Doc by the United States government. Perhaps Doc merely saw the staff car and Patsy as a desirable package that he was getting used to and very much coveted. After all, it seemed that in Washington, D.C., every officer in the Armed Services from the grade of major on up had his own staff car and driver. Why shouldn't Doc?

The old Buick back in California was getting mighty tired. Not only had it become rather shabby to look at, having suffered at the hands of a dozen drivers of various skills, but its parts were wearing out one by one, and even with Doc's access to priority rationed items auto spares weren't always easy to find.

There was something special about being driven around in an

olive drab staff car, piloted by a snappy driver, that appealed mightily to Doc. Now that he had this car and driver at his exclusive beck and call for a week, Adams didn't want to let the package go.

Doc spent another two days in Washington trying to wrangle a permanent assignment of car and driver. He didn't succeed in getting the car, but he did win the other half of the battle. I don't know whether or not Adams really wanted Patsy without his wheels or whether accepting him alone was merely a face-saving gesture, but that's what he got. And we now inherited Scarface's ex-right-hand man in the bat unit.

Except for size, for Patsy was only of moderate stature, Al Capone's man seemed to have everything else it would take to fulfill the bizarre requirements of his former role. He was brash, outspoken to a sometimes embarrassing degree, with a hard-stocky-square kind of physical toughness that you knew would stand up on two feet in any kind of a scuffle and be impossible to knock down. He had curly black hair and used words like "rub out," "gat," and "hit-man," just as a Chicago gangster ought to. Patsy wore his trousers so high above his hips that his crotch looked like a butcher's apron, and the gold buckle on his GI webbed belt made a shiny center of gravity mark closer to his ribs than his navel. He'd picked up one phrase of GI lingo that he used liberally intermixed with his Windy City gangster's dialect, the ubiquitous military expression of the time: "yer fuckin' A." The exclamation punctuated nearly every sentence and was useful for either positive or negative affirmation.

Patsy had smooth hands, with a huge diamond and gold ring on fingers that looked iron strong like the rest of his body; except for the curly mop under his starched overseas cap and his black eyebrows, there didn't seem to be another single thread of hair on his swarthy body.

Doc loved him. With his colleague and starboard escort, Bobby Herold, in tow, he had now added a port escort and the means for additional maneuverability. Henceforth, the three of them sailed like an armed convoy through the seas of military bureaucracy.

This was one explanation for Doc's interest in Patsy. Another, probably equally true, is that Doc was intrigued with Patsy as a human being. People fascinated Doc, and here was a kind he'd never known before. Not to *use* the man but merely to *know* him is a more charitable and doubtless a truer motivation. With all his Italian charm and curious background, Patsy rounded out Doc's growing army of oddballs—he played a valuable role and played it well.

Thus we gained another name to add to the muster list, to the reveilles and roll calls we never had.

Everything that *could* go wrong *did* go wrong at the Muroc tests.

The Texas caves were remote, and we didn't yet have a ground support setup in the state. The Carlsbad bat colony, however, was logistically easier to deal with, and we were able to collect enough bats from the national park to carry out the Muroc tests. Also, there was an Air Force base near Carlsbad; we had only to fly in with hand nets and carrying cages, requisition a car from the base, drive out to the cave, catch as many bats as we wanted, and fly them fresh and strong to where they were needed. The Park Service was cooperative and issued permits to take bats whenever they were required. Because the underground chambers where the bats lived were off limits to tourists, we could carry out limited catching in complete privacy.

Eddie and Bobby Herold and I flew down to Carlsbad to collect bats in the B-25 assigned for the tests. Because of their differences in physique, one could not confuse the brothers. Their faces, however, had uncanny similarity—identical white translucent skin with the same shadow of subcutaneous dark bristles on indistinguishable chins, noses alike, with a hook where a hook didn't belong, down near the bitter end, rosy dots on smooth cheeks like the red rouge of 1920s flappers, and straight dark hair parted with a sharp line dividing east from west, combed and stuck down smoothly with pomade, gave them the interchangeable faces of painted wooden soldiers.

The bombardier in the plane's crew was a young lieutenant named Tim Holt, who as a civilian movie actor had achieved stardom in a popular film called *Hitler's Children*, about the Hitler Youth, an organization of young men and women indoctrinated into fanatical worship of the leader. His father was the western star Jack Holt, and after the war Tim was to play the role of his life as Curtin in John Huston's cinema masterpiece *The Treasure of the Sierra Madre*.

Tim had a fascination with learning about new things. Because he'd never been around anyone with a natural history background before, he was interested in me. I saw that it was difficult for Holt in the service—there seemed to be an assumption with its attendant resentment that as a famous film star he achieved his military status through influence, and he inevitably had to break through this stigma to develop a relationship. But Tim had earned his bombardier's wings in the same school as any other flight officer and knew his job so well that he was trusted for this special test assignment. Following the Muroc tests, Holt was permanently assigned to the Adams Plan as executive officer to oversee the administration of those of us who were in the Air Force, as well as Fletch and Williams, who were on detached service from the Marine Corps.

On the way to Muroc with our bat cages full in the bomb-bay, Tim allowed me to ride in the nose cone, the clear plastic gunnery and bombardier's station that formed the transparent bow of the plane. As I lay on my stomach in the clear bubble, nothing but space around me from waist to head, I felt like Superman tearing through the sky. It was an incredible feeling that I have never experienced before or since, and I was mesmerized. All on my own I dove through clouds, winged into the canyons between their walls, watched the landscape moving past far below, and lost all connection with the plane that was propelling me. It felt as if I was doing it all myself.

I knew it was going to be hot at Muroc on California's Mojave Desert in mid-May, so we carried along enough ice to keep the bats cool. I didn't want to chill them so much as to make them torpid, however, so I frequently adjusted the ice to achieve the best results. I put pieces of ice wrapped in a towel into the bat boxes, took them out, and varied their sizes and output of cold strictly through intuition. It was a primitive way of doing what we would eventually design a sophisticated device to control, and I felt it was a foreshadowing of all the other half-baked methods I was afraid we would be required to utilize for this highly important test.

But as it happened, we never got that far. The Muroc tests were a bust from the first try. Fortunately, top brass did not attend, saving us the embarrassment of snickers from the sidelines. Doc and Fieser made no bones about the deficiencies in their official reports. We simply hadn't been ready. Even the incendiary was not fully perfected. Its fire-starting capabilities were impressive, but Holt pointed out that it was woefully lacking in dependability. If the igniter malfunctioned in the plane it could cause a disaster, and he wouldn't allow one aboard. Fieser ultimately agreed that some sort of safety device, perhaps a removable pin that would automatically activate at the time of launching, would have to be devised and incorporated into the unit.

The cardboard bat containment shell, which was a full-scale model of the one that would eventually be fabricated from sheet metal, blew apart in the plane's slipstream the moment it was launched, so experiments with the bat release device and the parachute which would lower the container were a write-off. It was back to the drawing board for all hands, and a new test was scheduled for late the next month when everyone optimistically declared we could be ready.

Doc made arrangements with a small manufacturing and engineering company owned by Bing Crosby, the popular singing star, and his brother Larry to fabricate the bat bomb carrying shell to his design. The five-foot-high sheet metal container, which superficially resembled an ordinary aerial bomb with its fins and cigar shape, would hold the compartmented cardboard egg-trays of bats with their attached incendiaries, along with environmental controls—cooler and heater—and a parachute with its deployment device.

Wiswell and I got a lift in the Buick with Patsy from Crosby headquarters at Del Mar, California, where we had been in conference with the engineers. Patsy was in his usual gruff mood of disrespect for the world in general. This time, his target was the chemist. Along with his plebeian manner, Patsy had all the keen character perception of a boy who grew up street-smart.

"Whaddya think of this *Doctor* Fieser?" he asked of the rear view mirror. "I don't think he's a *real* doctor, do you? I mean, not like Doc Adams, an honest to God genuine *Dental Doctor*. Ungh-ugh! A phony from the word go."

"He is not a *medical* doctor," Wiswell said. "If that is the category you require to fulfill the designation."

"What other kind is there?" Patsy snorted, oblivious to the fact that Wiswell held a doctorate in physiology. "Me, if I was Doc, I'd put out a contract on him. I had me a gat, I'd rub him out myself."

"You actually would?" Wiswell stared mockingly at the ex-gangster in the mirror.

"Yer fuckin' A."

"Come, come, Patsy," Wiswell said. "I believe that's mere hyperbole."

"You trust that egghead?" Patsy looked at Wiswell in the mirror. "Pardon the expression, Prof. Present company excepted."

"Tell me," Wiswell said. "What specific duties did you actually perform for Mr. Capone?"

I saw what was coming. Wiswell seemed to take great pleasure in exciting Patsy's evocations of his dubious erstwhile profession.

"I was his . . . " Patsy's brow wrinkled in thought. "What do you highbrow guys call it? His *colleague*," Patsy said. "Yeah! His *associate*."

"His disciple? An alumnus of the gangster school?"

"That's it. On the nose, Prof."

"Were you in fact a hit-man? Did you actually drive a get-away car on big jobs? Did you perform rub-outs for Scarface? Is that what you called him? Did you truly employ the concrete casket and utilize Lake Superior as a clandestine cemetery? Did you pack a gat? Were you an enforcer? A goon?"

"Yer fuckin' A, Prof. All of that. I was the big man's Number One. *Número uno.* Just like I'm Doc's Number One. And I got very bad feelin's about this Fieser bird. I got a feelin' I ought to break his knees."

"Well, if you did," Wiswell said, "you'd be performing a great disservice not only to a distinguished scholar and noteworthy chemist, but to the war effort, as well. My suggestion, Mister Batista, is to cool it."

Patsy nearly choked on a laugh. "Honest to God, Prof, you sure got a beautiful education. 'Cept you don't know yer ass from yer egghead when it comes to common sense. You can't even see what's written all across the wall. I learnt more in kindeegarten than you know about stiffs like Fieser. Too bad they didn't teach you some street smarts in the university."

The depth of Patsy's knowledge, as it turned out, was in its way more profound than the lettered Wiswell's.


The site chosen for the next test was Carlsbad, New Mexico. Carlsbad had the twin advantages of an operational base at the Air Force flight center and the close proximity of bats which could be tested while fresh-caught and not debilitated by handling and holding for an extended time. Even with Wiswell's guidance, we could not hope to solve the problems inherent in the forced hibernation of the carriers in only a month of research and preparation. These experiments were on the back burner, as it were, until the coming flight tests were concluded. For now, we could only pretend the hibernation problems didn't exist and use bats in prime physical condition for the tests with the hope that the results would still be valid after we'd completed the physiological experiments.

In the secrecy of the Crosby factory, located in converted rooms beneath the grandstands at Del Mar horse racetrack, the bat bomb carrying shells were assembled, complete with parachute, automatic barometric opening device, and a small warming unit to bring the bats out of hibernation prior to the drop. The performance of the new sheet metal shell would be an essential part of the Carlsbad test.

Doc had designed the container himself—the cardboard prototype was the one that had been torn to pieces by the slipstream at Muroc—and it was during the blueprint stage that Adams, in a private moment incidental to the greater work, took a family picture into a shop for framing. As he waited for the proprietor to cut the matt and put the frame together, Doc struck up a conversation in his ever affable way. As they talked, Adams watched the skillful way the framer went about his work and noted the adept use of his hands. Doc came out of the shop with the framed picture under his arm—and with a new recruit.

Andrew Paul Stanley was just the person to cut and glue the cardboard model of the bombshell with its many-compartmented accordion of paper trays. Later he would work with the Crosby Company to make the metal shells and their cardboard contents.

Each shell would hold 1,040 bats with their attached incendiary bombs. Each bat would fit snugly into a cubicle in a tray much as an egg fits into an egg crate. There would be 26 of these round trays about 30 inches in diameter in each shell.

The trays were to stack one on top of the other with the open sides down, all connected together with strings at the edges so that, when suspended from a parachute, the set of three-inch-long strings between trays held one tray above the other like an open accordion. When a shell was dropped from the bomb-bay of an aircraft, it would fall for a while like an ordinary bomb, tail fins guiding it down from the stratosphere in vertical descent. At a designated altitude (optimum for the bat's benefit to be determined by future testing), the barometric device—which was no more than an aircraft altimeter—would signal a parachute to deploy and at the same time set off a device that split apart seams on opposite sides of the sheet metal carrier, jettisoning the shell. The egg crate–like trays would then drop to the ends of their strings, hanging from the slowly descending parachute in a column some eight and a half feet long.

As the stacked trays separated and fell the three inches from tray to tray allowed by the strings, short wires attached to each little bomb would be pulled, activating the time-delay mechanisms of the incendiaries, and at the same time each bat would fall out of its upside-down cubicle onto the top of the tray below, which then became its launching platform.

Swinging down through the sky on a stable level surface, the bat could pause to orient itself before crawling off into space and flying down on its fiery mission. The safety pin of each incendiary would be secured to the bottom compartment in which the bat was housed; when the bat launched itself, it would pull the pin.

A fully fueled and combat-armed two-engine B-25 could carry 25 shells or 26,000 bat bombs. A four-engine B-24 or B-17 could carry many more, and a B-29 (not yet in use in 1943) more yet.

The concept of the contraption as a whole was novel, but except for the easily manufactured trays and sheet metal shells all components to make it work were standard off-the-shelf parts. For that reason, Doc was sure that Paul Stanley and the Crosbys could have enough shells ready to meet the test date.

Fieser, on the other hand, was under more pressure. He had to devise a safety device that would work without glitches, and he was dissatisfied with the original acid-eating-metal design of the time-delay device. He was working on a tiny model that would be entirely mechanical. Not only did these elements have to be designed, but enough units had to be built to conduct the tests.

In the six weeks between the tests at Muroc and the forthcoming one at Carlsbad, there was little we in the bat unit could do to push ahead our researches. We were stymied by General McClelland's directive that step one must be completed with satisfactory results before we could move on to step two. The mechanical aspects of the plan had to be satisfied before further bat research was authorized. Thus our future was up to Fieser and the Crosbys. All the bat unit had to do was to catch bats the day before the operation, attach Fieser's incendiaries—or dummy noninflammable bat bombs for most tests—and pack them into the Crosbys' shells. Meanwhile, it was a frustrating time of waiting. We played pinochle.

It had now been several months since my basic military indoctrination. Superficial as my training had been, I did not acknowledge the inadequacy at the time and thought of myself as a completely educated, full-fledged dogface. Well, almost. In one aspect of life's experience, in that realm of carnal lore which a soldier was expected to know and proficiently serve, I was woefully behind my peers.

Throughout high school, when most of my chums had steady girlfriends, I remained a girl-shy wallflower. When one young lady (who often was involved in my midnight fantasies but came no closer to real intimacy) disappeared from school under mysterious circumstances and reappeared a few weeks later just as enigmatically, I naively found it impossible to believe that this vision of my dreams could have been away, as was widely acknowledged among my more worldly classmates, for an abortion. My sex experiences were strictly secondhand; I heard about the pleasures of the flesh only in the lurid recountings of my chums, tales of romances consummated in the back seats of Model A Fords and customized hot rods. I had made a few frustrated attempts at courtships, I even knew two or three girls well enough that I could utter a few well-rehearsed words of conversation without falling over backward with embarrassment, but when those practiced words had been spoken, I was at a loss for more. Mine was a classic case, the situation of countless plays and novels, yet this made my personal yearning no less severe. In retrospect, I realize that once or twice sex was even offered to me on a silver platter, as it were. But I lacked the perception to know a seductive invitation when it was being made. Where are you now, Maida Johns?

Surprisingly enough, my initial experience, as horrible as it was, did not completely dampen my enthusiasm for all time. The big event happened shortly after Muroc, thanks to an encounter at the Rodeo Inn. I was in uniform and wore my sergeant's stripes. The regulation dress made confrontations with MPs easier to handle, although with von Bloeker's letter in my pocket there was no danger of a replay of my visit to the Fort McArthur stockade. It wasn't obvious that my rank was "Acting," and I was probably at the time the only virgin sergeant in the entire United States Armed Forces—or so I thought. I met a pretty brunette at the bar, we had a cocktail or two, and I managed a conversation. I even pulled together enough self-confidence to imagine that I was a barrel of laughs. Presently, she invited me to accompany her home.

The house was only a short walk away. On entering, she cautioned me to be quiet, giving the impression that somewhere in the darkness someone was asleep. If so, it didn't seem particularly to inhibit the girl. We sat down on the couch in the living room and necked. After my first introduction to this delightful activity went on for a while, I noticed that her clothes were beginning to peel away rapidly like feathers from a goose in summer molt. I was utterly surprised—and terribly pleased.

It was really happening! After all those fantasies, after all those years, at last I was going to get laid! Was it really as great as Eddie Herold made it out to be? Soon I'd know. She went to her adjoining bedroom; I saw her nude silhouette through the open door. I ripped off my shirt, flung off my shoes, stumbled out of my trousers, and followed.

In bed at last, warm soft skin touching, all mysteries there to be revealed, I realized that I didn't really know quite what to do. I tried first from an impossible position on my knees. She must have thought me kinky indeed.

"What are you doing?" she said.

I replied with utter truth: "I don't know."

As virginal as she looked, she didn't seem to lack experience.

She showed me. At last, we lay satisfied. It was wonderful. Then I rolled over. A light from the previously dark living room was showing from the crack under the door.

I reported this latest development.

She sat bolt upright. "Oh, damn!" she said. "My nosy grandmother can't mind her own business."

"My clothes are in there," I said meekly. "On the couch."

She got up with another expletive, put on a robe, and went out.

The half-heard sounds of unintelligible conversation slithered coldly under the door. I listened, heart pounding. What was going to happen? How deep was our sin?

She returned in a momentary glow of backlight as the door swung open and closed, my clothes bundled in her arms. Unceremoniously, she dropped them; my shoes hit the floor with an earthquake's crash.

I put on my uniform and walked out into the revealing brightness of the living room, profoundly remorseful.

A stone-faced woman sat on the couch glaring at me.

"I'm sorry," I said.

"A soldier!" she hissed with contempt vomiting from her lips. "I might have known."

All pride in my uniform vanished. I wished I'd worn my boots and Levi's. What would she have said then? "Welcome, cowboy"?

Her reply to my shrug was a red hot glare. It burned a hole through me, searing so deeply into my heart that I can still feel its heat. Fortunately, the wound left no permanent scar, and I doubt that the incident created a repressed psychological trauma in my soul. Yet since that night, I have never taken a sexual encounter lightly—there has to be something more than lust, and I have not the nature for a one-night stand. Perhaps I wasn't cut out to be a soldier—or maybe soldiers aren't exactly what they're thought to be, as much as they'd like to be.

# 13

# *Carlsbad*

THE CARLSBAD TEST was to be attended by an Air Force captain and a Chemical Warfare Service colonel, with orders to report results back to their superiors. Recommendations would then be made to General McClelland of the Air Force, the senior officer who had requested the experiments. Also present aside from the bat unit and Fieser's men were a stills photographer and a motion picture cameraman from the photographic unit of the Signal Corps, with which Doc now had his spurious relationship as technical advisor.

Doc may have been put off by the mid-grade level of attendance proposed by the Army and Air Force. The fact that there would be no official observers above the rank of colonel could have seemed to him like a putdown. At any rate, Adams advised his personal contact with the Navy, Admiral King, of the upcoming tests. King clued General Louis DeHaven, USMC, who showed up unannounced as an observer. As things would turn out, DeHaven, who was so unobtrusive we scarcely knew he was there, was our most important visitor.

We assembled with our various equipment at Carlsbad Air Force Base, then moved on out to the remote test site, a newly constructed but as yet unoccupied auxiliary air field complete with control tower, barracks, offices, hangars, and various outbuildings.

Fletch, Eddie Herold, and I drove to the site in jeeps with bats freshly caught from the national park. We would attach capsules to them for the various tests as needed at the site. Tim Holt with the fully crewed B-25 bomber and an observation plane were waiting on the runway when we arrived.

The first disappointment was that Fieser had been overly optimistic in agreeing to this test date. Neither his new mechanical time-control device nor the safety mechanisms were ready. He came, however, adequately armed with enough of the original napalm capsules and their chemically controlled firing mechanisms. While adequate for basic tests of fire-starting effectiveness, these lacked the dependability to be carried in armed mode aboard the aircraft. "Never mind," Doc said. "Most of the tests will be carried out with dummy capsules, anyway. We don't want to populate this part of New Mexico with fully armed incendiary bats flying wherever they feel the urge."

We began with an experiment to test the effectiveness of the Crosby canister shell. Fletch, v. B., Wiswell, and I loaded it with bats carrying the dummy noninflammable bombs. The black sheet metal casing with its load of 1,040 bats was hung in the bomb bay of the B-25 and flown by Holt and his crew to high altitude. The B-25, paced by the smaller observation ship, circled in the sky far to the south, then it straightened its course and headed in for the drop. Far away, through binoculars, we saw the bomb-bay doors open in the plane's belly. The plane closed the distance quickly. Now we were craning our necks, looking straight overhead. But the expected bomb didn't appear. We knew that Holt up there would have his eye stuck to the bomb sight and knew what he was doing, but he seemed to be overshooting the mark. "Damn!" v. B. said. "He's going to blow it!" Then, when it already seemed the moment to drop had passed and we were about to lower our binoculars, Fieser said: "Bomb away!" and we saw the black shell separate from the ship and fall toward us. The chase plane with Doc and a photographer aboard broke its course paralleling the B-25 and circled the falling bomb, following it down.

We on the ground watched it come toward us through our binoculars. Anything could go wrong, as we knew from previous tests. The black canister plummeted, rapidly losing altitude, and nothing happened to slow its descent. Surely it had reached the optimum height to deploy the chute—but from the ground it was impossible to calculate the altitude accurately. We began nervously thinking of places to take cover; the drop was precisely on target, after all. It was going to crash to earth right on top of us. Again, there seemed to be a screw-up.

"Stand by to get out of here!" one of the officers shouted. "It's coming straight in!"

Then at about 4,000 feet above us the chute blossomed and the trays deployed, hanging beautifully in a long swinging chain against the clear blue sky. Spontaneously we all cheered. A slight wind aloft carried it toward the north as it fell. Soon tiny motes began to flutter across the sky, flying in all directions, most borne northward in a fluttering clump by the breeze.

Von Bloeker watched for a moment, then shouted: "We're going to have to chase 'em. They're going to touch down miles from here."

We leaped into jeeps and with the observers—general, colonel, and captain—hanging on with white knuckles bounded wildly in the direction the bats were flying, driving across country, dodging around larger bushes, plowing through smaller ones head-on. The bats were being carried farther by the breeze than we had expected. They had been hard enough to see through binoculars with two feet planted solidly on the ground. From a jeep bouncing cross-country, it was nearly impossible to keep them in sight. After half an hour of chasing, we lost them. Then, as we drove over a hill, to our dismay we saw buildings ahead, a ranch headquarters. Still driving flat out, we hit a graded dirt road and rumbled across a couple of cattle guard grids. Houses, barns, outbuildings, and corrals were ahead. I glanced at Fletch, who was driving my jeep. He shook his head, shrugged, and swerved into the wide yard between buildings. A weathered rancher with brown blotches on his skin stood on the porch of the main house watching the three jeep-loads of soldiers and military brass careen through his gate and slide through a dust cloud to stop at the picket fence outside his door.

With what must have required the utmost control in the western pretense of nonchalance, he slouched sleepily against a porch pillar, looking out from under the sweat-stained brim of his Stetson, and coolly watched us disembark. The observation plane circled low, around and around, the noise of its engine and prop causing all sorts of agitation in the corrals.

A grimy general, colonel, and captain climbed out of the jeeps and slapped dust out of their uniforms. Bobby Herold slid up in another cloud of dust. Doc was still circling in the sky bothering the livestock.

Bobby approached the rancher, who was eyeing the plane with a great deal of mistrust. "Good morning, sir."

A nod. "Mornin'."

"Ah, did you see anything, ah, that you might call unusual flying around here?" Because of the secrecy, Bobby wasn't about to let anything out of the bag if he could help it.

"I see a noisy airplane." The rancher watched Doc's ship, still circling low.

"I don't mean that. Something, ah, smaller."

The rancher eyed Bobby warily. "Maybe."

"We're conducting experiments . . . " Bobby glanced around nervously, not quite knowing how to proceed. All of us now stood listening at the picket gate. "We're from the air base," Bobby glanced in the direction of Carlsbad. "You know, over there . . . "

A nod, acknowledging.

"The United States Air Force."

The rancher listened, unimpressed.

"Experiments with, ah—well, highly secret experiments. We didn't expect them, that is, anything, to come this far. Probably didn't. But if they did, ah, well . . . I hope we can depend on you to keep the confidentiality. You know, under your hat."

The rancher listened, shifted his weight.

Again Bobby probed the noncommittal air. "As I said—asked, that is—Did you see anything . . . ? Unusual?"

At last a slow drawl: "Like bats flyin' 'round in broad daylight? Unusual like that? What'd you give 'em? No-Doze?"

"Yes. No. You saw them, then . . . ? Bats?"

The rancher raised the brim of his hat, glancing up into the rafters overhead. "Like that one?"

Bobby looked aloft. "Yeah. Just like." He waved toward the men at the fence. "There's one here. Right on the porch." To the rancher: "Mind if they have a look?"

"Go ahead. There's another bushel of 'em flapped into the barn." He squinted up to the bat, peering down from a crack between a roof joist and the ceiling boards. It straddled the dark dummy bomb still attached to its belly. The rancher squinted closer. "Looks to be serving a black filly."

"Well, that's the secret. The point of this whole operation, this test I was telling you about. Can we depend on your discretion?"

"Listen here, young feller," the rancher said as if his patience could finally break. "I got two sons somewhere in Europe fightin' the Hun. If you tell me that what yer doin', however damned fool as it looks to me, is a military secret, nobody's goin' to get me to say a peep even by puttin' bamboo splinters under my fingernails and alightin' fire to 'em. You and these boys have a good look around as much as you like. You can have all your bats and their mounts back. I already got a few of my own and you can have them, too, if you want 'em. But I do wish you'd tell that blessed airplane to fly away and stop spookin' my livestock."

"Yes, sir. We'll get busy on that right away. And thank you very much. You're a great American." Bobby turned to Williams. "Get down to the jeep and get on the blower and tell Doc we'll meet him back at the air strip. Tell him he's spooking the hell out of this man's livestock."

The rancher grinned. "And when you're through with whatever you're doin', there's a pot of coffee on the stove and plenty of beer and soda pop in the Frigidaire, so you can wash down some of that dust before you leave."

Back on the runway, Doc had been in a dither until we arrived back with the bats we'd collected and the notes on the invariably inflammable places we'd found them. All the mechanisms of the container shell had worked perfectly, just as Doc had planned—and Adams's eyes sparkled and his cheeks were flushed with excitement. The success eased the burden on Fieser, too. If we didn't accomplish another thing at Carlsbad and stopped where we were, we'd have been way ahead.

We should have packed up at that point and gone home. Instead, the photographers said they'd like to stage a few setups for the cameras. They tried taking half a dozen bats loaded with dummy bombs up in the observation plane so they could drop them out and film them soaring down with their loads in flight, an exceedingly difficult, if not impossible, undertaking. To try to film a bat flying at 5 or 6 miles per hour from a plane traveling at over 150 was hopeless. We saw from the ground that they were getting nowhere in their endeavor. Then one bat, when it hit the fast-moving slipstream, broke a radial bone in its wing, spun to earth, and crashed onto the runway. Doc called the plane on the ground-to-air radio and broke off the exercise.

To confirm the earlier results, Adams wanted to deploy another dummy-loaded shell from the B-25, which took a couple of hours to prepare and get under way. A weather balloon rose in the sky and became invisible; with his tracking device a meteorologist told us that winds aloft were still and we could proceed to drop the bomb.

The mechanics went as before. This time there was less wind and the distribution of the bats flying under their own power was more definitive. We estimated their dispersal as accurately as possible in this bushy country and decided that for any future testing of distribution our original choice of Muroc Dry Lake, where the bats could be seen from great distances, would be the best site.

Then Fieser said he wanted the photographic record of bat bombs actually going off in various realistic situations, "with complete verisimilitude," as he put it—in other words, attached to the vectors. In the doing, he also asked the photographers to shoot some pictures of himself with the bats and their attached bombs. He was playing now; if there was ever to be a training film made, he wanted his face to be a prominent feature.

We, of course, sniggered at this bit of vanity—but what the hell, we'd made enough snapshots of ourselves going into and out of dangerous, adventurous-looking caves, so we could hardly fault Fieser for wanting a few pictures of himself with his spectacular creation.

It was this apparently innocent exercise that led to our first serious mishap. The bats that Fletch and Williams and I were fitting with live incendiaries for the photo session were cooled down to a semitorpid state. But it would take less than ten minutes on this warm afternoon for the chilled bats to heat up and become completely active, and we cautioned Fieser and the cameramen about the danger. Once we turned the bats with their inert fixed bombs over to Fieser, the bats became his babies, so to speak.

We attached a half a dozen unarmed capsules of napalm to half a dozen bats for Fieser to have his fun. We did not expect him to inject so haphazardly the chemical that would start eating the wire of the time-delay trigger. Once injected, the capsule became a ticking bomb, a firecracker with a short fuse.

Fieser put the corrosive copper chloride into the pencil (his nomenclature for the time-control device) of one capsule, into another, and into another, until all six were armed. The cameras snapped and whirred to record the preliminaries to the puff and flames. Then, chemicals still "ticking" within the pencils, all the bats simultaneously began to come to life.

"Hey!" I heard Fieser shout. "Hey! They're becoming hyperactive. Somebody! Quick! Bring a net!"

By the time I got there with a hand net, Fieser and the two photographers were standing with looks of awe, staring helplessly into the sky.

"Those pencils were set for fifteen minutes," Fieser said. "We've got to catch them again quickly."

We in the bat unit looked at each other with dismay. Fletch shook his head and got pinker. "When we locate those bats," von Bloeker said, "I'm afraid it's going to be by the smoke that leads us to them."

And so it was.

The airstrip control tower with its conspicuous structure was like a magnet to one bat, the barracks to another. Exactly fifteen minutes after arming, a barracks burst into flames; minutes later the tall tower erupted into a huge candle visible for miles. Offices and hangars followed in order corresponding to the intervals between Fieser's chemical injections. The conflagration wasn't meant as a test, but Fieser had confirmed the accuracy of his time-control device to the minute.

To get the entire picture of the events that occurred with such panic-inducing rapidity after this, I have to go back to the days preceding the event when arrangements were being made for our use of the new auxiliary field. The field was the brainchild of the commander of nearby Carlsbad Air Force Base and was to be occupied as a manned flight training station. Construction had been completed and personnel were about to move in, but orders to hold off on staffing pending our temporary use disrupted the base commander's plans. This did not please the commander at all—and when he was informed that *his* new auxiliary field was to be under the command of an Army officer of lower grade than his own Air Force rank and that the operations at the field were to be confidential and he wasn't even allowed in on the secret, he was doubly troubled.

He had made his displeasure evident when we arrived; even a contingent of guards to man the station's gates was granted only with extreme reluctance. Grudgingly, the Air Force colonel had to submit to the Chemical Warfare Service lieutenant colonel's request—and to his junior's order that he would not be allowed on his own field while we were present.

When the fires erupted, sending black pillars of smoke curling high into the sky, there was nothing we could do but sit and watch the flames eat up building after building. Quite unprudently, it had been decided that fire-fighting equipment would not be assigned— the result, of course, of the secrecy involved. It hadn't been considered necessary because no armed bats were to be used for the tests. With a crew of firemen hanging around doing nothing, or so it was thought, it would have been impossible to keep what we were doing confidential.

Back at the air base, the commander was alerted to the curls of smoke climbing the sky in the direction of his auxiliary field. Suspecting the worst, he arrived at the locked gates in company with three fire engines. The entire auxiliary field was by that time ablaze—fires not ignited by bats had leaped from building to building and started on their own. The commander stood between his fire engines and the still-padlocked gates, raging to *his* guards to let them in.

Our officers held a quick conference. There was nothing the fire fighters could do. It was clearly too late to quell the flames. Nothing could be saved: the blazing torch of the tower was already done for, and many buildings were now smoldering ruins. There was no point in adding to the physical damage by hurting the project itself—by compromising the confidentiality of what we were doing. If we let the strangers in, it would be impossible to keep the secret.

It took a brave lieutenant colonel to stride to the gates, order the guards away from the padlocks, face a raging superior officer through the chain-link wire, and tell him to go away.

"That's *my* Goddamned field," the colonel roared. "What the hell do you mean, 'go away'? Let this equipment in or we'll break down the gates."

But it was obvious, even to him, that the time for fire-fighting action had passed.

Our next request only added to the insult—a bulldozer to grind into the earth any charred evidence of what might have started the fires.

From the point of view of the ballistic feasibility of the Adams Plan, the incineration of Carlsbad Auxiliary Airfield proved something. But it also proved that this was a most potent munition and had to be treated with all the caution and respect due such dangerous hardware. More importantly, it very nearly spelled the end of the Adams Plan.


To say that Fieser was embarrassed would be to say a mouthful in a word. Not only had he shown up for the tests without the materials from his department that were to be tested, but his careless mistake had brought about a costly and humiliating accident. One might expect him to back off in discreet humility. On the contrary, the calamity prompted him to leap to his own defense, an unwarranted overreaction since Doc was keeping a low profile, Bobby Herold was successfully employing his utmost guile to smooth things over with the Air Force, and nobody was accusing anyone of anything.


Warren C. Lothrop, who was to become an important player in the story of the Adams Plan, held the title technical aide to Division 19, Office of Scientific Research and Development. It was to Division 19 that the chemical and bomb design aspects of the bat project had been assigned and to which Fieser reported.

In a memo describing his role, Lothrop wrote: "Division 19 has been handling this [the development of the bat bomb] in cooperation with Dr. Fieser because of [Division 19's] experience in problems involving delay elements." Although Lothrop was the man in charge of this important phase of the Adams Plan, Doc apparently had never met him, had never communicated with him, had never even been advised of his involvement. WCL (as Lothrop signed all of his memos) was, however, very close to Fieser. He was the one, for example, who increased the stipend Fieser had requested for his work on the bat bomb. A considerable correspondence had been carried on between Fieser and WCL, and eventually they came to address each other in memos with their first names, Louis and Warren. As early as April 2, 1943, WCL wrote a memo to SAC-6T, summarizing a meeting at the Pentagon attended by at least four top brass. The subject was the Adams Plan—Doc was conspicuously absent and evidently not even sent a copy of this important communication. Lothrop, in short, was a man Fieser was keeping close to home.

On July 2, 1943, following the Carlsbad tests, WCL wrote to SAC-6T and the Office of the Chairman, NDRC:

> Thought you might be interested in this informal report. Has the Air Force given a formal one yet? On June 23rd, WCL interviewed Dr. Fieser on the [Carlsbad] tests. LFF [Fieser] reported that a cooperative group of Air Corps, Chemical Warfare Service, Dr. Adams and himself had spent several days in the far West testing out Adams' plan.

The omission of General DeHaven, USMC, from Fieser's report speaks either for the unofficial nature of the marine's visit or for his unobtrusive observation of the tests. But he wasn't so lost in the background that Fieser didn't know he was there. His exclusion is difficult to explain, and, in view of later developments, Fieser's lack of mention of the general is ironic. Lothrop's account of Fieser's report continued: "These tests had shown that the bats were not as easy to catch as had been supposed, that they were more delicate than had been supposed, that they were much more difficult to cause to hibernate than had been supposed and that once in hibernation they were not as easily aroused as had been supposed."

These reports by Lothrop of LFF's conversation with him appear to be Fieser's pure fabrication. The bats had not been difficult to capture, and if Fieser meant that they were delicate because the photographers weren't able to toss them out of a fast-flying airplane successfully, that should have surprised no one. The hibernation tests still lay many weeks ahead; but in contrast to LFF's statement that they were not easily aroused from hibernation, it had been their quick arousal from a semitorpid state that had been the main cause of the Carlsbad fiasco. The whole subject of hibernation that Fieser attacked was yet to be the subject of research and was still scientifically speculative—although grounded in what we all believed to be workable parameters. WCL's informal report of his conversation with Fieser continued: "Furthermore, release of the bats from aircraft was an item which would require considerable experimentation. Some bats, if sluggish, plummeted to the ground, others if put out of the plane at high speed apparently had their wings broken."

Again, Fieser was using details from the photographer's misguided activities to draw unscientific conclusions. The releases from the container shells had gone off as planned. No one expected to throw unprotected bats from fast-flying planes. In the first place, Fieser was wrong; in the second place, he was not expected to comment beyond the chemistry aspects of the tests. Now he was making behind-the-scenes biological evaluations which were outside his expertise.

WCL, speaking for Fieser, went on to say: "Lastly, the bats were not able to carry the load expected (18g) but would carry successfully a load of 11g."

Had the chemist already forgotten the considerable success the bats had in carrying an 18-gram armed load into the buildings of the Carlsbad airfield? And that these had taken off from a position on the ground rather than from a more advantageous high altitude drop? He later contradicted himself on this statement by developing a 17.5-gram bomb which he considered ideal as a bat load. WCL, speaking for Fieser, continued:

> On the other side of the ledger, the bats, once properly gotten into the air, would act as gliders and covered a vast area, many of them not being located afterwards. Moreover they were found in some cases to have entered barns and to have climbed under the eaves of buildings. Because of the wide dispersion, the group did not try to run actual tests using an incendiary for fear of damaging private property.
>
> In the later stages of the experiment, there was a disaster in which hangars and outlying buildings of the small airport used burned down. The cause of the fire was never ascertained, but it served to discourage the group.
>
> A report prepared by Captain Wiley Carr and a Colonel at CWS, it was understood, had been sent to the Air Corps. This report more or less coincides with LFF's [Fieser's] own opinion and recommended that the experiments be dropped and that the idea

was probably impractical. No final decision had yet been made so far as LFF knew.

As shocking as it would have been to Adams (fortunately, he was probably never made privy to the above, nor to the following documents), it now seemed that his chemist was prepared to dump the whole project to save himself personal embarrassment over the fiasco he had caused at Carlsbad. Had Doc known, he would have called Fieser's undermining sabotage.

Lothrop continued his attack, stimulated by Fieser's claims, in official correspondence to a Colonel Millard F. Peake, of Technical Division, Chemical Warfare Service.

> From a recent conversation with Dr. Fieser, I have learned that tests were performed in the Far West sometime ago and that a formal report on the feasibility of the Adams' plan has been issued. I gather that this report is not favorable and that it is likely the idea will be dropped as impractical.
>
> If this is so, I think Division 19 would like to stop work on the special delay which was to have been part of the incendiary unit. Would you be good enough, therefore, to advise me whether there is further need of our continuing the development of this special element?

In a brief note to Fieser, addressed "Dear Warren" and written the day after his request to stop work on the time-delay, Lothrop seemed to take the decision to cancel for granted. "If the plan has been abandoned, as seems evident, I imagine you are through with this . . ."

He must have been surprised, then, three weeks later when Lothrop received a letter from Colonel Peake, speaking for his boss, flip-flopping General Kabrich of Chemical Warfare: "The development of a small time delay element for use on the incendiary used in the Adams' Plan should not be stopped at this time. The Army Air Forces have gone over the experimental results of the tests conducted in the West and have come to the conclusion that additional work must be done . . ."

Following the debacle at Carlsbad, Fletch and Williams headed for California by way of Carlsbad Caverns to collect bats for a high-altitude pressure test. The park naturalist suggested they meet a young man who was hitchhiking across the country visiting bat caves. The visitor's unusual itinerary was surprising enough; when Fletch and Williams learned his name they were astonished. Not only had they heard about Denny Constantine before, but they knew that Doc had been trying for months to get in touch with this peripatetic young man. They found him at the cavern entrance that evening, enthralled with a rapture that only a ratified fanatic could attain while staring at a black column of bats fluttering toward heaven.

This ghost who had materialized from the caverns was bound east in search of other bat caves, but Fletch and Williams persuaded him to drop his plans and accompany them back to southern California, where he'd come from. There the marines released their rare catch to Doc Adams. Doc enlisted Denny in the Adams Plan on the spot: Constantine enrolled in a nearby high school and moved into the Adams compound, where he was available to join the crew for emergency or major operations as school allowed. Had Denny been recruited as a full-time member of the project, he would have usurped my claim as youngest member of the team—he was my junior by half a year. Denny wanted to drop out of school at once, enlist, and get on with the bat project, but Doc seemed satisfied for him to maintain the status quo.

Adams was especially interested in Constantine's earlier studies with free-tails, wherein Denny had investigated the time required to make them torpid and how long it took to revive them at various temperatures, a surprisingly relevant experiment in view of the secret needs of the Adams Plan. Perhaps Doc's reluctance to encourage Denny to enlist in the Armed Services was because his new recruit was providing a lot of labor at the Adams School in return for a place to live and meals with Doc's sisters. Or, to be more charitable, maybe it was because he wanted to spare the young scholar a unwarranted interruption in his education. Constantine joined in many later experiments and collecting trips; but in spite of his new role as part-time bat researcher, Denny did not participate in the next test, which took place at Santa Ana Army Air Base, where there was a decompression chamber.

Fletch remembers the test as proving that free-tails could withstand the pressure and diminished oxygen of high altitude flight.

We put the 250 bats from Carlsbad into the chamber and simulated an altitude of 25,000 feet. We could watch the reactions of the bats through a porthole. They were hanging from curtains of burlap fastened to the ceiling. Then after a certain time, the pressure valve was thrown open and the air roared in, a rather inaccurate simulation of being dumped out of a plane nearly four miles up. The shock caused them all to fall down, but only a very few suffered any damage. That's when it was decided they could stand the pressures and make the flight to Japan without supplemental oxygen.

# 14

## *Bandera*

WE NOW HAD GENERAL McCLELLAND'S authorization to proceed with the next phase of testing, the all-important study of how to control the bat's hibernation processes. Doc was assigned his long-coveted staff car; with the ex-gangster driving, Doc, Bobby, von Bloeker, and Wiswell headed for Texas. I took off after them with Fletch, Williams, Eddie, and the Benish brothers, from Santa Ana, California, where Holt signed the requisition forms for the command car and two jeeps that had been assigned to our outfit. Tim would follow on the first available military flight to San Antonio after we arrived. It was the beginning of our intimate look into the lives of the bats.

We drew tents, beds, and blankets from an Army base at Hondo, Texas, bought pots and pans and the other household items we would need to be self-sufficient, and divided our forces between Ney Cave and Bracken Cave, some ninety miles apart on opposite sides of San Antonio. Fletch and I paused for a night in Bandera, renewing acquaintances and making new ones at the OST Cafe. Then Fletch and I set up camp at Ney; Williams, Eddie, and the Benishes at Bracken. V. B. and Wiswell would shuttle back and forth on their errands of data collection and supervision. Holt ensconced himself where there was a phone, with Doc and Bobby in Bandera. The three of them, involved as they were in the politics and business of keeping the brass from forgetting us, traveled often to California and Washington.

Wiswell had brought with him a crate of environmental monitoring equipment, with sets for each cave consisting of barographs, recording thermometers, and wet-dry thermometers to check humidity. The humidity test, the only one not automatically logged, had to be made by hand four times a day from various stations within the caves. It meant that somebody—in the case of Ney,

126 ]

Fletch or me—had to climb in there every four hours, all the way to the last station, 1,000 feet from the mouth to the very end of the cave, whirl the instrument on its swivel handle like a bull-roarer, and jot down the data.

Winter, with what we believed to be its attendant hibernation time, was approaching and Wiswell wanted to gather enough environmental statistics over the period of transition so he could chart the atmospheric changes that presumably (along with other as-yet-unknown factors) would cause the bats to hibernate.

Fletch and I, who took turns recording the data from within the cave, each drew from Hondo Army base supply a set of mechanic's coveralls; when tied tightly at ankles and wrists, they stopped most of the bugs. A cowboy hat kept the rain of guano out of our collars and ears, but there was nothing to do about the smell. That we merely endured—a discomfort we eventually got used to, if not fond of.

As Rugh said, "You can't spend yer life in a bat cave, wallerin' in ca-ca, and hate the stink. Else you'd go plumb batty yerself."

Even today, when I pass a building with a bat colony in its attic exuding its distinctive smell—and there are more of them around than one would think—my nose tics with nostalgic recall and aims me like a setter toward a quail. I feel as if I should cock my right arm in perfect point.


On the way east from California, while exploring a potential bat site under a highway bridge, I had come upon a clump of bats of a different kind. I plucked one from the mass and studied it in my light. It proved to be a rather uncommon species of little brown bat—*Myotis thysanodes*. The Latin name sounded like a Greek god, with a stylish ring, and its common moniker—fringe-tailed bat—had connotations all its own. Someone when contemplating this animal's nomenclature had come up with a rather mellifluous designation, most lyrical for a bat, whose usual names—lump-nosed, yellow, leaf-nosed, vampire, pocketed (provocative, if not flattering), big-eared bat, hoary—were all somewhat vilifying.

It's not easy to wax poetic about a bat. With features hardly appealing and few kittenish aspects on which to dwell—no cuddly attributes such as a mewing voice, soft pelage, large blue eyes of mellow charm, furry paws, tickly whiskers—my subject was anthropomorphically decidedly unappealing. Yet everything in God's world is relative, and observed generically the little bat in my hand, in comparison to hideous Flamethrower, was ravishingly beautiful.

Her face lacked any of the ugly protuberances for radar receiving so characteristic of her kind—no lumpy nose bumps, no fleshy folds of naked skin or leafy ornaments on her proboscis. She had no ears of extended length or curious shape, no grossly exaggerated physical features of any kind. Yet she was not plain. Her upturned nose, in fact, was *pert*, even cute. It slanted up in that saucy way that if she could talk—or so I fancied—would reveal a clever sense of humor. She was the Kathleen Turner of batland, the young Katharine Hepburn of her nocturnal kind. And ears! When compared with Flamethrower's dragon's lobes, they were exquisite. Her eyes were small, even tiny, shiny black beads surrounded by short russet fur and long black lashes. At first glance they seemed inexpressive, but upon closer examination one could see character in their mischievous twinkle. The wing membranes of chocolate color were as pleasant to touch as a baby's skin, accounting for the expression used in the backwoods of Texas, where a well-worn dollar bill— having achieved the ultimate in limpness through age and careless pocketing—is called a bat-wing. If my newfound bat didn't meow or sing, at least her squeak was subdued and not unpleasant to the ear. No loud shrill like Flamethrower's grating radar outbursts, her locator electronics were tuned to a more pleasant pitch. And there was, of course, that beguiling fringe along the trailing edge of her tail membrane that provoked her name, soft like the lacy hem of an Indian princess's skirt.

I called her Princess and in empathy with Flamethrower's lonely bachelorhood decided to impose on her the life of consort. I was sure my solitary captive would appreciate his new companion. In fact, however, due no doubt to their dissimilarity of species, they showed not the slightest compatibility. Not antagonistic, they were merely aloof. Still, I hoped that, over time, constant association would bring about tolerance, if not passion. Such proved to be the case, but no love was ever to blossom between this vastly dissimilar pair.

There was ample room for two in Flamethrower's den—they hung, alike only in their upside-down positions, in opposing corners. The squeaks that issued from the box on occasions that I fancied might indicate amorous advances were only loud complaints when one bat ventured into the sacrosanct space of its neighbor.

In spite of her decidedly more acceptable appearance, Princess never did aspire to the theatrical stardom achieved by her male companion. She got off to a bad start, for one thing. Doc had his patter down the way he liked it, and Flamethrower's now perfectly rehearsed act never failed to achieve the desired effect in the introduction to Adams's presentations. I tried slipping Princess into the act, but she just didn't fit. Perhaps beauty wasn't what was wanted or expected in a bat. For all his ugliness, Flamethrower had personality. Not that Princess was a clod; it was only a matter of appropriateness, and the big mastiff simply *had it* when it came to making an impression. Having a fringed tail just wasn't enough.

Doc's associates in subterfuge, the overzealous photographers from the film unit, pitched up at Ney Cave one day shortly after our experiments began with the news that they wanted to film the bat flight and scenes of the animals at roost inside the cave. I volunteered to guide them around and help set up the lights for motion pictures. They brought with them a small generator with enough output to burn eight or ten photofloods, stands for the lamps, and a long coil of cable.

They filmed the sunset flight as the bats made their exodus from the cave. Then when the chambers were empty we set up the generator near the mouth and began to lug down cable and lamps.

These two were not at all expedition-type photographers, having probably run portrait studios or shot wedding pictures in big cities somewhere in civilian life. They had prepared themselves by reading up on bats, dipping into the rather superficial popular literature of the times. If they had been able to peruse the postwar publications of Dr. Denny Constantine I doubt if they would have made the trip from Washington.

Probably no one else has spent as much time in caves studying free-tailed bats as Constantine. His description of a typical visit into a cave accompanied by assistants to study health problems associated with bats, made many years after our venture, is worth repeating for its scientific accuracy as well as for its goose bump–inducing imagery.

> The boulder-strewn floor of the cave was blanketed by bat guano, which varied in thickness from several inches to several feet and in consistency from muddy to dusty. The guano presented dangers of slipping in some areas and of floor collapse in others where the guano had bridged over holes in the floor. . . .
>
> Massive areas of sloping walls and ceiling . . . were whitened with mites, layered as a blanket about one-eighth inch thick. These very tiny glycyphagid mites, *Nycteriglyphus bifolium*, though probably not parasitic, are sometimes so abundant that it would seem that sheer weight of numbers would suffocate

the bats. . . . If the layer of mites was disturbed at a point, that area seemed to boil with activity, which radiated outward as a wave. Air space under the mites was subjected to a constant fine shower of their falling bodies; thus, everything in the area became [infested] by them. . . . I have been contaminated with a near-continuous layer of these mites. The most evident effect was a burning sensation about the edges of the eyes, as the mites were especially dense there, possibly attracted by or trapped by the moist conjunctiva. They also created a burning sensation in the nostrils, which seemed another preferred site, although ear cavities and the mouth edges were also invaded.*

When the stills man sank in a soft place and realized he was bogged down knee-deep in guano that was teeming with the kind of creepy-crawlies Constantine described many years later and that the burning sensation around his eyes was made by *Nycteriglyphus bifolium* attracted to the moisture of his conjunctiva, his reaction, even though he wasn't aware of the scientific explanation, made it difficult for me to keep a respectfully straight face. He engaged in a series of odd spasms and tics, flapped his arms, jerked his knees, made a quick assessment of the situation, hurriedly fired off a couple of face-saving flash bulbs, said, "Great stuff! I've got everything I need," and disappeared in a hurry back toward the mouth of the cave.

The more intrepid movie man and I pressed on alone. As we descended deeper into the cave we encountered more of the fauna Constantine so chillingly described.

> Parasitic streblid flies, *Trichobius major*, and *T. sphaeronotus*, were frequently exceedingly annoying, attacking in buzzing, stubborn, biting swarms.
>
> Small hordes of milichiid flies, *Leptometopa*, attracted by our head lamps, joining the streblids in buzzing into ears, eyes, and nostrils; and the milichiids would accumulate on whatever was illuminated by the light, which was usually one's face, nose or hand. Both fly species were occasionally inhaled, and they were frequently trapped under eyelids.

The cameraman moaned and groaned and cursed and slapped and brushed his way deeper into the cave until we arrived beneath a

---

*Denny G. Constantine, *Rabies Transmission by Air in Bat Caves*, pp. 2–5.

place on the ceiling where I knew, when daylight came and the bats returned, there would be a spectacular mass of squirming furry bodies and leathery wings. Now we had come into an area inhabited by a new kind of fauna:

> Arthropods ascended anything available, presumably to regain access to the bats. Fallen bats endeavored to follow the same pattern. . . . Guano pellets under the bats were often frosted with mites, [and] mites, fleas, and fallen bats concentrated on the tops of gummy boulders or other projections. . . . Such areas sometimes bristled with fleas. When standing in such a place I have observed fleas, *Sternopsylla texana*, advancing blanket-wise up my trouser legs.

There the cinematographer finally took enough time away from picking off the hordes of arthropods swarming over his clothes and skin to set up his camera on its tripod and cover it with a waterproof bag, ready for the next morning after the bats had returned.

"I can't stand another second of this," he said, swatting at a horde of *Sternopsylla texana* and breathing in the odd milichiid fly. "I'm getting the hell out of here. Set up the lights, will you?"

"How?" I asked.

"Any damned way you want," he said on the run. "Just point them at where the bats are going to be. I'm sure it'll be fine."

I loved it, my chance to be creative. I fussed with the lamps, adjusting and readjusting, the sound of the distant generator thrumming through the cave, imagining the bats in their places, picturing in my mind the great cinema we were going to achieve.

To protect himself from dermestid beetles and their larvae, glycyphagid mites, streblid and milichiid flies, and *Sternopsylla texana*, the cameraman appeared the next morning so completely swathed in rubberized rain ponchos that I was sure he would suffocate before the job was done. If he had been privy to Constantine's publication, I doubt he would have prepared himself as he did. Breathing was difficult enough without putting a plastic bag over one's head.

> Ammonia is sometimes very strong . . . at times our eyes burned as if filled with excessively chlorinated water; breathing was momentarily impossible at first and later had to be forced. The carbon dioxide concentration was surprisingly high and presumably contributed to early fatigue. Guano dust collected in

one's respiratory passages. . . . I have experienced an immediate headache in the presence of excessive guano dust, and coughing resulting in discharge of guano particles that continued for three or four weeks. . . . [In some places] water . . . stands over the guano. . . . This fluid has a corrosive effect on human skin.

The penetrating odor of guano was eventually accepted by most workers but there was one phenomenon that seemed to retain its nauseous properties: the hot blast of bat breath . . .

We plowed on down into the cave through the guano and arthropods. This time, of course, the bats were present, adding a whole new element to the cameraman's horror.

Free-tailed Bats were attached as a continuous mat over areas of the ceiling. They maintained a constant din, composed of individual squeaks, in response to elbowing by neighbors, retaliatory bites, and departures and arrivals of individuals. This sound elicited apprehension and excitement in human observers, possibly as a result of ultrasonic components in the bat utterances. On occasion I have experienced head pains in phase with squeaks of individuals of this species . . .

Now I noted my companion performing an energetic dance, raising clouds of unwanted dust in a patch of dry guano. I knew there was a technological explanation for this underground ballet.

[Some] bats are white with starving, flattened bloodless mites, many of them running with unusual speed and quick to spread over a warm hand. While still active, such bats routinely alighted or crawled onto us, ascending, sometimes inside a trouser leg. If the worker's hands were occupied, the bat might reach the worker's head before endeavoring to fly. Or it might rest there. A bat would occasionally get lost under clothing and have to be left there until removing it became less objectionable than leaving it where it was.

At last the photographer stood behind his camera, panting through the rubberized sheets, and pointed the lens at the dark ceiling. Through the folds of fabric he called for the lights to be turned on, illuminating the inside of the cave for the first time in its primordial history. The cavern had been born in darkness. Ages ago the limestone had seeped away to make its chambers, an ever-continuing process. Never before had illumination more brilliant than an exploring lantern or flashlight or flaming torch played on the great stalactites. I knew the bats would react to the sudden light. I had no idea *how* they would react.

When I had told Fletch about what we were going to do and how the photographers (who were not our favorite people after the fiasco they had accomplished to our embarrassment at Carlsbad) had reacted to their first steps into the cave, he laughed and said, "I wouldn't miss this for anything." He stood beside us now, ready to help in any way he could, but more interested as an observer than as an assistant.

The cameraman checked his machine with a shielded flashlight, set f-stop and focus, and said, "Okay. I'm ready. Now, what are they going to do when you turn on the lights?" His voice was muffled and strange through the layers of rubber sheeting. It sounded as if we were filming underwater rather than underground.

"Search me. What do you think, Fletch?" I said.

"I haven't the foggiest," my partner said. "But it'll probably be something fairly interesting."

"Okay, lights!" the cinematographer said from the pseudo-watery depths.

Off in the darkness I heard the metallic click of a switch— Fletch snapping the first light. It came on with surprising brightness. Even though I was expecting it, the brilliant light came as a shock. I moved quickly, joining Fletch in turning on other lights— *snap, snap, snap!* I heard the camera motor whir and stared up at the motionless bats. They had frozen, stunned by the sudden shock of dazzling light. For several seconds there was no movement. Then with spontaneous vigor they all seemed to come alive at once, squirming, crawling over and under one another, trying to escape the glare. The whole ceiling began to surge like waves rising with a sudden squall on a placid lake. It looked like a beehive at swarming time.

Again, Constantine's as yet unwritten paper can illuminate scientifically what was about to happen to us as laymen.

> When a human intruder excited great numbers of resting bats in a relatively small space, the entire group would endeavor to fly at once. . . . Bats were everywhere immediately, striking everything, dropping in confused masses to the floor. One found himself being pelted with bats, many of which would cling and crawl in confusion, others taking off again, many falling instead at one's feet to join the horde climbing up his body. Carbide lamps would be extinguished by the bats. Flashlights were useless, for if the intruder could force his eyes open, he would see

nothing but hurtling bodies. The bats seemed not to bite intentionally or frequently under these conditions, though the intruder might suffer scratches. . . . These scratches were hardly
noticeable except when the cornea was scratched. Unless the
intruder moved, the result would be an ever-increasing pile of
bats until his body would be covered. . . . Persons do not usually
stand still that long; they generally endeavor to remove themselves at once.

"Oh, *shit!*" the cameraman said with incredible awe, a statement loaded with more meaning and double-entendre than any
other possible choice of words more profound.

Another light came on. Now they all were glowing.

A few bats dropped away from the mass, falling through space
toward us, then catching themselves in midair and fluttering away.
The lights playing on the thin membranous wings, caught in a cleverly placed backlight, had an eerie effect. I was immensely proud of
my modeled lighting: the chiaroscuro effect was perfect, I thought,
very Rembrandt. I awaited words from underwater, complimenting
me. None came.

The ripples of crawling bats became storm waves, turned to a
tempest. For half a minute he filmed—beautiful footage, marvel-
ously cinematic, I thought. Then I felt a wet drop strike my upturned forehead. Another splashed on my chin. And another. In the
glare of lights the drops sparkled like glittering jewels as they fell.
They came faster. The occasional drops turned into a steady drizzle,
changed to rain, burst into a downpour, erupted into a cloudburst.

Each bat had come awake simultaneously. Each bat, now awake,
at the same moment felt the need to urinate. Until a few seconds
ago the colony had been asleep. It was only to be expected that now,
suddenly roused from slumber, they must answer nature's call; a
million bats above our heads must simultaneously empty a million
turgid bladders. It was not, as one prone to anthropomorphize might
speculate, an indiscreet or disrespectful comment from the wild. It
was simply basic physiology. Ozro would understand.

I stood face turned downward in the deluge while the cameraman attempted to film. In seconds his lens was inundated and useless. Pools began to form in the lens shade. Truly, he *was* filming
underwater.

On the floor of the cave the photoflood lamps, exposed bulbs
pointing upward, began to radiate heat from the energy of making
light. The downpour sizzled on the hot bare bulbs. Beside me, there
was a sudden explosive sound—as if a pistol had been fired. It star-

tled me, but I realized its cause at once. Another loud report sounded from across the cave. One by one the lamps were bursting, detonating with sharp reports as the cool rain came down on the hot thin vacuum tubes. They went off in rapid sequence now, reaching a final climax of firecracker popping before they left us in the terrible absolute of total darkness.

I felt the peak of the flood begin to slacken. Then a new surge sprinkled down, growing in intensity as it had done before. But this time the rain was different. Now solid objects were pattering off our heads and shoulders. I knew, even though I couldn't see them, that they resembled small dark grains of rice—the rain of moments ago had changed to hail!

The bats swarmed off the ceiling now, the agitation of one quickly transmitted to the next, as panic seizes a mob. I could hear the close flutter of millions of leathery wings, the high-pitched voices; ultrasonic vibrations tingled our nerves. With so many on the wing at once in the confining cavern some were bound to fly into us. Many began striking our bodies as they surged and whirled through space.

We turned on our flashlights. The air was a living mass of creatures, suffocating in its density, closing in, surrounding. We were immersed in fluttering wings.

"My God!" the cameraman shrieked. "They're attacking!"

Pressed by the mass of their brothers, bats flitted across our cheeks, bounced off our backs and heads. The meager beams of our flashlights that heretofore had been nearly lost in the absorbing blackness beyond the stalactites suddenly closed in on us. Now our lights threw back a glow, reflecting off the many wings, closing in, closer the mass came, whirling swarming bodies, a kaleidoscope of light and movement flashing and driving by us as in a wild disco.

More bats circled the huge vaulted chamber, a dense cloud, lowering as more and more bats came off the ceiling, crowding the ones already in flight below. We couldn't see beyond the curtains of wings closest to us, a condensed turbulent mass of life—as if we were bagged in the same net with a huge school of swarming herring. Around and around they flew, gaining in momentum and volume as more and more took wing. They choked the room—there was hardly space for all to fly at the same time, hardly space for air to breathe.

The bottom wave of bats formed a dense layer, and the cave's ceiling seemed to come down on us, lowering like the canopy of Poe's smothering bed. The living curtain hovered at head height, then continued down. Now even more bats were flying into our faces, striking our shoulders as thousands of wings collided with each other and with anything that stood in their way. It was useless to try to fend them off or attempt to protect oneself from their blind confusion. Every foot of air space in the grotto was filled with a churning maelstrom of squeaking, fluttering bats. They flew into our bodies from heads to knees and surged up over our feet and legs. It felt as if we were being sucked into a surrealistic living quicksand. The only order to the seeming chaos was that all flew in the same vortex, swirling as a whirlpool guided by the same centrifugal force. Colliding bats clung to our clothes, more came; they built squirming layers one on top of another over our bodies. Their natural tendency was to crawl upward, seeking the highest place. Our heads and shoulders rapidly became heavy with layers of bats. Some, having achieved the peak, took off again, but for every one that flew, two collided—in the way a rolled ball of snow gathers more, our burdens grew. We couldn't see each other. Our flashlights were useless. There were only flapping wings and hurtling bodies, a compact mass of movement that stifled our breaths. The sound of wings and squeaks was deafening. I was aware that someone was screaming, but had no orientation as to where the cries for help were coming from. We were drowning in bats—feelings of excitement, approaching panic, seized us. The weight of bats seemed to exert a pressure, pushing us down. We were engulfed in a chaos of bats.

We could only crouch under our burdens of bats and wait for the onslaught to recede. At last, as the tide diminished, I heard a whimpering sound beside me, then what I thought was a muffled sob. "They're going to kill me." I turned my flashlight toward the underwater sound. I saw a moving mound of bats which I was barely able to recognize as the cinematographer. Slowly the seething mound moved and became erect. As a dog comes out of a lake, he shuddered, shaking off a few hundred bats as spray.

The whirlpool of life was spinning away, filling other parts of the cave or alighting again. With our flashlights we could see once more. Suddenly the rubber-wrapped cameraman sprang into motion, a toy puppet, arms and legs seemingly out of control, flailing on broken strings, swiping uselessly at the flapping wings. He ran, fell, got up, windmilling his arms, and stumbled away alone in the direction of the cave's mouth.

It was worth every horrible moment. Soaked by urine, pelted by defecation, hair crawling with vermin, giggling at the cameraman's terror, we followed for a way until through the fluttering screen of wings we saw him far ahead, running as best he could through the unstable guano, windmill arms still pumping, slipping, driven from beneath the earth, a frightened blind mole. At last, sweating within his plastic bubble, he disappeared into the glare of daylight at the cave's door, convinced that we all were mad and that he had barely escaped from hell with his life intact.

Fletch and I went back, picked up his camera and lights, and stumbled after him, nearly falling over with diabolical mirth, toward the glow of sunlight still dimmed by swirling bats.

Fletch and I soon found that we had time on our hands. Our only official duties were the four-times-a-day treks into the cave to record data, followed by the four-times-a-day baths in the creek that flowed past camp. We found that a quick wipe-off with a kerosene- or diesel-soaked rag, followed by a good soaping and rinse, performed with pails of water on a rocky ledge well back from the banks where we would not foul the stream, finished off the biting things at not too great a cost to our skins. We realized that by trading off on the duty we could arrange our lives to suit ourselves. A two-days-on, two-days-off schedule agreed with both of us. And we had, all to ourselves, our own Army jeep.

Thus on alternating two-day periods we made second homes of one or the other of the several dude ranches in the area or went to our favorite home-away-from-home, the OST Cafe, where we flew like lost lonely bats to the companionship of their favorite cave.

Although I had never learned to dance, I was introduced and eventually learned to participate awkwardly in a lively terpsichore of the Old West called *Put Your Little Foot*. It was a square dance of sorts, at least it was in that league, and was the nightly favorite of the crowd at the OST Cafe. When beefsteaks were finished for the evening, the tables were pushed aside to clear a wide floor, a fiddler or two and guitars appeared, and the caller came forward, a colorful habitué with a lean cowboy's face and a rim-stained white hat. He appeared to be about ninety years old, yet still spry as a goat, and he half-sung in a happy cadence that really got the folks to smiling.

> Put your little foot,
> Put your little foot,
> Put your little foot right out.
> Put your arm around,
> Put your arm around,
> Put your arm around her waist.

Put your little foot,
Put your little foot,
Put your little foot right out.

And on it went with lively, increasingly racy verses, long into the night.

It was in the OST Cafe, obeying the caller's phrase "Put your arm around her waist," that I met Arlie.

My fascination with her was extreme. She was built just like a girl ought to be, slight boned and petite. But her hands looked like any other cowboy's—rough, weather-beaten, callused, with nails broken-off and rimmed with dark arcs of horse sweat and fence post oil. Her hair was cut short like a boy's, and she wore men's Levi's and the ubiquitous pearl-snap long-sleeved cowboy shirt. Her lips were red as wine, but she didn't affect lipstick or makeup of other kinds so far as I could tell. Arlie was an odd mix, at the same time boy—and all girl. With her freckles and perfect teeth, she was cute as a pin.

She told me that her pappy had wanted a boy, gave her a boy's name, and raised her like one. But I was sure she felt all of a girl's urges.

One Sunday, I took Arlie out to the Rocking-W Guest Ranch where I was introduced to a cowboy friend, Jay-R George. There were still a few genuine cowboys around Bandera, because the work they did was considered essential to the war effort and they were exempted from the draft. Jay-R was about as cowboy as you could get. When he took off his hat, which he had been known to do in public on only one or two occasions in his life, one of which I was privileged to witness, he had a sharp line at mid-forehead, pure sickly white above, brown as an old leather bridle below. At about age twenty-five, he was a champion calf-roper and wore the huge silver trophy buckle to prove it. Jay-R couldn't walk very good, having grown up in the saddle, but he rode like he was floating.

A couple of other cowpokes hobbled in on their bent legs and high-heeled boots and joined us for a beer—and then for a couple more. At about three o'clock in the afternoon it was decided to stage an impromptu rodeo. (And be sure to pronounce it *rodeeo*, if you want to sound like a real Texas cowboy, sort of *sing* it. Not, ro-*deh*-o, which, although probably correct for the word's Spanish derivation, is all wrong to a Texas cowpoke.)

Not to be made a fool of in front of Arlie, who spurred her pony, flung her rope, and flipped her calf just as well as any other man there, as she would put it, and came within a couple of seconds of taking Jay-R's belt buckle, I accepted the challenge to rope a calf. I still had not been convinced of the dangers of face-saving as a motive, and thought I'd employ a bit of one-upmanship on these cowpokes and cleverly manipulate established rules to suit myself. Perhaps a trace of Doc's teaching was already influencing my peachy clean scruples. I couldn't ride for beans, and I knew it. What I didn't know but was soon to learn is that a dude doesn't beat a cowboy— ever—at his own game.

I knew I wouldn't have half a chance playing by real rodeo rules, so I said I'd accept a bet with Jay-R on my terms. He didn't figure there was any way in the world that he couldn't rope and tie a calf quicker than me, so we each handed a fiver to Arlie to hold and headed for the corral.

"My rules are," I said with tipsy self-confidence, "no horses."

"No horses? Whaddya mean? They ain't no calf ropin' without a horse. Hell, man, the pony does all the work."

"That's it, nevertheless," I said, knowing by his outrage that I'd outfoxed him. "By my rules, as agreed. No horses." I knew I had him. I didn't have much experience at twirling a lasso, but Jay-R would be an absolutely helpless fish out of water trying to run down a calf on his wobbly legs.

Jay-R's standard roping time was something around 10 seconds flat. In that 10 seconds a lot happened. The calf was released from a holding pen through the starting gate; it came out full bore. The roper, from a dead stop beside the gate, had to spur his pony and overtake the streaking calf, throw the loop of his lariat while at full run, circling the lasso accurately around the running calf's neck, while the pony, as if taking it for granted there would be no miss, began to throw on the brakes, sliding on all four hooves to a stop so the rope which was attached to the saddlehorn came taut with a jerk and flipped the calf all with one continuous movement, as the cowboy was swinging off his pony. He hit the ground running, guided into the dust by his hold on the rope, came out of the cloud to the calf, now on its back due to the horse's steady backing away, which kept the rope taut, grabbed a foreleg, yanked the short tie-rope out from between his teeth, looped a front ankle, pulled up a rear leg, quickly wound the rope tying front foot to rear, leaped back, and threw both arms in the air, signaling to the timer to stop the clock. It takes about four times as long just to tell it, as it took for Jay-R to do it during a championship rodeo.

Not to be a quitter, spurred by the beer in his belly, Jay-R begrudgingly took his lariat, slogged out in his pretty red and white Sunday boots into the muddy corral, gamely chased a calf around the fence, finally threw, and tied it in the time of three minutes-six.

Not bad under the circumstances, but I knew I had him. The fiver was as good as mine—and all the glory that went with it. For I had a plan.

But I was about to be taught a lesson about cowboys. I stood in mid-corral awaiting the release of my calf, figuring that from this central position I could close in quickly no matter what direction it took, make my throw, snub my rope to a fence post, and nail it in less than a minute.

I stood ready, lariat swinging in a slow loop over my head, and made that little nod that experienced cowboys make to signal the gateman for the release.

The gate swung wide and, prompted by a hard slap on the rear and a couple of loud "Yahoo"'s, out came my calf with a bellow. But this was no ordinary roping calf, no hundred-pound daughter of a Hereford cow. What came charging and bellowing out of the chute was the mad son of a Brahma mother, about three-quarters of the way there to qualifying as a full-fledged bucking bull—he aimed his head, tossed his horns, and came at me like a freight train. I didn't have the time or the presence of mind even to move. Fortunately, my calf's horns weren't yet as developed as his spirit; the boss hit me square in the middle and I took off on a flying trip to the moon. When I came back down flat on my face in the mud, I didn't ever want to be a rodeo star again.

Arlie handed my fiver over to the winner, and my cowboy friends, full of commiseration, helped me to my feet and back to a seat by the fireplace where we all had another beer, no hard feelings. I was still a dude, but now an acceptable dude. I had paid my dues—playing the good loser, I bought.

A young cowboy at the bar of the OST Cafe had seen Tim Holt in a western film where he had played the role of a fast-drawing gun-slinger and posed the question "How do they make impossible tricks look so real in the movies?" A snigger of derision made the clear point that the statement to follow was meant to be an embarrassment, for surely no Hollywood cowboy could really do what this Texas cowboy had seen Holt do in the film: "Things like *you* fast-drawing a gun in *Comanche Pass*." The emphasis he gave the "you" was clearly a verbal sneer.

"No tricks," Tim replied. "I learned to fast-draw when I was twelve."

"Naw!" his heckler said. "Don't joke me around. They speed up the film, right? Some kind of camera foolery?"

Tim shrugged. "My dad taught me." Tim's father was the retired western star Jack Holt, veteran of more shootouts than Wyatt Earp.

"I don't believe it," somebody said, backing up his buddy at the bar. "You don't look to me like you could handle a gun at all. Sure, they do it with trick photography."

Tim, not looking for trouble, shrugged again. "Whatever you say, pardner."

Then someone pulled down from where it decorated the wall an ancient Frontier Model Colt .44, dusty in its holster and belt. Now, Holt was far from being a showoff, but the locals ragged him so persistently that he finally buckled on the weapon, took a few practice passes at the butt, slow and not impressive, only to get the balance and feel of the piece, then proceeded to astound the gringos at the bar. When an able person has practiced just about anything requiring the use of hands, arms, or body to near-perfection, particularly something requiring the physical dexterity of gunplay, the dance can become a joy to behold. Like a champion gymnast on the bars or a diver from a board, Tim Holt would have won the gold in gunslinging at any Olympic competition. He drew in a flash and the .44 became a part of his hand—it spun on its finger-guard, flew in the air, came down in deadly aim. The hammer clicked on an empty chamber; it reversed its spin, reversed again, and slid back into its holster with such grace and fluid movement that the old .44 that hadn't been off the wall in years seemed to have accomplished its feat with an energy of its own. The room full of locals, both friendly and hostile, stared in speechless awe.

Then an old cowpoke said, "Hot damn! That's right pretty."

"Do it ag'in, Tim," someone said.

Holt didn't have to be coaxed, and now that he was getting warmed up he performed an extended repertoire even more impressive than the last. The old handgun came alive and flipped and danced and did somersaults and twirls and just exalted in the joy of getting off the wall.

If my amateurish encounter with the Brahma had cost our standing in the community a few points, Tim handily won them back. By riding on Tim's coattails we were all redeemed. From that evening of Holt's demonstration of six-gun dexterity, we were accepted as bona fide members of the community, and Tim's grace—not only in handling the gun, but in his warmth with the people—rubbed off onto all of us.

That was Sunday. On Monday Fletch took his couple of leave days, disappeared in the jeep, and came back bearing a wild card that no one who gave a fiddler's damn about keeping a sense of propriety among his Texas cattle and sheep rancher hosts would have the gall to play. Relationships with our cowboy friends definitely seemed to run in cycles, on and off, hot and cold. Fletch's next contribution decidedly turned the cold water onto our alliance.

I heard the jeep coming up the track, put Flamethrower and Princess back into their box from their exercise of tidying up an accumulation of flies and yellowjackets that had been buzzing around inside my tent, and opened the flap to see Fletch pull into camp. Sitting beside him on the front seat was a passenger that even I, knowing Fletch's penchant for the bizarre, found hard to believe.

I walked out, scratching my head. "Is that what I think it is?" I asked. "Or am I seeing things?"

Fletch grinned. "If you think it's just a tiger, maybe. But if you think it's a *Royal Bengal Tiger*, six months old, then yes, it's what you think it is."

The tiger cub hopped out of the jeep, strolled—all big-pawed and long-tailed—over to me, and began to rub his face against my leg. For a six-month-old kitten, I thought, he had a lot of push. His strength was impressive. I glanced at Fletch with a look of doubt.

"It's okay," Fletch said. "He's a pussycat. Loves people, kids. He grew up with a dog. Go ahead, he wants to be petted."

I rubbed the tiger's ears. He nuzzled my hand, as affectionate and playful as a puppy. "How many ranchers took potshots at you on the way here?" I asked.

"None!" Fletch seemed mortified at my reaction. "Do you think they would?"

"I'm pretty sure of it," I said. "What's the story?"

"I spent the morning at the San Antonio zoo," Fletch said, "and I saw this tiger." He rubbed the cat's ears and hugged it affectionately. "It was love at first sight—mutual. I found the superintendent and told him about the plight of the Texas Tigers."

"Texas Tigers?" I asked. "What's that?"

"Us, stupid. That's the name of our outfit."

"It is?" I shook my head.

"You don't get it, do you?" Fletch said impatiently. "I told him we were a unit of GIs and marines stuck out in the wilderness—we call ourselves the Texas Tigers, and we want a mascot for our unit. He gave us Top Sarge."

"This is Top Sarge?"

"Sure. Don't you see all his stripes?"

"Jeez, Fletch," I said. "Did you learn to be such a conman from Doc or Bobby?"

Top Sarge had been handed over to Fletch in a large crate that now perched empty in the back of the jeep. Fletch discovered right away that the tiger preferred to ride in the front passenger seat, with his head out the side, like a car-happy hound, ears flapping in the wind.

As a kitten, Fletch told me, the cub had been a favorite in the petting zoo and the children had loved him. But Top Sarge had outgrown his role as cuddly stuffed toy, and the zoo man had been only too happy to place the tiger in a good home where he was sure to be loved and well cared for. That, along with the patriotic motive of presenting a mascot to an outfit so obviously right for it—Fletch's inspiration in instant entitlement, Texas Tigers, indeed!—seemed a divine answer to the zoo man.

But when Fletch pulled proudly into Bandera with his new friend, the first act of tigerly indiscretion was that our mascot saw the town's mascot, crept out of the jeep, and began a belly-against-the-ground, fixed-eyed killer stalk with that deadly intensity common to all feline predators. He went after Billy like a cat after a rat, and the flustered goat had to scramble for refuge on top of Emil Rugh's old pickup. "He went up the front bumper, across the hood, and onto the roof in three easy jumps," Fletch said. "Amazing! Then Billy showed Top Sarge what those curvy things on top of his head are all about. I don't think Top Sarge will try having goat ribs for lunch again soon."

Fletch collared Top Sarge before any blood was let, but the incident had been observed by half the town of Bandera, most of whom were cattle or sheep men. The idea of a meat-eating tiger invading their ranges, a domain that had been laboriously cleared of mountain lions, coyotes, bobcats, eagles, and every other real or imagined predator half a century ago, didn't appeal at all to these wildlife reactionaries.

There was more head-shaking around Bandera than at a convention of lizards taking the sun, along with considerable speculation as to what was going to happen "when that man-eater grows up."

In the meanwhile, Top Sarge took over Fletch's tent as his den, and from behind the dark flaps at night I occasionally heard my partner grumble: "Move over, dammit. Do you think you own the *whole* bed?"

# 15

## *Project X-Ray*

FOR TWO AND A HALF MONTHS Fieser did nothing to follow up on General Kabrich's directive to continue work on developing a new time-delay device. Then, on September 14, he wrote to his friend Lothrop regarding a recent meeting with his chemist partner, William Young.

> Dear Warren,
>
> I heard some further developments on the bat problem from Bill Young at the Pittsburgh meeting. He has been in touch with Adams and is completely sold on the feasibility of the plan and hopes very much that NDRC will help move it along. He says that Adams has perfected completely satisfactory methods of transportation and release, that the bats in practically any season but that involved in our first tests [when our vectors had not yet recovered their energy after a long migration] are very husky and strong and do all the things they should do. He has scouted around and located what promises to be a suitable location for conducting full tests with incendiaries. He was willing to make a survey of this location if given authority. According to Young, Adams has completely sold his plan to several Generals and Admirals. Probably the matter will be brought up again shortly and the problem of supplying incendiaries presented to Edgewood [Arsenal, CWS Headquarters] and then probably dropped on us. We, of course, have done nothing on the perfection of the small delay device since June. On the other hand, I believe Leeds and Northrup [engineering and manufacturing firm] continued work and I would like to be informed of their progress and present status.

Fieser continued with a brief review of his own doubts about the project, but in the final analysis he rode the fence by reserving judgment until he could see more of the animals' performance. He queried his boss on what steps should be taken and wondered if his partner Young (now favored by Doc) should be authorized to make a survey of the proposed new test site. Fieser concluded by expressing doubts about his partner's qualifications for this important study.

> Although I have great respect for Bill's judgement on chemical matters, I am not sure that he has seen enough of incendiarism to judge of the suitability of the place for the tests in view. Another possibility would be for me to go out and see Adams and his new device and then proceed with Young to explore this test location. The task would be made definitely less arduous by the fact that there is some good fishing about seventy miles away.

Any keen fisherman could appreciate Fieser's yen, but it seems a bit contrived and not at all charitable to use his partner's supposed inadequacy for an excuse to go on a fishing trip. Did the fact that his once-esteemed partner seemed now to have thrown his support behind Adams color Fieser's opinion of Young's expertise?

Fieser's letter to WCL was answered by Lothrop's boss, Harris M. Chadwell, chief of Division 19, NDRC.

> Dear Louie:
> Your letter of September 14 to Warren about the bat problem was very interesting. I do not know Bill Young to whom you referred.
> Upon receipt of your letter I checked with Mr. Allen Abrams, in the absence of Stanley Lovell, in OSS [Office of Strategic Services], and was informed that so far as he knows there is no further interest in OSS on the Adams Bat problem. I feel that it would be unwise for NDRC to spend any more time, money and effort on the Bat problem unless NDRC's aid was solicited by some recognized branch of the service.

A summary of work completed to date on the incendiary followed, then: "In regard to the small delay device for this unit, Leeds and Northrup did develop such a unit in the early summer to such a stage that it was shown that a suitable unit could be produced easily. The work for that company on this subject is now inactive but could quickly be resumed if it was needed."

Chadwell's departmental equivalent in Division 11 of NDRC, Chief Earl Stevenson, who was sent a copy of Chadwell's letter instructing Fieser to lay off work on the incendiary, followed up with his own repudiation and orders to Fieser to quit work on the Adams Plan.

It is my understanding, though not through official channels, that there is no further interest in the problem referred to [the Adams Plan], in this letter and I am in agreement . . . that Division 11 should not spend any more time of its associates on this project. I would, however, qualify this position to the extent of saying that if CWS made any request of you in this connection the above should be reconsidered.

In view of General Kabrich's very specific letter from CWS to NDRC—his official request for continued research and support of the Adams Plan—the lack of activity and negative attitude of NDRC are difficult to explain.

Here we had two chiefs of separate NDRC divisions writing orders for the suspension of work with Adams *unless requested by CWS* in the face of the fact that General Kabrich of CWS had very specifically made just such a request. It didn't make sense. Once again, the head didn't seem to know that the tail was wagging.

But Doc was not one to let sleeping dogs lie. If the Air Force couldn't stir itself enough to keep NDRC interested, he would go elsewhere.

General Louis DeHaven, the marine who had so unobtrusively observed the Carlsbad tests and had wryly watched our bat bombs burn down the Air Force's installation, had been more impressed with the bats' performance than any of us knew. Fieser had been so casual about the unassertive general's presence that he hadn't even mentioned the marine in his report of the tests. Surely no one in U.S. Navy Headquarters was sitting back watching our every move and waiting for the moment when the Army would blow it. But General DeHaven had made a highly favorable report to his superiors, Gen. Holland Smith and Navy secretary Frank Knox. When the Army opted to pass on the Adams Plan, the Navy quickly stepped in.

As the result of Doc's bulldog tenacity and DeHaven's favorable report, a one-sentence-long order was issued that was to profoundly change the fortunes of the Adams Plan.

Dear General Kabrich:
It is requested that the Chemical Warfare Service cooperate with Lieutenant Colonel R. H. Rhoads, U.S.M.C., and Dr. Lytle S.

Adams, in the development, preparation and acquisition of the incendiary adopted for use by Dr. L. F. Fieser for the "Adams Plan."
> Very truly yours,
> D. C. Ramsey
> Rear Admiral, U.S.N.
> Chief of the Bureau of Aeronautics

The Navy had taken over the project and assigned a crusty Marine Corps lieutenant colonel as our new commanding officer. Instead of Fletch and Williams being the Ugly Ducklings—marines serving with the Army Air Forces—the situation had been turned topsy-turvy. Now they were members of the dominant command and the rest of us were assigned under the "Detached Service" designation to the Marine Corps.

Our outfit even had a new name. It had just enough flair that I was sure Doc must have dreamed it up. No longer to be known as the Adams Plan, our project henceforth would be called Project X-Ray, a suitably mysterious-sounding moniker for a supersecret operation, we all agreed.

And Adams, for the moment at least, was gratified to see Fieser put in his place by Naval Ordinance.

Dear Dr. Fieser:
> Your letter of l October, 1943, stating that six (6) dummy Adams project units were being shipped separately, has been received by the Bureau of Ordinance.
> These devices have been examined thoroughly. They do not fulfill the purpose which we had in mind. Accordingly, we shall require no further samples.
>> W. H. P. Blandy
>> Rear Admiral, U.S. Navy
>> Chief of the Bureau of Ordinance

If Fieser was to stay on the project, he would have to go back to the drawing board. Indeed, that is what he did. Fortunately, problems with the time-delay pencil, which were the chief stumbling block in the design of the total incendiary bomb, had been worked out in the interim by independent contractors, the Leeds and Northrup Company. Fieser would continue to mastermind the total concept of the incendiary, but now his aim was to pull together different elements from various sources into one overall package rather than do it all himself. Under the new urgency demanded by the Marine

Corps program, he had to do it rapidly. Only three weeks after the marines became involved, they were requesting an order of 3,000 incendiary capsules for a test. Because the design of the new automatic pencils was still being refined by Leeds and Northrup, original models with chemically activated starters were again to be provided as temporary substitutes. They were to be shipped to the Marine Corps Air Station on the desert at El Centro, California, our new base of operations.

In spite of Doc's growing disenchantment with Fieser in favor of Young, Fieser's friends at NDRC kept him in the fore. Now Fieser had twin urgent activities to occupy his prodigious mind—his official development of the incendiary and his unofficial exercise in intrigue.


The OST Cafe was quiet. It was Tuesday evening. Only a couple of loudspeakers with coils of wire and empty plugs for amplifiers stood in the corner for the Saturday night band. Connie brought me a mug of beer with a head running over onto the frosty glass. Behind me, Wiswell was placing the nightly call to his wife from the pay phone on the wall. He chatted up the operator while she rang through. I couldn't figure how he could afford to call California every night— he sure couldn't do it on a private's pay.

The call went through.

I didn't *want* to listen, but it was dead quiet in the cafe, and I sat only about three feet from where Wiswell was hanging on the wall. In respectful decency I could have gotten up and taken a different table, but I didn't bother. Besides, I'd heard this same conversation a dozen times before, at least this end of it.

"Hello, sweetheart, honey grapes. How's my little frog tonight?"

*Little frog?* I thought of Wiswell's wife. Not the most apt comparison—on the other hand, I visualized a frog, long jumping legs shaped a lot like a Las Vegas showgirl's graceful limbs—not such a bad simile at that. At the time, the pinup painting by George Petty was the first page to be turned to in any issue of *Esquire*, the *Playboy* magazine of the day, and it would not be an exaggeration to say that Petty art hung on the walls of every U.S. Army barracks and in the lockers of every U.S. Navy ship on all the high seas of the world. The smooth-muscled legs of Petty girls in all their overstated length were shaped a lot like those of a skinned frog if one could imagine a pink amphibian and see through the other obvious dissimilarities. So, I conceded, Wiswell had imagination in addition to his scientific bent.

"I miss you, too, Poggy. I don't know how *I* can live all this time without you, either."

It wasn't *what* he was saying, it was *how* he was saying it—a slice of toast with too much honey dripping off. Poggy, of course, was his sweetheart's diminutive—Little Frog. Honey Grapes was synonymous with Poggy. Even keeping Petty in mind, I could barely accept the comparison.

"I don't know when I'll be back, Honeybunch. I miss you so, precious love."

Without turning around I could see Wiswell listening with rapt attention, eyes closed to shut out existing environmental realities—stark empty tables and chairs, used mugs amber with dried foam, the smell of stale beer.

"Yes, little frog. I love you *more* than you love me. Yes, *more* Poggy. Even *more*! Oh, you're in bed? Don't! I can feel it when you say that. Stop! You mustn't." He giggled hysterically.

I glanced over my shoulder toward the wall. Wiswell's face was flushed and, as expected, his eyes were blissfully closed. I'd heard all the billing and cooing I could stand. I got up, took my mug, and selected another table out of earshot across the room.

Later, when Wiswell had joined me to cool off with a Dos Equis of his own, Holt came in off the street and strolled to our table. He nodded a greeting to me, then glanced Wiswell's way. "Hi, Poggy, how're the bats keeping?"

Thus was the scientist christened with his durable *nom de guerre*—Poggy.


Our new CO, Lt. Col. R. H. (Dusty) Rhoads, ordered us to report from Texas to El Centro for summary briefings and to conduct yet another test. The marines wanted to sort out firsthand all the contradictory data accumulated so far.

We would be away from our statistics-collecting chores for only a short time, and Wiswell was sure that except for the personally logged humidity tests the automatic recording instruments in the caves would continue to provide all essential information.

Detachments of Marine Corps infantry were assigned to guard both Ney Cave and Bracken Cave. Before we departed for El Centro, Fletch instructed the sergeant in command of the encampment at Ney in the care and feeding of Top Sarge. The caretaker promised me he'd throw a handful of mealworms every evening into the bedroom box of Flamethrower and Princess. I had been exercising my pets frequently by flying them in Ben Gerdes's barn. I hoped that their muscles wouldn't atrophy too much, but I didn't trust the marines to let them out of their box while we were away. These leathernecks from Corpus Christi, five at each location, were not expected to enter the caves, only to keep people away. All were combat veterans of the Pacific campaign, incapacitated in one way or another and disqualified from more duty in the war zone—most suffered from combat fatigue or shellshock, as it was sometimes called.

Because of the distance and frequency of travel required between our two bases of operations—from Texas to California—and as if to prove commitment to Project X-Ray, the Marine Corps assigned a full-time aircraft with crew of pilot, co-pilot, crew-chief, and assistant to our unit. A twin-engined Lockheed Lodestar, Navy designation R-5-o, was our full-time air transport; the chief pilot was Captain Hulls. Captain R. N. Smith, the co-pilot, would also serve an administrative function as Colonel Rhoads's executive officer when not flying.

Lt. Tim Holt, who remained with the unit as our Air Force administrative officer, was confronted with what must have been a most unsettling obligation in introducing his corps of military misfits to Lieutenant Colonel Rhoads, USMC, the hard-assed marine commandant called out of retirement to head up Project X-Ray. Rhoads had little time for the Army to begin with and he projected a brusque air of superiority, as if he considered us wimps at best.

We stood in a ragged line in the thrown-together wooden building at El Centro Marine Air Station assigned to us as headquarters, awaiting the arrival of our new CO with trepidation. Then Holt barked "Attention!" and Rhoads in stylish greens ablaze with a chest full of colorful ribbons strode in, returning Holt's smart salute with an arm-jerker that ripped through the air with the hiss of a fired bullet.

Holt introduced us by grade, beginning with von Bloeker, Master Technical Sergeant, Acting. Rhoads stood before von Bloeker and inspected him with a suspicious eye, trying to discern just what species of top sergeant he had inherited.

"Von Bloeker?" he said. "What kind of name is that?"

V. B. was puzzled by the question. "German origin, sir. If that's what you mean."

"Mmmm!" Rhoads said, continuing to study his top sergeant. Rhoads knew that a command could thrive or die on the shoulders of this important member of his team.

In the contemplative silence, von Bloeker seemed to feel compelled to fill the vacuum. "A long time ago, sir," he said apologetically. "Prussian . . ." as if hoping the military genes of his ancestors would favorably impress his commander.

"Mmmm," Rhoads repeated. If the colonel drew any conclusions or harbored any wartime prejudices, he did not make them evident. His face was as closed as a shut military manual on how to fire a cannon.

Holt continued down the list, adding the "Acting" suffix to every rating as he ticked them off. "Master Sergeant Wiswell, Sergeant Couffer, Sergeant Herold, Sergeant Williams, Sergeant Benish, Mark, Sergeant Benish, Frank, Corporal Batista . . . " He was interrupted by the entrance of the last military member of our team, late, as usual. "Sergeant Fletcher."

Fletch stepped smartly into line, straightened his shoulders, and saluted with a flourish. He was a splendid saluter.

Rhoads's eyes bored at Fletch from under their bushy brows.

Fletch stood rock steady at military attention—in Levi's, Tony Lama boots, and pearl-snapped shirt.

Rhoads glanced at his clipboard and muster sheet. "Fletcher, Harry J.," he said with profound disgust. Then looking closer at his board, the lion roared: "It says here you're a *marine!*" He glowered at Fletch, eyes flashing up and down, bare head to booted heel. "You don't look like a marine to me. You look like a fuckin' cowboy. A *sissy* cowboy!"

He handed the clipboard to Holt. The veins in his temples seemed to swell. "From now on," Rhoads growled, "this unit will dress according to the *book*. So I can tell the fuckin' dogfaces from the fuckin' civilians from the marines." He shook his head, a bit sadly, I thought. Or was it with bewilderment? Decisively sharp, he barked: "Got it? *Regulation!*"

With perfect unity we all saluted, incredibly militarily. "Yes, sir!" in faultless chorus.

Then Dusty Rhoads strode into his cubicle office and closed the door. I wondered if his quick disappearance was so we wouldn't see his tears.

We looked at each other, speechless. Fletch raised his brows in chagrin, made a grimace, and shook his hand on a limp wrist in a gesture that spoke a loud "Whew!"

We all knew that in that moment, from this day onward, life would never be the same for the bat men.

Northwest of El Centro lay a vast tract of uninhabited desert set aside as an aerial gunnery and bombing practice range. In a flat valley near a dirt landing strip bulldozed into the creosote bush, rocks, and sand, we began to set up a dozen boxlike structures, mere frame and plywood cubes with empty squares and rectangles to simulate windows and doors, the targets for the bats. Here we would conduct our demonstration for the marines.

On one occasion, before we got well acquainted with our swarthy chief pilot, Captain Hulls, he offered to fly me out to the test site, then under preparation. Rather than bounce my way across the desert in a jeep, I happily accepted—so kind of him, I thought.

I already knew a little bit about Hulls from the scuttlebutt. He was a combat veteran of the Pacific Theater, where he had been decorated as a top fighter pilot with many Zeros chalked up to his credit. He killed the boredom of hanging around El Centro Air Station by taking up a Piper Cub observation plane, a tiny two-seater that was like a toy compared to the hot gull-winged Corsairs he had flown in combat. I knew Hulls had a reputation as being wild, but I didn't know that his favorite recreation was taking aloft any young marine rookie who didn't know better and scaring the pants off him.

We were airborne and out of sight of the gunnery range, when suddenly the bottom dropped out of my seat. The little Cub winged over, climbed abruptly, stalled, and then fell into a gut-wrenching spin that made me lose all my bearings and very nearly the lunch I'd just eaten. Hulls had lost control and we were goners for sure, or so I thought. We were caught in a maelstrom of dizzying spirals for a very long time. I had no orientation whatever, didn't know up from down, but I assumed that we were falling. The feeling was sickening, terrifying.

It was only when I felt my fanny pushing through my seat and saw the tops of trees flashing past our wings that I realized that somehow Hulls had managed to save us. But he didn't seem a bit perturbed—rather, he was chuckling and looking back over his shoulder to see if my heart had survived his first test.

Next I was aware that we were zigzagging in more or less level flight, that the ground was frighteningly close, and that telephone poles were zipping by first on the right, then on the left.

Hulls flipped a switch and chattered merrily to me on the intercom: "I call this maneuver Threading The Needle," I heard in my earphones. "You've got to look straight ahead to appreciate the effect."

Flying under the telephone wires, Hulls was holding the ship only a few feet above the ground and at the same time weaving through the poles, passing one on the right, the next on the left. One instant there was a dirt road under us, the next an irrigation ditch. The poles ran in a line between, and our wingtips, when we banked to make the next tuck between poles, barely cleared the ground below and the wires above. I was sick with fear. My reaction must have pleased Hulls immensely. I was just the kind of chicken he delighted in skewering.

Then, before he could begin to inflict some new torture on me, an unfamiliar voice sounded from the ether into my earphones. "What ho! Could that be Killer Hulls down there in the Piper?" I heard: "There are three cats up here, Hulls, just itching to drive a mouse into its hole." I didn't know what it meant, but the words on the airwaves were obviously a challenge of some kind and it sounded ominous.

Hulls to me: "I know that voice. A wise-ass second-looey just out of flight school. Thinks he's a hotshot."

Hulls to the sky: "Not this mouse, pussycat. I've got a passenger to deliver all in one piece. Can't waste time playing silly games."

We had been gradually climbing and were now flying at a thousand feet over the desert. Hulls was craning his neck like an owl trying to see where the enemy was lurking. "Where the hell are they?"

As if reading his words, a voice on the radio said: "Behind you, Hulls. Classic shot, right up the ass."

I twisted around in my seat harness and looked behind.

"Got you! Bam, bam, bam." A Corsair, gray-blue and ugly and huge as it overtook us, flaps and wheels down to reduce speed, came flying close alongside. Wingtip to wingtip, cockpit to cockpit, the two planes flew for a moment side-by-side, pilots looking at each other. The second lieutenant grinned; Hulls's return sneer was diabolical.

"Little game of pat-wing?" Hulls said innocently into his mike, quickly maneuvering the Cub into a partial dive to pick up speed to stay with the faster Corsair. With a sudden sideways slip he was on top of the fighter and the bottom surface of his wingtip gently tapped the top surface of the Corsair's wingtip, three distinctly jolting pats, then we peeled off. He giggled like a child getting away with a naughty trick. "Whaddya think of them apples?" he muttered nonsensically into the intercom.

Then, instead of the expected ground-hugging ploy of the cowardly that made the game so much fun for the cats, Hulls pulled back the stick and we began to climb. Again he spoke into his mike: "Don't much feel like a mouse today, flyboys. I feel like a *bulldog.* Bulldogs chase cats!"

Hulls pointed to the Corsairs dropping from high, out of the cloud where they had been hiding, out of the sun, strung out in a line the way they had been taught to attack in flight school. He said to me, "It's the unexpected that wins. Watch."

Watch was all I *could* do. That or close my eyes, and Hulls was about to take that option from me.

I heard his voice speaking professorially to the enemy: "I thought I told you flyboys. This mouse don't feel like playing silly games today. So buzz off or be eaten."

He flipped the Piper around, and again I felt the pressure of G forces on my seat and the giddy disorientation of a sharp turn. Then we straightened out into a steady climb and I saw to my horror that we were headed straight at the lead Corsair. Hulls spoke coolly into the mike: "Warning! This mouse is *not*, repeat is *not*, turning. This mouse is now closing its eyes. Converge at your own risk. Radio off."

And close his eyes he did. "Tell me when he's gone past," he said to me into the intercom.

We flew straight at the attacking Corsair. Unwavering, both ships bored ahead. I couldn't believe I was here, the last place on earth I wanted to be. I couldn't believe that I was about to die in this way.

At the crisis moment, collision imminent, the Corsair banked abruptly and sailed by, incredibly fast and close. The next fighter in line was closing quickly. "He's past," I squawked obediently. "And another one coming!"

Hulls opened his eyes and trimmed slightly left to head straight for the next gull-winged Corsair. I had no doubt of his resolution, no doubt that he would hold true to the course until the planes' props ate each other up. In quick succession two more birds tipped their wings and roared past.

"Damned fool! He's crazy!" came into my earphones.

Hulls watched them, grinning, as they sailed away and arced into a climb, came together, and headed away in the direction of the base. He laughed to himself and flipped to air-to-air: "Cluck, cluck! What happened? Cats become chickens? Cluck! Cluck! Bye, bye. Cluck-a-doodle-do."

I didn't fault the Corsairs for their change of tactics. Instead of fear, I reckoned they had merely shown good sense, and thank God for that. As for myself, all I wanted was my feet on solid ground with a nest to collapse into. Hulls and his games could go to hell. I was ready to lay an egg, I was so chicken.

It was around eleven P.M., a couple of nights before the demonstration, when a marine wearing a Shore Patrol armband came into the barracks and shook us awake. He said that Lieutenant Holt could use some help. It seemed that he had borrowed Colonel Rhoads's staff car for an evening on the town. Whether or not its use was authorized did not enter into the conversation, but we assumed that it was not. The fact of importance was that it was at the moment roof-deep in an irrigation canal on the west side of El Centro. Tim and the girl were okay, a bit soggy, the SP said, but the dunking had sobered them up. The car, however, was an unholy mess.

It was this episode that, as much as it cemented the bond of comradeship between Holt and his crew, brought us equal satisfaction in realizing what good friends the marines could be—how true their motto *Semper fidelis*, always faithful.

Within a half hour of the news, Fletch and Williams had roused the dispatcher at the base motor pool, who assigned a tow truck and crew. By two A.M. the colonel's car was under bright lights in the base garage, where with a crew of eight mechanics we dried it out, straightened, filled, sanded, and spray-painted the dents, and added a coat of polish. When Rhoads called for his car the next morning, he complimented his puzzled driver for having brightened it up so neatly. "Well done, corporal," he said. "Very spiffy. I hope these batty dogfaces of ours take note. That's the kind of spit and polish I expect to see from a marine."

We were all terribly proud of ourselves, of the Marine Corps motor pool, and of Tim Holt for giving us the opportunity to know and appreciate our hosts so well.

Again we went through the familiar test procedures, dropping the bats in their containers with their dummy bombs from high altitude, and again we scored success. Fletch and Williams had all the fun that day. They got to drive jeeps carrying the marine brass who were observing the flights of bats—as Hulls had treated me to the ride of a lifetime, they took revenge on the officers. The crosscountry bat chases were like modern motocross, and the jeeps became airborne at the summit of every anthill or gopher mound. The operation was as much a demonstration for Admiral J. S. McCain as it was a test, because there was nothing new to try out.

Colonel Rhoads alone of the officers seemed to enjoy the experience and complimented Fletch on his hairy driving. Back in the saddle again after retirement, Dusty Rhoads was happily dusty once more; after chasing down a couple of dozen winging bats and watching them crawl into the darkest recesses of the plyboard target houses his spirits were high.

The bombs were dropped from a Marine Corps B-25 manned by its regular crew with Holt as bombardier. Once again, Hulls was left to hang around the base, bored and restless with nothing to do. He took up a young flight crew trainee in the Piper Cub and put him through the usual belly-wrenching paces.

When returning from our successful day of testing, we met a Shore Patrol jeep on the dirt road. They informed us that there had been a plane crash nearby. A Captain Hulls and a boy had been killed. Rhoads ordered us to detour to the crash site. As we approached and I saw the familiar row of telephone poles between the road and the irrigation ditch, I knew what to expect. It had happened exactly as I had visualized it from my seat in the Piper. Road, irrigation ditch, telephone poles, wires: the sequence was clear. Hulls had been playing Thread the Needle and a wing had caught under the wires, guiding the light plane along a straight course, smack into a pole. The wreckage was sickening, and I could only think that just a couple of days ago I had been sitting in the same seat. The poor kid. I wondered if he had been as terrified as I was.

The members of Project X-Ray attended a memorial service for our late chief pilot, where we heard a summary of Hulls's remarkable combat record. It seemed incredible that a man so experienced in flying could wipe out his life in such a silly way as Hulls had done, almost as if his end was the fulfillment of a death wish. Why had he played his desperate games when he must have known that the odds were so heavy against him and he would lose the gamble one day? We hadn't been acquainted with Captain Hulls long enough to know the answers to the tragedy, but this touch with sudden death cast a pall over the gladness of our otherwise successful mission.

On the eve of our departure back to Bandera, to be flown by our new chief pilot, Captain S. R. Leigh, von Bloeker was working late, rapidly banging away in his two-fingered typing style, squinting through his smoke, doing up Rhoads's reports on the tests. Until now, the colonel hadn't cottoned on to the spurious nature of our ratings, an oversight easy to understand in view of the unorthodox way in which we had achieved promotions. No hard-line military officer could possibly expect such a flamboyant break with tradition and would naturally assume that sergeant's stripes on a sleeve meant the wearer was a sergeant.

This evening as he glanced over the orders for tomorrow's travel signed by his top sergeant, Rhoads casually asked, "What is this 'Acting' crap, anyway?"

Von Bloeker, now so used to the deception that he took it for granted, casually justified the long-standing rationale of our pseudo-ratings. He explained that Doc had felt uncomfortable commanding a staff composed exclusively of privates and had upgraded us forthwith to our present more substantive "Acting" ranks to add a little class to his corps.

The crusty marine colonel looked at von Bloeker as if he couldn't understand what had been said. As v. B.'s explanation gradually penetrated, he began to redden. "Do you mean to tell me that you're not a top sergeant at all? That Adams just assigned you the rank? Out of the blue? All on his own? That you're really a *fucking private*?"

"That's correct," said v. B. innocently. "By the book, I suppose we're all privates."

"By the book? I *live* by the book!" the colonel barked. "Let me get this straight. Adams has been jerking off the Army, the Air Force, and the United States Marine Corps all this time and nobody tumbled to it?"

"Well, 'jerking off'? I don't know. That may be a bit strong."

Rhoads glowered at von Bloeker. "Send a memo to all officers, Project X-Ray," the colonel roared. "That's Smith, Holt, and Leigh. There's to be an officer's staff meeting at eight o'clock tomorrow morning. Here. In this office. And don't sign it fucking 'Acting'! Sign it fucking 'private'! You got that?"

"Yes, sir," von Bloeker said. He saluted and stepped out.

Rhoads's voice thundered after him. "And get me Adams on the blower. I don't give a damn if he's in some shitty bat cave in Texas or at the Pentagon. Get him now!"

We were never to be privy to the exchange that followed, but thus began the first drift in a current of mistrust that Rhoads developed toward Adams. The colonel was furious with Doc's breach of military procedure. The inventor's resourcefulness outside his area of authority had been carried a step too far, and the colonel would never forgive Adams the gall, which Doc probably thought of as much as a joke as genuine subterfuge. But if Doc saw the humor in it, our CO didn't think it was funny at all. It was possibly the potentially most embarrassing thing that Rhoads had faced in his entire military career.

How did one approach Marine Corps Headquarters and announce that one's total staff of noncoms were in fact all privates? Just how did one say: "I've been hoodwinked by a fast-talking Santa Claus and made to look a fool"? Was there any way of getting out of this coffin he'd been nailed into by a grandfatherly civilian without seeming a simpleton?

After his original flush of outrage subsided, Rhoads had a serious think about the situation. If tomorrow morning every noncom in Project X-Ray—and that meant every member of the team—showed up with empty sleeves where all those stripes had been, with ragged thread-ends sticking out to show where rankings had once been sewn—as conspicuous as the light patches on a wall where long-hung pictures have been removed—there would inevitably have to be explanations. Questions asked would have to be answered with the embarrassing truth. Soon the whole Air Station would hear through the scuttlebutt, which traveled wide and fast like jungle drums. It would be only hours until the entire Marine Corps would be in the know, for this was the kind of boner that was material for legend—and Rhoads didn't want to be the butt of it. What terrible crime had Rhoads's noncoms committed to warrant such all-inclusive total demotions? He could hear the answer now: "Well, they merely pulled their stripes out of a hat, sewed them on, and for half a year they got away with it!" This answer, Rhoads knew, would make him the laughingstock of the corps. No, the colonel decided, he wouldn't get drawn into the humiliating situation half-cocked. After all, he rationalized, his team had been successfully performing the duties of noncoms for all these months, they hadn't embarrassed anyone with gross military blunders, they didn't appear to be in over their heads; they had, in fact, done a thoroughly commendable job.

So, in his troubled mind, Rhoads began to capitulate. Yes, the simplest and most effective way to handle this potential embarrassment would be to carry on as closely as possible with the status quo. But he couldn't stand—ever—to see that offending designation "Acting" again. And if he allowed things simply to drift along as they had been, when the duplicity was eventually discovered, as eventually it must be, he would seem to be even more an ass.

The answer to the dilemma was to write a letter of blanket

commendation, high praise for every "acting" noncom—God, how he hated that word—in the unit. Best just forget the offending qualification and straightforwardly request upgrades for all staff in view of a job well done, work accomplished in grades below the standards expected of the MOS (military occupational specialty). Don't make any reference to the fact that these jokers had been pretending to be noncoms all this time and probably no one at headquarters would notice. Then, once the ratings were made official, he could breathe normally again.

But he'd write the letter himself. He couldn't face that whiz-kid von Bloeker with his annoying two-fingered rat-a-tat-tat with this one.

And so Colonel Rhoads labored into the night, pecking out alone on the big Smith Corona at von Bloeker's desk the official request for advancement in grade, from private to noncom, straight through the roster. And because of the special nature of Project X-Ray with all the secrecy and mystery attached, no one questioned his curious request that skipped right past the usual step-by-step raises in grades—orders sailed through channels with record speed. Now we not only wore our stripes with official sanction, but we all got a healthy raise in pay, as well.

But Rhoads was never to forgive Adams for bringing him so close to the ridicule of his peers.

# 16

## *The Other War*

THE LOCKHEED R-5-0 was equipped with hard wooden benches along both sides of the fuselage with a wide aisle amidships for the stowage of cargo. The plane had been fitted out to carry neither passengers in comfort nor goods in quantity, but in the most functional way possible to accommodate any contingency. As a compromise carrier, it would serve neither role perfectly, but either adequately. Cargo, however, would definitely be cozier than passengers. The ship stunk with the pungent odor of aviation fuel and the roar of the engines was undampened by soundproofing, nor was the chill of high altitude lessened by insulation. Parachute packs were stuffed under the benches along with green oxygen cylinders and red fire extinguishers. "Doc" Savage, the burly crew chief, sat at the end of the bench closest to the pilots' compartment and Chuck Hubbard, his mechanic-assistant, sat opposite. Captains Leigh and Smith, of course, occupied the cockpit with its formidable array of instruments and switches. The rest of us made ourselves as comfortable as possible on the hard seats or by lying on our duffelbags on the floor.

The entire bat unit was aboard; Rhoads remained in El Centro to choreograph the combined efforts of our work with that of Fieser and Young. Doc was headed for Washington by commercial airline.

After what seemed a very long time underway, Leigh leaned back through the cockpit door and shouted above the engines' racket. I couldn't hear what he said, but from his hand motions pointing down and catching the word "Bandera" I gathered that we were about to fly over our favorite spa. Fletch went forward and asked the pilot to drop down for a closer look.

"So that little burgh with the water tower is the famous Bandera I've been hearing so much about?" Leigh shouted. "We'll just drop in and say, 'Howdy!' "

He put the Lodestar into a steep dive and I had vivid recollections of the last time I had been airborne. Had we drawn another Hulls as our chief pilot? Or were *all* Marine Corps pilots lunatics?

We approached Bandera with our belly skimming the pecan trees along the Medina River and roared into town with wings just about ripping the roofs off both sides of Main Street. Cars screeched to a halt in mid-road, Billy stampeded, pedestrians dove for cover, and white laundry turned instant brown from the dust. At the last moment near the south end of town Leigh tipped one wing barely enough to clear the water tower, then dipped it back down again on the other side as we zoomed past.

"Just to let them know you're on your way home," he cackled, then pulled back in a climb so steep our bottoms smashed into the hard seats and our stomachs were sucked down to our toes. He circled as he climbed, leveled out, wobbled our wings in greeting, and I looked down. Half the population of Bandera was already out on the street looking up, waving and pointing, and the rest were still pouring from doorways. They must have thought the world was coming to a sudden end.

"It'll be 'Put Your Little Foot' tonight," Fletch shouted. "And I can't wait to see how much Top Sarge has grown."

I nodded, agreeing. But I was thinking less about tigers than about how nice it was going to be to see Arlie again.


A week later, Patsy Batista picked up Tim Holt at Hondo Air Base and drove him in the staff car toward Bandera. Patsy put on airs about being unimpressed by Holt's civilian status as a movie star. After all, he'd been on staff of an even more famous individual. Yet he couldn't hide a bit of awe.

Patsy opened the conversation. "You movie stars know all about how movies are made, I suppose?"

Holt, ever modest: "We just do what the director tells us, Patsy. Why?"

"You must know all about trick photography. Special effects and that stuff?"

"A bit," Holt admitted. "I didn't know you were interested in movie technique."

"Yer fuckin' A, I am. I'm interested in a lot of things. Very technical minded, I am."

"I see . . ." noncommittal.

"I saw this flick . . . *The Abdominal Snowman.* A monster show. Looked real as hell, but of course it couldn't be."

"*The Abominable Snowman,*" Holt corrected. "Matte shots and miniatures, I think."

"You see? That's what I mean. Like can you put a different head on someone else's body?"

"Anything's possible. It's been done, sure."

"In, like, those *blue* movies? Where they put a beautiful woman's face on someone else's body? I mean if the beautiful face doesn't have a great body? That's what they do, huh?"

"I doubt it," Holt said. "More likely they'd just find a beautiful head and a beautiful body all on the same person."

Patsy let that sink in for half a mile, then: "But they do enlarge the tits? You know, the breasts . . . ? Like I heard they do? With trick photography?"

"I don't think so, Patsy. Some of those Hollywood girls come already very well endowed."

Patsy shook his head dubiously. It was a bit too good to be true. But he accepted Holt's answer for what it was worth and thought it over in silence with an occasional sage nod. He drove without speaking for another half mile, deep in thought, then: "Have you ever, ah, acted in a blue movie?"

"Unfortunately, no," Tim said.

That was the most disappointing thing that Patsy had heard since Al Capone got sent up by the FBI for tax evasion. Tim Holt's rating as a movie star just fell by 50 percent in Patsy's opinion.


The Coleman gas lantern burned brightly in my Ney Cave tent, attracting a myriad of moths and crane flies that swarmed in through the open flap. It was by far the easiest way to provide a banquet for Flamethrower and Princess. When I figured that about a tenth of a pound of succulent insects had collected inside the tent, I closed the flap and opened the door to my pets' sleeping box. The tent was too small for Flamethrower to fly. He crawled along the canvas and took a position hanging near the ridge pole, where he grabbed moths out of the air or from my fingers as I handed them to him. Princess flew back and forth through the swarm, catching on the wing. She had her favorite corner to hang upside-down and dewing moths between catching forays around the lantern. On the floor beneath each feeding place, piles of wings collected. They would have to be swept up in the morning. After an hour or two, when the bats had their fill, Flamethrower and Princess would return to their box, which was hung, door open, from the ridge pole at the back end of my tent.

When I grew tired of watching, I shut off the hissing lamp and lay with my head against my pillow, listening to Princess's wings fluttering in the darkness. I realized that I had grown quite fond of my pets. In the case of Flamethrower, I felt that my feelings were at least partially reciprocated. He seemed completely content with his new life, and a couple of times before the arrival of the female, when I had forgotten to close the door of his box in the morning, Flamethrower had made no effort to leave my company. Princess, on the other hand, remained forever aloof, and I knew that if given the chance she would depart. Neither Flamethrower nor I, with all our charm, held the slightest attraction for her.

Now that Doc was no longer required to sell his project at every turn of the road, Flamethrower's usefulness as a vaudevillian was redundant. It had been many weeks since I had tied the toy soldier with its awesome weapon onto his back. I was sure that the monstrous bat didn't yearn for his appearances as a performer, but I did suspect that when I was called away for trips to California, or when I disappeared for two or three days on leaves, he missed me. Not that Flamethrower had lost his spirit or was all sweetness and light, but when he bit me, as on bad-tempered days he was wont to do, he didn't bite as hard as he used to. This, I fancied, was about as close to showing affection as a bat could get.

On an impulse, I got up out of my dark bed and tied open the tent fly. In the morning, Princess had flown away. My analysis of the bats' characters had been correct. Flamethrower, as I suspected, was hanging contentedly in his familiar nest-box corner.

I looked closely into Flamethrower's face as I closed his door for the day. His appalling visage looked up as I moved, black beady eyes sparkled, and the rows of needle-sharp white teeth between his ugly lips were bared in a horrible smile. His squeaky voice chittered. I had no idea what he was saying, but I fancied that he was glad to be rid of his guest.

In our happiness to be "home," and with the exciting prospect of continuing our work under the truly committed auspices of the Marine Corps along with all the urgency that meant, we were unaware of the many problems that beset our leader.

Doc's last invention, the airmail pickup system, had proved worthy, but he had run into problems with the company management. By 1940 Adams had been gradually pushed aside by his partner and, under these unhappy circumstances, had sold out his interest to du Pont. Typically, he had closed the relationship with acrimony and mistrust. His method of departure was in keeping with his usual style. "The Wilmington Trust Company had prepared a cashier's check for the appropriate amount [$45,000], but Adams balked, demanding cash. Because it was already late in the afternoon when the two parties concluded the agreement, the trust company's vault was closed. After much scrambling about, the bank officials gained access to the cash section of the vault and Adams received his payment in ten- and twenty-dollar bills. He threw the money into a cardboard box, placed it in the trunk of his car, and drove off."*

Doc had been living comfortably in Irwin, Pennsylvania, in a lifestyle that cost most of his earnings as a dental surgeon and kept his savings low. At the time he had written to President Roosevelt proposing the bat project, his bank account totaled a modest $60,000. But now for more than half a year he had been supporting himself, his family back home, and a goodly share of the Adams Plan-cum-Project X-Ray with his own funds. So great was his faith in the project, and so keen his devotion to accomplishing something he sincerely believed would help the Allies win the war, that he was willing to extend himself all the way, further if necessary. Now the money was running out. Even the meager stipend supplied him by the government film unit as a technical advisor for a nonexistent training film was discontinued. The job came up for review by someone who wasn't clued in to the true reason for its creation—which had been merely a devious way to help reimburse Doc for some of his expenses.

Doc never mentioned his financial problem to us. We never thought of it. He seemed to survive and to keep us going with resources drawn from a bottomless pit. But this, of course, was not the case. His situation must have been a considerable worry and a drain on his seemingly boundless energy as well as his bankroll.

Another thing we didn't know was that Doc's bank account, which was now so materially depleted, had not been his alone. A considerable part of it belonged to the United States government. This was the portion due in income taxes. Doc's attitude about that, we were later to learn, was rather devil-may-care. He strongly believed that the U.S. government would eventually make good on its debts and repay him for all his expenditures. After all, his work had the tacit authorization of the president and he was working hand-in-hand with a great many top officers of the Armed Services and important government agencies. He kept accounts for all official ex-

---

*William F. Trimble and W. David Lewis, "Lytle S. Adams, the Apostle of Nonstop Airmail Pickup," *Technology and Culture* 29 (April 1988): 264–265.

penditures for which it was reasonable to expect reimbursement, and he had, as we shall see later, the assurance of a top government liaison officer that he would be repaid. Doc even expected to be paid some back salary or a fee for the time spent. But Adams had the unrealistic and naive belief that since it was the U.S. government's money anyway, the National Treasury would look at it in the same way he did—it all went in and came out of the same huge institutional pocket, so what difference did it make? He'd settle accounts with the IRS when the government made good on what he considered to be his temporary loan to them.

Doc was a visionary, a romantic; he could inspire immense loyalty with his amusing good looks, jolly manner, and winning sincerity—all of us in the bat unit were behind him 100 percent—but at the same time, in rather screwball ways that seemed irresponsible at times, he presented to those who didn't know him well the aura of being deceptive. Perhaps he was just too good to be believed. There was a common suspicion among those uninitiated people that in his beguiling manner Doc was basically a flimflam man. And a promoter he was, to be sure, but in the case of Project X-Ray, at least, it was the enterprise he was promoting and not himself.

Unfortunately, this unselfishness was not a trait common to Doc's associate, Fieser, whose ego split his interests between self-promotion and Doc's more benevolent goals. And in Fieser's way, perhaps this speciousness created an urge even more impassioned than Doc's.

When Fieser saw that the project had moved up from the on-again, off-again status as stepchild of a half-interested Air Force to an undertaking of top priority under the Marine Corps, he took the change of sponsors as his cue to reestablish the position in Doc's hierarchy he had lost to Young, who had moved up to top chemist in Doc's estimation. In a few solicitous memos to his junior partner, Fieser reconciled whatever differences had grown between them. Perhaps this device wasn't even necessary; Young probably wasn't even aware that Fieser had been putting him down. If he was, he was surprisingly forgiving, because he quickly responded to Fieser's queries and requests with all the promptness and subservience of any well-trained subordinate and accepted his minor role with gracious thanks.

With the strong support of his important friends at NDRC in Washington, who barely knew of Young, their distant California associate, Fieser solidified his position as top chemical man and was able to present himself to the new commandant, Colonel Rhoads, with all the proper credentials as team leader. For extra measure, he threw in the development of all hardware as his responsibility, too. Fieser made it seem that it was he, rather than Adams, who had been responsible for the successful design of the Crosby container shell. Rhoads didn't have reason to question this and took it for granted that Fieser was what he seemed to be, the man in charge of all chemical *and mechanical* aspects of the bomb. Besides, Rhoads was disenchanted with Adams because of the inventor's mischievous handling of the military ratings system.

Just as the chemist had proffered his unasked-for opinions about the biological aspects of the project, he now intruded into another area outside the expertise for which he had been brought aboard. But in this case he simply took credit for work already done by Adams and the Crosby Company. Fieser successfully moved Doc out of the one technical niche in which he was qualified.

Little did anyone realize it then, but Fieser was out to get Doc's position in totality. The infighting had begun, but so far it was a one-sided war, with only Fieser aware that the first salvo had been fired and the battle joined. If I had realized the intrigue that was building at the time, I would have thought back to our first meeting—and the suspicion I felt because of the way Fieser wore his watch.

Now that we had a definite project with all the resources of the United States Marine Corps behind us and Fieser was reestablished as leader of the chemical and now mechanical wings, he began a cunning series of maneuvers to move himself up to top position overall. His memos no longer hinted at the many doubts he had expressed before; now he was all-supportive and threw himself behind the project with complete belief in its potential. So unqualified was his support that this opportunistic change went unnoticed. His opinions of the merits of Project X-Ray changed direction with the tide of political current. If the flipflops of General Kabrich of CWS had been motivated by indecisiveness or the promptings of his junior staff, at least they had been well-intentioned. Fieser's devious maneuvering for position, however, came out of a personal hunger for power.

His chief method of achieving increased prominence was to bombard with correspondence all interested departments, from his several contacts at NDRC, to the Chemical Warfare Service, to the Marine Corps, to OSS, to Leeds and Northrup. He never wrote to Adams and rarely mentioned the inventor in his correspondence elsewhere. Copies of a Fieser memo to one office were sent to all—thus everyone got a steady stream of paper. His missives flew like bats released from on high and sought out every nook and cranny to spread their devastation. With this steady flow of memos Fieser kept his name in the fore.

Quite possibly, Doc was unaware of the device of paper bombardment Fieser was using to bury him. With rare exceptions he couldn't know it was happening because he was never sent copies of the communications; because every paper was marked "Secret," none was distributed beyond the specific recipients. If Doc was aware, there was little he could do about it. The project required input from Fieser—or someone with his knowledge—and he was perhaps the most distinguished authority in America on incendiary materials. Doc would have preferred Young, but the senior chemist had seen that coming and had forestalled any attempt at replacement by solidifying his relationship with his assistant. Perhaps Adams was content merely to see his baby grow. Maybe he would have been happy enough accepting a secondary role, anyway. Although the idea had been his, he lacked many of the technical skills required to bring it to fruition, and he must have realized this. He now generally accepted the findings and recommendations of the bat unit as an administrator, without meddling in the science—as a director and not a hands-on investigator, which he left to von Bloeker and Wiswell.

In the meanwhile, only vaguely aware of what was going on with our brother unit, we in the bat section dug into our researches, occasionally publishing our results in a memo, and concentrated on the work at hand rather than on the politics of internecine warfare. Even our prolific von Bloeker, who by virtue of custom as well as competence assumed the role of official correspondent for the biological unit and who attacked his huge Smith Corona with such amazing two-fingered speed, ran a distant second place in the memos race behind the literary verbosity of the frenetic Fieser.

Fieser's first correspondence which began to hint at an attack on Adams was a long letter written on November 26, 1943. It did not come to the attention of anyone in the bat unit until the file of the National Archives was opened in 1990. "I had a talk with Dr. Adams which, if anything, got me a little more confused, and Captain Carr [of CWS] and I are in hopes that you can clear up some of the points."

He went on to describe problems with the manufacture of the celluloid capsules which held the incendiary material, with Adams's objections to some of the design elements and his pointed counteropinions regarding the same. He said that Leeds and Northrup had come up with a time-delay unit that was 100 percent effective, then:

I had assumed that this lot of some three-to-five thousand incendiary units requested by CWS for the Marine Corps was for use in a series of practical trials of The Adams Plan. Dr. Adams, however, states that all the tests necessary had been completed and that no further experiments were required. This seemed very odd to me because certainly no tests have been made to show whether or not these small incendiaries are effective in setting fires to Japanese or other structures. I think the Marine Corps may have been taken in by perhaps a facetious report by the Air Corps, based on that nice job we did at Carlsbad Airport.

At least Fieser could now make a joke of the embarrassment in New Mexico, but whether Doc really said that all required testing was finished is problematical. If he did say it, it might have been a tactic intended to dismiss Fieser, throw him off the track of any tests Doc might have wanted to conduct on his own. Perhaps Doc still thought he could pick up the pieces with Young. If he did, he was very much mistaken. Young had committed himself to Fieser.

Fieser was no fool, and this letter addressed to Young, with copies to officials at NDRC and Chemical Warfare, who were the significant readers, was undoubtedly a turning point. The chemical and mechanical conclusions that Fieser expressed in this letter were all sound, and many of Doc's design and developmental ideas, if accurately reported by Fieser, were expressed in such a way as to make Adams seem dense in this highly specialized field, where the more scientifically educated chemist from Harvard had the upper hand. But the fact remains that, in spite of the veracity of his design points, Fieser's letter was destructive for reasons of bolstering the chemist's status and ego as much as for improving the project.

# 17

# *The Hibernation Equation*

DURING THE THREE WEEKS of our absence from Ney Cave, Top Sarge had gotten himself into a pack of trouble. According to the marine guard left in charge, Top Sarge, all in the spirit of fun, had played rough with a visiting herd of sheep. During the game, the tiger had "accidentally" killed one or two. Even given the benefit of doubt and accepting the tiger's conduct as being merely a playful overindulgence, the act didn't sit well with the sheep's owner—nor with any other stockmen in the country, all of whom soon got wind of it—and a formal complaint demanding restitution was made to the Marine Corps. The deceased sheep, according to papers filed at the County Courthouse, had enigmatically become not one or two but four, and the most valuable per head of their kind in the whole state of Texas. The grievance, of course, quickly made its way to El Centro, and Colonel Rhoads was on the blower forthwith.

"What's this business about a tiger?" he asked Fletch with understandable suspicion.

"Yes, sir?" said Fletch, at a loss for words more illuminating.

"Yes, sir, what?" the colonel barked. "I said, what's this business about a tiger?"

"Oh, you probably mean Top Sarge?"

"I said, *tiger*," the colonel snapped. "T-I-G-E-R!"

"Yes, sir. That's Top Sarge, sir."

"Top Sarge is a tiger?"

"Yes, sir."

"You mean there really *is*? In actual fact, I mean? A tiger?"

"Yes, sir. The unit mascot of the Texas Tigers, sir."

"What in hell are the Texas Tigers?"

"Us, sir. The Ney Cave bat team. Well, Bracken Cave staff included. All of us," Fletch said, trying his best to spread responsibility around as widely as possible.

"Listen, Fletcher. If you've really got a Goddamned tiger there, and I find this extremely difficult to believe, or to understand if I could believe it, then get rid of it forthwith. Understand? Forthwith! I don't want to read another complaint about Marine Corps tigers killing Texas livestock. Or people, either, for that matter. Probably next thing I hear is that your damned mascot or whatever it is has killed someone. Now how would *that* sit with headquarters, eh? Now get rid of it. I mean immediately, understand? Forthwith!"

"Yes, sir. But it may not be that easy," Fletch said. "A tiger, you see, sir, is . . . well . . . a good home . . . I mean, not just anybody wants . . ."

"*Forthwith!*" Colonel Rhoads roared.

"Yes, sir. Forthwith."

"And no more mascots, get it?"

"No, sir. I mean, yes, sir. No more."

"Good."

This exchange took place the first day after our arrival back at Bandera. That evening, in a quandary over how to deal with our mascot, Top Sarge accompanied Fletch and me on a sojourn to the OST Cafe and later that night to the Rocking-W dude ranch where we retired for another beer.

There we met an affable young Air Force captain who had blown into town some ten days ago in the dudiest yellow Cadillac convertible seen around these parts in years. In Bandera, a three-year-old pickup with chrome-plated hubcaps was considered to be just about the smartest thing on wheels. This car was outstanding beyond imagination. The visiting captain, it seemed, was a hero of the North African and Sicily campaigns, where he had been shot down three times, parachuted twice, once behind enemy lines, and crash landed within walking distance of an Italian prisoner of war camp, where he had been interned for a month, eventually making his escape with the help of a beautiful Italian countess working with the Underground. After being wounded by sniper fire that killed the countess on their way through the lines, he was now on R and R (Rest and Relaxation) leave—that is, a furlough granted to exhausted veterans to allow them to recoup enough strength to return to active duty.

The captain and Top Sarge hit it off like long-lost pals from the jungles of Bengal. The tiger was treated to the biggest, tenderest, most expensive T-bone steak the Rocking-W had to offer—not one, but half a dozen of the prime cuts, enough to win the life-long love of any carnivore known to science.

When the captain heard that Fletch had been ordered to dispose of the beautiful cat, and to do it *forthwith*, he offered to settle Fletch's dilemma on the spot and without a hitch. With a page from a brand new checkbook filled out and signed in the amount of $500, the captain took possession, and that night Fletch again was sleeping alone.

Two days later, a military staff car bounced up the track to our tented camp at Ney Cave. It was driven by an MP, and out stepped another MP and a second lieutenant representing the provost marshal of an air base somewhere in Louisiana. They had been traveling around the country, it seemed, always only a step behind, chasing down a deserter who was masquerading as an Air Force hero. The fugitive was reported to have departed Bandera for an unknown destination in a stolen yellow Cadillac convertible, leaving behind about $6,000 in worthless checks. Did we, having been seen in his company at the Rocking-W a couple of nights ago, have any clues as to which direction he might have been heading?

We didn't, we told the officer, but an Air Force captain driving a yellow Cadillac convertible, doubtless with the top down to give the breeze to his traveling companion, a Royal Bengal tiger, shouldn't be too hard to find.

The MPs left with thanks, and a couple of days later Fletch got a message to report to the sheriff's office of a small town a hundred miles to the north.

"The provost marshal took away the prisoner," the sheriff said on the phone, "but told me to contact you about this damned tiger. Sweet-natured thing, but eating us out of house and home. Bring along enough money in cash to pay off the fifty bucks in beefsteaks he's already scoffed. And listen, he's incarcerated in the only cell in our jail. We can't put any other prisoners in with him, and Saturday night's coming up and we don't have a durn place for the drunks to sleep off the weekend. So shake a leg up here, will you?"

Except for his night in jail, Top Sarge had never been behind bars, and Fletch found a very humiliated tiger when he arrived to reclaim possession. Top Sarge wore a hangdog look and was off his feed, but when he saw his friend from Bandera he picked up considerably. When he saw the jeep, his day was truly made—riding in the open vehicle was, with the possible exception of playing with sheep, his favorite pastime.

But now Fletch was stuck again with the same dilemma. On his return through Bandera, he found a message from our CO.

Sgt. H.J. Fletcher, U.S.M.C.
Have you disposed of subject conversation, 4 Nov 43 yet? If not, urgent do so forthwith.

Rhoads

Fletch phoned the zoo superintendent at Top Sarge's former home. No, the tiger wasn't wanted there. Since he'd outgrown the petting zoo, there was no place to keep him. But the zoo man informed Fletch that he happened to know that the Los Angeles Zoo was looking for a male tiger to replace one that had died—if he had a way of getting him there.

Fletch fired off an official signal to El Centro explaining the situation. A brief dispatch came back. It said just what Fletch had been afraid of.

Fletcher.
Call me.
Rhoads.

"All right, Fletcher," the colonel said after hearing Fletch's story. "I'll advise Leigh that you can transport him aboard the R-5-0 on the next flight west. But under the following strict conditions, and write these down. Got a pencil? Okay.

"One. He'll be nailed inside of a good solid escape-proof cage at all times. I said, *nailed*.

"Two. You will personally escort him at all times. I said, *all times*.

"Three. You will be armed and prepared to kill if that damned latent man-eater escapes on the plane. I said, *armed* and prepared *to kill*. No guns, no shooting aboard an aircraft, of course. You got your K-Bar?"

"My what, sir?"

"Your Marine Corps issue combat knife, Mark-two, eight-inch blade? Right! That's your weapon, then. If that damned man-eater so much as shows a whisker outside its cage, if he even *hints* he's going to escape in the aircraft, you stab him. Okay? Good! In the heart, then. Good flight. And be careful."

Thus did Top Sarge journey under military armed guard to Los Angeles, where he met a beautiful tigress widow and lived happily ever after.

Prompted by the imperative of the marines to expedite the bat project, General Kabrich of Chemical Warfare picked up the pieces left by his previous vacillations and wrote to J. B. Conant, chairman of NDRC, asking that Fieser be given "authority to fully investigate the problem of designing the time delay incendiary capsule." The general wrote, "Some preliminary work has already been done, but it is now quite essential that the entire development be completed at a very early date."

He went on to formally request of NDRC that Bill Young be given full authority and sponsorship, with the financial support this implied, to cooperate with Fieser and Adams.

If Chemical Warfare was reacting emphatically to the pressure put on by the marines, Fieser responded in kind and with a typically wordy and technical memo, distributed for once to Adams as well as the usual recipients—Chemical Warfare, NDRC, and Leeds and Northrup. He addressed this letter, meant for all—to keep the pot boiling—to Colonel Rhoads.

"The units developed for the trials last summer had certain defects which can be easily remedied," he wrote. This switch in attitude was doubtless welcomed by all concerned. Previously Fieser had seemed to feel that the problems with the bomb would be quite difficult to resolve. Now in his letter to Rhoads et al. he listed the bomb's many inadequacies and described in detail the remedies he had in mind to fix them.

He also told Rhoads that Leeds and Northrup Company was perfecting a time-delay device that would "probably be capable of considerably greater accuracy." It was but another stone in Fieser's avalanche of correspondence, but this one bore the importance of his now unqualified support of the project.

While Doc attended to our affairs in Washington and California, and Fieser was at work developing the chemical side, Wiswell had been accumulating data in Texas. He now had enough knowledge of conditions in the caves that he thought we could begin building an artificial environment which would induce the bats to turn around their high season metabolism and enter into a state of hibernation. It was summer; the bats would not hibernate in nature until autumn.

The truck that had been built for the purpose at Wright Field, Dayton, Ohio, and driven out to the West looked like a meat delivery vehicle with its large walk-in insulated box body, completely fitted out with humidity and temperature control units. Poggy and v. B. designed, and we built on the spot, enough burlap-covered six-by ten-foot panels to fill the box. Similar to the rectangular frames on which worker bees build their wax cells, the frames hung side by side on brackets from the ceiling. Spaced three inches apart, the panels gave the bats many vertical surfaces, as a series of crevices, where they could easily cling and bunch up together as they liked to do while resting. Once their tiny claws were hooked into the burlap and the bats were cooled down and lethargic, even the joggling of the truck could not shake them loose.

An interesting balance had to be maintained. Unoccupied cave temperatures could be relatively low and constant, but the presence of active bats and the heat they generated brought up the cave temperature and kept the bats active. It was a self-perpetuating situation, created by the animals as they clustered together. When the bats were inactive for a time, they didn't sustain the cave's heat and it gradually cooled. This up and down condition was the one that must be maintained within our artificial environment.

Other subtle forces might also be at work in creating ideal conditions for hibernation. Poggy felt that that most outstanding natural feature of a bat cave, the one about which we all felt so much aversion—the guano, with its pungent odor and the constant transpiration of eye-stinging ammonia—was an essential part of the hibernation equation. Thus the floor of the truck's compartment was liberally spread with a foot of this aromatic material in the freshest bouquet available. We didn't need Emil Rugh's singular métier to accomplish this task—any of us could have bagged up a quarter ton of the stuff and brought it from the cave; but since Rugh had already fulfilled his primary role by disclosing the largest source of bats in the world, he was at loose ends. So with the thought that we'd keep him interested, we called on the bat-shit man to indulge his specialty and provide the wherewithal—to grease the hinges, so to speak, on which swung the hibernation equation.

For me, the weeks of instrument monitoring at Ney Cave were a holiday. My only duties were my four-times-a-day hikes down into the cave and a few minutes to write up the data—the rest of the time was my own. I spent the hours in between exploring the surrounding countryside and hiked as far as I could in the intervals between recordings, both ways along the meandering creek that wound through the limestone ledges at the foot of our escarpment. Not far upstream shelving layers of flat rock held an array of three-toed footprints, the tracks of dinosaurs of different sizes, and I tried to decode some story from the trails. In the brush up along the hillsides wild turkeys gobbled and bobwhite quail called. I made a bow and arrows and finally succeeded in creeping close enough to a big Tom to supplement our meals with the diet of our forefathers. I lay on a midstream boulder in the sun, watching a foot-wide soft-shelled turtle in the creek. It lay buried, barely outlined beneath a thin layer of silt, and in water two feet deep periodically extended its neck like a soft rubber hose, stretching all the way to the surface to suck in a breath of air.

Occasionally, I visited my neighbors, the managers of the ranch upon which we had intruded, Ben Gerdes and his wife and son. Ben allowed me the use of a barn for exercising Flamethrower. Sometimes I didn't even see my hosts when I came and went. Young Ben, Jr., never referred to his male parent by name or as "my father," but always as "him" or "he." I was sure the usage had some complicated basis in psychology beyond my limited comprehension. It fascinated me.

Fishing, hiking, picking pecan nuts, discovering a new world of nature, I was completely removed from the war in those weeks—except for the vicarious war I lived with the marine guards.

When Fletch was away my camp companions were the detachment of marines. They seemed at first to be a reclusive lot, living in quiet worlds of their own. They were not unfriendly; they were not friendly—merely neutral. I imagined that their exclusivity came from the common fortunes they had shared during combat, as if theirs was a private club to which no one outside their experience could belong.

The leathernecks had set up their camp apart from ours, large ten- by ten-foot wall tents with the luxury of wooden floors, commodious by comparison to our modest bivouac. They seldom ventured into Bandera except to buy provisions and were unknown at the OST Cafe or the dude ranches, which was just as well with Fletch and me. Perhaps *we* were the unsociable ones and jealously protected these places, which we regarded as our own private clubs.

Occasionally a different mood came over my mysterious reclusive neighbors and they became downright sociable and even invited me to share a meal with them in their mess tent. As time went on, these occasions became more frequent and I decided the marines were not intolerant; it only took time to become accepted. Always on these evenings of sociability their conversations drifted back to the war—as if the obsessions of their experiences couldn't be shaken. At these times they seemed to want me to hear it all; mostly they spoke of the badness, as if to shock me with their evil stars, all the most horrible torments of their private hells. And it was during these long nights that I absorbed vicariously the horrors of their lives and was transported by proxy to their bloody jungles.

It was the closest I was to come to the real war; sometimes their pictures were so vivid that I would awaken with the same nightmares that haunted them. As if trying to outdo one another, they recounted the commission of atrocities so matter-of-factly that it was impossible for me to discern whether they were speaking to shock me, to gloat, or to wallow in their own self-disgust, a way to purge themselves of the awful things they had seen and done. If they taught me anything it was that the inhumanity of the enemy was not the one-sided affair it was made out to be. The cruelty of warfare let no side off the hook. And most horrible of all was that the barbarism didn't end with orders home, for these marines were still in the jungles of their minds, still only a step from death, still cruelly fighting the brutal Japanese every night.

On the day of entry into the Armed Services, all soldiers, sailors, and marines were issued two dogtags, the standard identification pieces to be worn thereafter at all times. Dangling from the neck-chain of one marine hung a pair of these regulation metal tags, one inch by two inches, stamped with name, serial number, blood type, and a letter designating religion, the total personal data required to identify and properly dispose of a dead or wounded body. But also on his chain, conspicuously white between his dogtags, hung a large incisor tooth with a hole drilled through the root. It was his trophy of a particularly brutal hand-to-hand combat in the jungle, a symbol far more personal and deadly than any mounted lion's head on a living room wall. The fact that he still wore the decoration proudly like a medal and boasted most graphically of its acquisition was cause to wonder at the rehabilitative motives for these night sessions, which at the same time revolted, frightened, and fascinated me. Could these severely mind-wounded men ever be the same again?

One marine I thought was about my own age but seemed older began to speak one night as we sat inside the tent. His story, like most of those I heard, erupted in a flood, almost without punctuation, like the purgation of the main player in a psychodrama, an incredible tide of words and emotion that once started seemed imperative to be vomited out.

"It was in a Gook village in the Gilberts," he began without preamble. "We'd been shot up badly taking the ridge, couldn't tell the Gooks from the Japs in the jungle so we just took out anything that moved.

"We were crapped out in the village having a smoke after wasting the last of the Japs. The Gooks came crawling out of their huts like scared rabbits out of their holes, and we tossed them some boxes of K-rations. Not bad looking people in their way, pretty girls, clean, straight black hair, shiny like dark glass. Always combed. You wondered how they could come out of those ruined shacks made of sticks and mud, with pigs and chickens running in and out and crapping all over, and look like they'd just stepped out of some fine joint in the swankiest city in the world. Like some swell Honolulu whore.

"I was lying there on my side with my eyes half-closed when I saw this little boy—ten, eleven years old—about the size of my kid brother back home. He was sneaking up to pinch something, I could tell by the way he moved. He thought he was being very clever but his mission was as obvious as a cat stalking a mouse. A fatigue jacket he was after. Off the pack of one of my mates. I just lay there watching him through half-shut eyes, pretending to be goldbricking, till he reached out to take it. Then I jumped up and yelled.

"'Hold it!' I hollered. I thought it would be fun to scare the crap out of him, you see.

"But he didn't hold it. He didn't grab the jacket, either, I scared him so bad. But he was *going* to take it, you know. That's for damned sure. I know he was going to take it.

"But he ran away, scared as piss, flying down this long open slope. I stood up and grabbed a stone the size of a baseball and hauled back my arm to heave it. But then I didn't throw. He was only a kid, you see, about the size of my brother, and he was only going to steal a fucking dirty fatigue jacket and it wasn't even mine. But my fucking squad leader saw what was going on and while I was all set to peg the boulder but wasn't doing it, he yelled: 'Go for it! Go on. Throw! Hit the little fucker!' And I did. I threw the boulder and it sailed down, and I knew as soon as I'd let fly that I'd led him just right, and down it flew, and at the bottom of the hill they came together. Right in the ear I hit him. And the kid just dropped like a Nip taking a burst from a BAR, and twitched a bit, and my fuckin' squad leader said, 'Good throw, Johnson.'

"Good throw my ass!"

I saw that the narrator was on the verge of breaking up. His voice had a tremor of coming undone.

"Then this Gook woman came running up to the kid and screamed bloody murder and flung herself down on the top of him and lay there sobbing and clutching the kid, and I felt like shit. *Like shit, man*! 'Cause I'd *killed* him! I'd killed that little Gook kid who reminded me of my own brother back home."

And the marine was choked-up and full of tears and I wondered how many times he'd had to live through his experience and how much of this kind of flagellation it would take to beat the picture out of his mind. And I realized that all of these marines had nightmare stories just as close to hell as Johnson's and now I understood why they all seemed a bit withdrawn if not actually deranged and why as Williams remarked when it had been suggested they might help out by reading instruments in the caverns: "These guys are hard enough to get outside at night, let alone into the cave."

And that was as close as I came to the real war.

# 18

# *The Fistfight*

THAT FIESER'S JUGGLING of truth had caught up with him in at least one case was confirmed in a letter to the chemist from his old friend, Harris M. Chadwell, chief of Division 19, NDRC.

Chadwell reported that a Lt. Col. M. A. Fawcett, USMC, who was NDRC's liaison with the Navy and the Marine Corps in Washington, would search marine files and advise him if, in fact, as Fieser had quoted Adams's words, the bat project had now been completely tested and demonstrated. Chadwell also said, "If the rumor which you have passed along is correct—that . . . three thousand incendiary units are needed for an operation [as opposed to a test], Colonel Fawcett will take the necessary steps to straighten out the procurement."

It is inconceivable that Doc, however anxious he might have been to get his project operational, would consider it ready for an actual raid at this point of development—or that he could hope to bulldoze an improperly prepared project through military channels and pull off a half-cocked air raid on Japan at this premature point in time. But that was exactly what Fieser's rumor said that Doc intended to do.

Returning to Fieser's letter to Bill Young with its various copies for distribution, in which he had opened his attack on Adams and started the gossip, the senior chemist said:

> It seems to me that NDRC is not justified in spending money to supply these units unless they are to be used for experiments, for we are not supposed to be a procurement outfit. Also, I am inclined to think that CWS would not want to supply the incendiaries for a large scale operation without some evidence to show that the weapons are indeed effective.

Fieser's rumormongering was squelched in an unsigned note in Chadwell's hand dated ten days after Chadwell's letter. "Lt. Col. Fawcett telephoned that the . . . units were for the final development stage and not for an operation."

Thus it appeared that Fieser had been caught starting and spreading a false rumor. But this fact didn't get in his way or slow the groundswell of negative attitude about Adams.

Perhaps the most surprising aspect of this whole scheme to discredit Adams is that Fieser got away with it unchallenged. Except for Chadwell's note saying that he had seen through the rumor's falsity—an insight that apparently did not go beyond the chief of Division 19's private notepad—no one seemed to realize that Fieser's claim was patently silly. Was Chadwell in sympathy with Fieser's goal? Did he keep his mouth shut so as not to thwart the chemist's dirty tricks? We can never know.

Doc would never have requested only 3,000 units for an actual bombing raid on Japan. Adams visualized the eventual operation on the enemy as requiring at least a million incendiaries. The capsules ordered were clearly for testing.

Yet the tide of suspicion against Doc must have been running so strong in the upper echelons that no one came forward publicly to question Fieser's outrageous accusations. No one seems to have realized the absurdity of the charges, the impossibility of Fieser's claim that Doc was trying to force through an actual operation without definitive testing—and with a mere 3,000 capsules.

Chadwell's handwritten note—the single paper on record that reveals how Doc was set up—continued:

> Fawcett and Col. Rhoads went over the whole problem with HMC [Chadwell himself].
>
> Fawcett and Rhoads will see Fieser and Capt. Carr [of CWS] at E.A. [Edgewood Arsenal] tomorrow.

Just what "the whole problem" was is not clear, but the fact that all the principal players—except Adams—were about to hold a summit meeting at Chemical Warfare Headquarters was ominous.

While Doc was embroiled in his war with Fieser, a couple of us in the bat unit came up with a brawl of our own. I don't believe that the ugly blows of our alley squabble were any less dignified than the contest of words and paper being waged by the others. Maybe now that sword fights and dueling pistols are out of fashion, a knock-down, drag-out fistfight on mutually agreed terms is a more gentlemanly way to settle an affair than the sneaky artifice of back-stabbing and political intrigue currently in favor. But given the warm relationships of the contestants in the bat unit's fight, ours seemed a most unlikely match.

The bout happened, as might be expected, at that rough and ready place of libation, the OST Cafe, a shindy of ordinary occurrence in wild west honky-tonks on weekend evenings—the classic Saturday night chair-breaking. Except we didn't break furniture, we only tried to fracture each other's jaws.

The matching of contestants that at first glance might categorize this fight as something out of the ordinary was actually not unique at all, for the state of affairs in half the brawls in the OST Cafe was that the fighters were the best of friends.

Von Bloeker, in carrying out to the letter the stern orders of our hard-nosed Colonel Rhoads, by writing up the CO's commands and faithfully passing them on to his juniors, had made himself temporarily and unfairly unpopular with his crew. The latest order to be pinned to the office wall under the signature of our top sergeant was merely confirmation of a previous strong policy decision, one which had gone by the board in practice if not in policy the moment we arrived in Bandera. That order was: *No cowboy boots*, even in this cowtown! Fletch and Williams, who was visiting from Bracken and helping with the construction of the bat truck, took particular umbrage at this unpopular order, written and posted and signed by von Bloeker on command of the CO.

But before delving deeper into the strange action to follow, perhaps I should go back and explain a bit more about my special relationship with this exceptional man, for the unfortunate fistfight was between v. B. and myself.

For three years now, I had been von Bloeker's assistant, first at the museum and now in the Armed Forces. During this time we had grown very close. Von Bloeker, I felt, thought of me almost as a son, and he couldn't have been kinder and more helpful if I'd been blood kin. I felt the same about him. Back in Glendale, where I grew up, he had spent many weekends with my true family and knew my mother and father well. Ours was a relationship of mutual respect and love.

On many field collecting trips for the museum, v. B. had overseen my education in collecting and the delicate art of preparation of bird and mammal study skins for the research collections. On many midnights on hilltops with wide views, we had sat picking scarab beetles for his studies off the glowing screen of a stretched white sheet with a gasoline pressure lantern behind it, a luminous magnet to attract night-flying insects from miles around. We had tipped many a glass of beer together and had exchanged confidences one only discusses with the best of friends—and sometimes not even with them.

I don't know what it was on this particular Saturday night that got under v. B.'s skin, but I was having a swell time with Arlie, Putting My Little Foot, Putting My Arm Around, and obeying the other rhythmic instructions, all in the best of taste, that the caller sang out in tempo with the music. Meanwhile, v. B. sat morose and alone at his table staring into the foam on his glass. Just a temporary mood, I was sure; we all have them from time to time.

It was around one A.M., and things were just beginning to get interesting; there's no doubt that neither von Bloeker nor I was feeling any pain. He waved me to his table. Apparently he had called me aside only to make rude remarks about my girlfriend. "That particular beetle," he said, and he was not referring to an insect, but had sunk to the lowest Benish descriptive idiom, "that beetle has got a hard back—and a hard belly."

"Arlie?"

"And probably a heart of solid stone the geological hardness of the coldest granite—about Mohs scale ten."

"You mean Arlie?" I swayed unsteadily, under his unexpected vocal bombardment or from the lightheadedness of beer and dance.

"Yes, Arlie . . . *Personicus insectivorous*," he mumbled, inventing a pseudo-Latin epithet, a common von Bloeker nomenclature for things or people he despised. "*Cimex lectularius*, the proper name of the bedbug louse if you've forgotten the correct designation for that noxious bloodsucker."

"Are you trying in your clever way to say that Arlie is less than perfect?" I tried to joke.

"A notorious louselike species of *Hemiptera* of common habits, which sucks the blood of bats as well as humans. Did you know that it has been conjectured that the bedbug's association with man first arose when he, too, inhabited caves?"

"What's gotten into you, v. B.?"

"It's not *what's* gotten into me—it's *who* has gotten into *her*."

He went on in this vein longer than I wanted to stick around. Whether it was jealousy, as I suspected, or whether he really did think she was a bad influence on what he considered to be my lily-white and as yet uncorrupted person, I don't know. He even threatened to tell my mother!

He went from Arlie's blood-sucking propensities to the irrelevant fact that she was two years older than I was, as if that made her a woman running to seed, approaching menopause and out for a last fling with young boys on whom to feed a hunger of senile lust. At last, after enduring a long and slurred discourse on this subject, my pointed reply was a curt, "Go fuck yourself, v. B."

Sons shouldn't speak to fathers that way, not even surrogate sons to surrogate fathers, and buck sergeants in the Army don't give such explicit instructions to their top sergeants, even "Acting" ones, and v. B. wasn't "Acting" anymore. Perhaps one or the other or both of these snubs were the reasons v. B. got his hackles up even higher. Then my two likewise inebriated buddies, Fletch and Williams, who were already feeling more than a bit uncharitable toward our top sergeant because of his order regarding footwear, urged us to settle the dispute "outside," which meant the alley. Never being one to back down, bantam rooster that he was, v. B. said, "Yer fuckin' A. Let's go," and swerved to his feet.

So the four of us, with the best part of the honky-tonk's clientele behind us, paraded to the alley.

I was a half a foot taller with a correspondingly longer reach; I was stronger, younger, maybe I was even tougher, at least I thought I was—but I'll wager that I wasn't any drunker. The stakes would be odds-on in that bet.

A vivid picture of the next few moments flashes onto the movie screen of memory when I push the buttons of recall. I see von Bloeker swaying sharply rim-lit against the glare of an outside bulb, fists cocked like John L. Sullivan, and me, hauling back and letting fly a roundhouse punch. At least four hard blows landed with resounding effect before my mentor and best friend toppled and collapsed in the dust. He never threw a punch; whether from stupefaction or fatherly love, I'd never know.

Back at the bar I was back-patted and hailed as a hero, but already I was feeling considerable worry and remorse. The fight, if it could be called such—paying customers would have thrown us both out of the ring and demanded their money back—sure did spoil my evening as well as v. B.'s.

Late the next morning, when I saw my surrogate father at breakfast, both eyes purple and swollen nearly shut, lips that had obviously been stung by a nest of hornets, I felt no pride whatsoever. With a shirt cuff, I wiped away the tear I felt coming and went to von Bloeker. "God, v. B.," I said. "I'm so damned sorry. Can you ever forgive me?"

I had interrupted him trying to get a sip from his steaming coffee mug past his bee-stung lips. He looked up through the cigarette smoke, squinting with red eyes through the swollen slits in his head, and said, "What for?"

His reply puzzled me. "For that," I said, looking at his damaged face and wondering if it would ever be the same. "For punching you out."

"Oh," he said numbly. "Is that what happened?"

But the story didn't end there. Before the swelling went down, Colonel Rhoads flew in on an inspection trip. Von Bloeker had to come up with a reasonable explanation for his appearance without implicating me. He made some farfetched excuses that held as much water as a sieve. Rhoads saw through the explanations—as a Marine Corps colonel of many years he'd probably heard the likes of them many times before—and he made a big issue of getting to the bottom of his top sergeant's spectacularly changed profile. Of course he knew that v. B. hadn't *really* fallen out of a cornering jeep—but could he prove it?

My destiny hung on v. B.'s ingenuity. His improvisation stood between the status quo and the standard disciplinary action handed out for assaulting a superior, a general court martial. I was forever grateful that v. B.'s unexpected talents as an actor were greater than his skill as a prize-fighter. Maybe he got some tips from Tim Holt.


The next official communication of record was the back-breaker. Tim Holt's defection was a surprising disappointment, but he must have realized that the die had been cast—Doc was *persona non grata.* The decisive letter describing Holt's desertion came from Doc's old ally, Bill Young, posted from his office at the Department of Chemistry, UCLA, and was written on December 1, only a month short of a year since Doc's first communication with President Roosevelt.


Dear Louis:

I regret that I have been so long in getting the information which you sought in your letter of November 8. On November 19 I informed you of the difficulty I had in contacting the various interested parties. [Fieser had asked Young to obtain some technical information from "the El Centro servicemen" and Adams.]

Nothing further developed until the middle of last week when Dr. Adams came into town and called me on the phone.

He told me that he had been in Washington and that he had phoned you concerning the three-pronged clip. He also agreed to come out and see me late that afternoon. He did not arrive either that day or the next; and at the time I phoned his home I learned that he had left at five o'clock in the morning for parts unknown. Apparently, he just chases around from one part of Southern California to another without staying put long enough for anyone to corner him.

Doc's apparent evasiveness could well have been true and rationally justified. It was at the time that the Internal Revenue Service was urgently seeking Doc, and it is possible that he truly was making himself hard to find. It's also possible that Doc saw the writing on the wall insofar as the conspiracy against him. Perhaps he was deliberately avoiding a meeting with Young in some maneuver known only to himself to get back the control of Project X-Ray, which he saw slipping away.

Young's letter continued with the most damaging report yet, and from a most unexpected direction:

Last Saturday, Lieutenant Charles J. (Tim) Holt of the Marine Corps Air Station at El Centro came to Los Angeles to see me, and we had a very interesting talk. It seems that Col. Rhoads had been purposely avoiding me until he could get the personnel problems of the "Adams' Plan" under control. Everyone in the project seems to be in agreement that Adams cannot accept responsibility for the project and have it function. For example, he ordered Lieutenant Holt to prepare for a test to be held on the desert in which ten thousand assemblies were to be used. When Holt pointed out the tremendous hazard involved to the whole of Southern California by such a program, Adams was most indignant, and the Lieutenant finally had to tell him that such an experiment would not be performed even if he, Holt, had to stand in front of the Arsenal with a machine gun to prevent it.

Adams then complained to Rhoads that Lieutenant Holt would not accept orders from him and left for Washington, apparently to attempt to gain control of the situation. As soon as Adams returned from Washington, Col. Rhoads took a plane for the same place in order to try and settle the issue once and for all. Lieutenant Holt has suggested that we sit tight for a few days un-

til the Colonel returns, at which time we will know whether Adams is in or out, and make plans accordingly.

I did gather the impression that Lieutenant Holt is a first-
class man who has a lot of good ideas concerning the possibilities
of the project and its further development. I expressed the desire
to him that if the project is to be completely reorganized and established on firm footing, that it would be desirable to have you
come out here for a day or two and get everyone interested in the
plan together before any large-scale developments take place.

Young's letter continues with an analysis of his search for the
technical information sought by Fieser, then:

It amazed me to learn that Lieutenant Holt had been on this
project since last July, and he had never seen the Fieser unit, except in the photographs furnished him [from] our previous expe-
ditions. Adams had taken at least two dozen of those units from
this laboratory with the express purpose of showing them to the
Marine Corps officers at El Centro. I have no idea what he did
with them, but certainly Holt was not approached.

If you learn anything further concerning the project, kindly
write me at once and I will do likewise.

Best Regards,
Bill

There appears to be no pat explanation for the charges brought
by Holt and Young. Either the combined pressures of financial crisis
and a paranoia induced by Fieser's undermining brought Doc to the
point of emotional irrationality or the conspiracy against him insti-
gated by Fieser and seconded by Rhoads now included Holt, Young,
and everyone else in the upper hierarchy.

Perhaps Doc saw his impending ruin coming and desperately
sought time and any way out to save his baby.

It's strange, thinking back, how some things stick in your memory
that in hindsight don't seem to be so very important, but these now
insignificant-seeming details once carried such impact that those
brain cells where the information was put hung on to the recollec-
tion, while other more important things have sloughed away. So has
my cellular filing system inexplicably clung to the vivid memory of
Arlie's hands.

Arlie captured my heart. Looking at her pretty face and fine figure in jeans and cowboy shirt that showed teasing gaps of bare brown skin between the buttons was inspiring. She was as playful as one of her colts on a rainy morning. I yearned desperately to try out with Arlie all and more of what I'd learned from the girl with the grandmother who hated soldiers. Once in the jeep down on the bank of the Medina River, a chorus of amphibia yodeling frog Mozart and all the lights of heaven winking in the autumn sky, I put down my bottle of Dos Equis on the step of the jeep and took her in my arms. It was dark enough that I couldn't see her hands so I thought it was the chance of a lifetime. If she would only keep them in her pockets it wouldn't have to be dark, but it's hard to do much serious necking with your hands in your pockets, and I didn't think I could tell her about the uneasy feelings aroused by a look at her hands.

The top surface of Arlie's hands was brown, wrinkled by twenty-one years of exposure to the Texas sun. Her fingernails were broken off short and showed dark crescents where the mixed blood of dehornings and castrations, yellow tick-dip, black fence post creosote, and purple cattle, horse, and sheep ointment made their non-erasable stains. The insides of her hands were the hard palms of a working stiff, callused by the grips of hammer handles, axe handles, fencing pliers handles, scarred by sharp staples and barbed wire, tempered by leather reins. They were two man's hands sticking out of the sleeves of a pretty girl and they fit the rest of her like a patch of black wool yarn on a white lace petticoat.

There in the Texas night, the sky ablaze with Texas stars, my arms around my girl, on the banks of the Medina River with the frogs croaking Mozart, she touched me—and I died.

A few days later, I made a trip over to Bracken Cave to deliver a new recording instrument to Williams. He met me with a sheepish grin. "We got an urgent message from Colonel Rhoads. Said he had to know how many bats were in the cave. Very crisp memo," Williams said. "'Determine accurate number of carriers your area. Suggest assignment to each counter of defined area of sky as in grid-search survey. Add all area counts together when individual counts completed.'

"So Eddie and me took a section apiece, we had a Benish each on two pieces of sky, and all of the guards had sections. We set up some stakes like gun sights so we wouldn't overlap and started counting when the first bats came out. We stuck with it until the last ones were coming out and you could hear the 'whooshes' of the first ones to return diving back in.

"We each had our section of sky and were counting when it began to get dark. Then it got *really* dark and we couldn't see any more so we started guessing. We finally counted and guessed thirteen million which was what I put in the report. Fletch and the guards counted bats at Ney and guesstimated eleven million, and everyone accepted our figures as the gospel. That's what went into Rhoads's official report. So much for trusting Fletch and me and a bunch of battle fatigued marines to play biologist."

It was reassuring, at least, to know that Poggy wasn't working by such crude methods.

But the near-accuracy of Williams's method is surprising. Recent researchers have been faced with the same numbers problem. Constantine solved it by mapping the ceiling of a cave into-one square-foot sections. "The entire ceiling area occupied by bats was used as an index of numbers of bats present. . . . Direct measurement . . . indicated that each square foot of bat-occupied ceiling contained 300 bats. . . . Population estimates were obtained by multiplying bat-occupied square feet by bat density per square foot."

Constantine found different densities in autumn when female bats were present than at other times when the caves were occupied by males, which cluster separately. Seasonal differences also occurred when females were pregnant, and when there were suckling young of different stages of growth. Another group of researchers estimated 10 million bats at Ney Cave, 20 million at Bracken, and "at least 100 million [free-tails] in all the guano caves of Texas."

Now that the bat truck was fully primed with Rugh's contribution of guano, we proceeded with the next biological experiment— inducement of hibernation and monitoring of the bats' health while in that state of suspended animation.

We grabbed active clumps of bats with nets off the walls of Ney Cave and placed them in the artificial hibernation environment. Wiswell checked their condition daily, weighing and examining the now-torpid little creatures to check for weight loss or any other deleterious signs.

Late in the afternoon of the tenth day he removed a few and placed them in a warm box for an hour and that evening released the once again active, squeaking little mammals. They seemed unaffected by the hibernation that had been forced upon them and flew off quickly, joining the other members of the colony already emerging from the cave. He also tested the weight-carrying ability of the dehibernated bats and found that it had not diminished.

Now, nearly fifty years later, it is frightening to think of the careless way we handled the Mexican free-tailed bats of these caverns. The offhand methods by which we explored the swarming caves and picked up live, squeaking, biting little bats with our bare hands, suffering countless tiny wounds, could not be used today without troubling thoughts of the considerable risk—even of an agonizing death.

In the early 1960s, long after Project X-Ray was a nearly forgotten memory, our erstwhile associate Denny Constantine was a well-established and respected medical researcher at the U.S. Public Health Service's Centers for Disease Control, at Atlanta, Georgia. Dr. Constantine had become a leading authority on the disease rabies, one of the most frightening of the deadly viruses. Because of his longstanding interest in bats, and because bats had suddenly become implicated in the spread of rabies, Constantine undertook a medical study of our Texas caves. By placing larger mammals prone to the disease—coyotes, skunks, and foxes—in bat-proof cages deep within the caverns, he discovered for the first time that the rabies virus is not transmitted exclusively through saliva via animal bites as had previously been believed, but can also be contracted through the air.

By the year 1959, five persons in the United States were known to have died after exposure to bats, and two men had died of rabies after only brief entries into Frio Cave, one of the Texas caverns where we had worked on Project X-Ray. Both victims, a mining engineer surveying the guano deposits and a health service worker, declared after contracting the disease that they had not been bitten.

We in the bat project spent many hours in the caves where Dr. Constantine performed his experiments with such astonishing results. All of us not only breathed the apparently rabies-contaminated atmosphere, but were also bitten dozens of times. The first conclusion one is tempted to draw from the fact that none of us contracted the disease is that the virus did not exist in these bat populations at the time we were working there. Otherwise, the consequences are too frightening to contemplate. One could imagine all of us foaming at the mouth, biting each other with our teeth instead of with mere words.

But Constantine believes the disease was present at the time of our studies in approximately the same degree as today. "Data available . . . do not support popular belief that an increase in bat rabies cases has occurred since the disease was first detected in the

West in 1954." Less than 1 percent of bats that show no symptoms—a higher ratio for sick-looking individuals—are found positive for rabies infection. This ratio has not increased over the years since its first discovery. The explanation for there being more known cases of bat rabies today than there were then "seems to be that increasingly greater numbers of sick or dead bats have been submitted to health departments as public awareness of bat rabies has grown."

There are many strains of rabies, and the one infecting free-tailed bats may be less consistently lethal for humans than the canine virus. Rabies virus from gregarious bats like free-tails differs in several ways from other strains, one being that the infected animal does not go through the furious phase of symptoms so frighteningly dramatic in canines. No unprovoked attacks by infected gregarious bats have been recorded. Nor does the bat virus kill its host with the same near-invariability with which the more deadly strain kills canines and humans. Constantine has found that approximately 80 percent of healthy-looking free-tails carry antibodies, indicating that they have been exposed and have recovered. Carnivores infected with the strain common to their kind nearly always die, while those experimentally infected with the bat strain often recover. Denny believes that, like those bats carrying antibodies, those of us who worked in the bat caves could also have been naturally vaccinated. Perhaps, he speculates, the small percentage of bats that die of rabies, along with the few people who have died of the disease, had something wrong with their immune systems. When I pressed him to theorize further on why Project X-Ray personnel showed no signs of the disease he said: "I knew about this, of course, when I first went to work on the rabies problem. I was so impressed with the lack of mortality in Project X-Ray and that there had been no known bat-associated deaths in the general population that I thought the bat virus must be a strain that wouldn't infect people. I even volunteered to be inoculated with the live virus, figuring it would probably do no more than immunize me. Then shortly after that off-the-wall suggestion, the first person died."

Bat rabies does not seem to be a serious threat to humankind at large. Because of their habits, bats do not frequently come into contact with humans. Exposure most often occurs when a curious person picks up a sick bat—in the common reflexive reaction of any wild animal, the bat bites. But any bat that a person can pick up off the ground is probably sick and automatically belongs to the high-risk group. "Rabies is nearly always fatal in man after symptoms appear," Constantine says, "so any possibility of exposure should be investigated without delay." Fortunately, an exposure to rabies can be dealt with by inoculations, and bat rabies has even been treated with success (in one case) after symptoms appeared.

A more serious threat is from vampire bats. Vampires feed by biting other animals or humans during sleep and lapping up the blood. They do not commonly occur in the United States and are controlled in Mexico and Central and South America, where their economic impact on the livestock industry as well as their threat to human health is real. The annual blood loss caused by each vampire is about 5.75 gallons, a sizable portion for an animal the size of a mouse. During their southern migration, free-tails often occupy the same caves as vampires and are subject to their bites. Now that rabies is known to be a part of the vampire constitution, another element of fear is added to their already disquieting way of feeding, a mystique even more scary than that of Count Dracula.

Because a first-glance appraisal might condemn free-tailed bat colonies as public health hazards, their control could seem prudent. But, as in the case of any tampering with established natural ecologies, hidden problems lurk in the idea. With only rare exceptions—three known cases outside of cavers up until 1969—the threat of bats to human health in the United States involves primarily those few people who go into bat caves. If one has the masochistic urge to explore these places, one should do so with self-contained breathing apparatus and after appropriate vaccination. Human health in the long run is enhanced by free-tailed bats—consider the tons of potentially disease-carrying insects they consume every night. The economic benefits are equally in the bats' favor. Not only do bats eat malarial and encephalitis-spreading mosquitoes—they also feed on moths, the adults of crop-destroying caterpillars. The tradeoff for the tons of insects free-tails eat every year would require the application of vast quantities of insecticides, whose poisonous attributes are far more widespread and sinister than the chance of catching bat-borne rabies.

Curiously, despite the skin-crawling descriptions of hordes of mites, fleas, and ticks within bat caves, Constantine reports that "no diseases in man are known from ectoparasites of bats or the urine of bats. . . . Ordinary repugnance tends to preclude massive exposure to them in crowded bat caves. [Nor are bats] carriers of rabies; evidence indicates they either survive exposure to the virus without spreading it or they succumb like other mammals."

Denny Constantine's probing of the rabies situation in bats brought to light a side-issue of concern to cave exploration. Several dangerous gases were found in bat caves. In addition to the carbon monoxide that miners guard against with the proverbial canary in a cage, other toxic gases are produced indirectly by the bats.

> Bats live in concentrations of ammonia that would soon kill persons, and . . . in carbon dioxide concentrations similarly lethal to people. Therefore it cannot be assumed that the presence of bats signifies a safe atmosphere.
>
> Government agencies have recommended limits for human exposure to various harmful gases. Bat researchers are advised to heed these standards or risk life-long debilitation, such as brain damage or permanent pulmonary impairment, if not death.

Free-tailed bats can live in 100 times the concentration of ammonia established by the National Institute of Occupational Safety and Health as safe for humans. Curiously, ammonia is produced less by the bats than by the insects they attract. Constantine says that ammonia develops in proportion to the numbers of dermestid beetles and their larvae, "which were found experimentally to produce astounding concentrations of the gas." Bats cluster in caves where their body heat warms the rooms. Urine (which also contains ammonia), guano, and exhaled moisture contribute to the climate of cave rooms favored by dermestids, which feed on the guano and on fallen bats. In their modification of cave climates, the bats provide perfect conditions to support dermestids, whose production of ammonia reaches such strong concentrations that it bleaches the bats' fur, causing them to take on different colors depending upon their exposure to the gas. A comparison by a taxonomist of bleached and nonbleached free-tails showed such gross differences that the study produced the false impression that the bats were of different species, a dark and a light-colored variety.

Constantine's description of a dermestid population in Frio Cave reads like someone's nightmare:

> [Dermestid] beetles and their larvae were abundant under places where bats clustered on the ceiling. Here a continuous agitation of guano was maintained by beetle infiltration and surface movement. Larvae and discarded casts collected in depressions up to six inches deep. Bat droppings generally were attacked by dermestids as food as they struck the floor. Sick bats fell to the floor, as did young bats which lost their hold on the ceiling. Bats falling or wandering into pools of dermestids were skeletonized in minutes. . . . Some dermestids attacked the hanging bats; lar-

vae scaled the walls to reach them, and adults flew to them. They also attacked humans.

My experience repeatedly showed that shortly after the first beetle alighted on me, I was surrounded by a small swarm of buzzing beetles which alighted and rapidly ran about seeking exposed flesh. The first swarm was followed by increasingly greater numbers of beetles. . . . The activities of the dermestid beetles were attended by production of ammonia. . . .

Other dangerous gases recorded by Constantine in bat caves include methane, produced by the decay of organic material, hydrogen sulfide, sulfur dioxide, and oxygen deficiency. And another disease found in bat caves, histoplasmosis, acquired through inhalation of the spores of a fungus that grows in the guano, is a threat reckoned as dangerous to cavers as rabies.

After reading Denny Constantine's 1988 publication, *Health Precautions for Bat Researchers*, it seemed incredible that the members of Project X-Ray all survived. That we are now probably naturally vaccinated against bat rabies is small consolation. We didn't dodge bullets like our mates at the front, but our duty in the bat caves was life-threatening, even if we didn't know it.


Wiswell's experiments with bats from the artificial environment truck were repeated after two weeks of forced hibernation, a week longer than the maximum time anticipated to conduct an actual air raid operation. Again, the bats performed to expectations. Our trials so far were on target. We kept them in hibernation for another week, then Poggy detected a falloff of condition. That evening we swung wide the heavy insulated doors and let the remaining captives fly into the night to join their brothers.

Adams was jubilant.

Recent studies have proved that our hibernation experiments were only partially valid and that we had been operating under a basic fallacy. We did not know that nearly all free-tailed bats migrate to Mexico during the winter, and, contrary to the belief of the time, the few that remain in southwestern states do not enter into profound hibernation as do some other species of bats. If wintering free-tails are caught by cold weather, they merely become lethargic, sometimes torpid, until the next warm period; then they get active again and resume foraging.

But in spite of the errors of data available at the time of our research, the end result of our method was entirely feasible. "Free-tails are opportunists," Constantine says. "They can put themselves into a lethargic state when conditions require it." We were merely calling for the occurrence through artificial means, and the bats' preparedness for natural climatic contingencies applied whether their bodies held energy reserves for hibernation or for migration, as was actually the case.

Other results of the newer studies revealed that bats live up to twenty-five years and that free-tails breed in early March in Mexico. They return to the north in spring, when 90 percent of females produce their young within a period of only fifteen days, usually in early June. Young bats can fly at about six weeks of age.

The next experiment on our list was to confirm the practicality of Doc's idea of the way we should collect vectors. Once an actual attack was scheduled and put into motion, everything must happen with quick precision. Adams imagined a whole fleet similar to the prototype bat environment truck already in operation. On the first evening of the hypothetical operation, the trucks would line up outside the caves and bats would be funneled into them as they emerged from beneath the earth; one truck after another would pull into place at the funnel's end, fill up, and move on so the next one could take on its cargo.

To make the cave-end attachment of the funnel easy, Adams decided to screen the mouths of the two caverns with removable panels of wire netting. The frames could easily be set into place or taken away by one person.

Wooden frames with stretched wire netting were prefabricated at Hondo Air Force Base, while members of the bat unit turned to carpentry and masonry. Stuck to the mouths of the caves, casements to hold the panels across the cavern mouths were built. Ney Cave was the first construction. When the screens were in place, there wasn't so much as a crack where bats could escape. Then we took away the panels and stacked them against the cliff, awaiting their day of use. With the screens removed, the bats were free to fly at will into and out of their home.

Adams felt it was necessary to test the funnel method of capture. So far as we knew, nothing of the kind had ever been done before, and we didn't want to leave anything untried until the fateful day, then to discover that, for some unforeseen reason, theory didn't work in practice.

But the season was now approaching when the hills of south-central Texas would feel the frost. Already we had noted a tapering off in the numbers of bats that emerged from the caves each evening. Then suddenly one cold night there was no flight at all.

Doc talked to Rugh about this worrisome situation, and the cave man told him that it happened thus every year. As intervals of cool weather hit the country, the bats' activities decreased. Then with the advent of a few warm days they flew again, on and off, as the weather changed from warm to cold and back, until the continued chill of late September told them to hang up or get out for the rest of winter.

When the prolonged season of real cold came over the land the flights would cease completely for several months. Some of the bats, Rugh thought, migrated to the warm South. The remainder, he believed, crawled back deep into the honeycomb of crevices and potholes within the cave and there they disappeared to hibernate.

No one at the time knew for sure what portion of the colony migrated—or if *any* of them did—or if *all* of them did. There had never been a comprehensive scientific investigation into these habits of Texas bats. Maybe all stayed torpid within the caves, maybe all migrated. The single fact that Rugh knew for sure was that during the months of coldest weather there were no flights. During these times of inactivity when he went to work with his guano miners, only a few thousand, or perhaps a few hundred, torpid bats could be seen hanging in cold bunches on the ceilings of the caves.

This phenomenon we had known from the beginning. It was the limiting factor insofar as choosing a time to carry out an incendiary raid against Japan. No operation could take place during the northern winter, when we would be unable to collect large quantities of vectors. Also, tests had shown that during the early summer birthing season (following spring migration, as later proven) the bats' vigor was diminished and their load-carrying capability insufficient to fly with the incendiary. Because Griffin's first load-carrying measurements did not tally with later studies, the misleading data had thrown confusion into our earliest statistics. Then the factor of seasonal weakening, from whatever cause, became clear, making it possible to state the optimum weight of the bomb load accurately.

In addition to the five months out of the year when bats were unavailable, the disruptive "weak" season cut another month from the potential schedule for an operation. Still, even with these shortcomings, bats with sufficient stamina, in practically unlimited numbers, could be taken during approximately half the year.

With all the pressures caused by Fieser's ploys for power and by Rhoads's attempts to get the managerial friction—now out in the open—settled once and for all, and with Doc's personal financial problems becoming acute, Adams was obliged to make another sojourn to Washington. He would be away only four or five days. As usual with Doc, he wanted to be present for the next experiment—to add his personal input if any hitches to the funnel-capture test developed.

It was still early in the autumn season. Although there had been no bat flight for nearly a week, a walk through the cave revealed masses of bats, lethargic but not yet completely hibernating, clinging in bunches and layers to the walls and ceilings. When the next warm weather came, it was reasonable to expect bat flights to resume—then we could test the funnel before the bats hung themselves up for winter. In the event of a warm spell before he returned, to hold the bats inside preparatory to the forthcoming test, Doc ordered the screen panels to be placed in position.

My instructions during the short time Adams was to be away were specific. I was in charge of the bats at Ney Cave with orders to keep the doors closed until Doc returned, then, at the next break in the cold weather, the funneling test would be carried out under his supervision. In the meanwhile, we didn't want to lose a caveful of bats suddenly taken with the urge to migrate. If Rugh was correct, the whole lot could disappear to Mexico in a single night.

After Doc's departure, Fletch left for Bracken Cave to help with the construction of containment doors. Except for the guards, I manned Ney Cave alone.

Sometime deep in the night, I was shocked to instant wakefulness by rapid bursts of machine gun fire. Then a shout: "Halt!" Another machine gun burst banged in the night.

I leaped out of bed, ran outside, and bumped into four jittery marine guards who had also been asleep. The corporal on shift hurried in out of the darkness and reported to his shocked superior. "Infiltrators . . . Three or four, couldn't be sure. I think I winged one."

It was the first time we had been confronted with the real possibility of spies. The guards had been sure from the beginning that enemy agents could be lurking behind every bush, but to Fletch and me the possibility seemed remote. Now I was suddenly confronted with the reality. Shots had been fired; someone was hit.

"Okay, men," the sergeant said with brisk efficiency. "Corporal Rubinski has made contact with the enemy. Get your weapons and we'll make a recce."

Five men in skivvies and boots, flashlights in one hand, Reising submachine guns loaded, cocked, at ready, disappeared into the night. I sat in the darkness in front of my tent and waited.

"They should have left one guy behind," I mumbled to myself. "What if there *is* somebody and they come snooping around here?"

From the darkness I heard the voices of the guards, checking back and forth so as not to shoot one another. Then at last a shout: "Hey! Here's somebody. You got him all right, Rubinski."

I watched the wink of flashlights converge on the hillside.

"Where?"

"Over here. Under the bush." Streaks of light from the hillside probed, a flashlight flared toward my eyes, darkness.

I could hardly believe it. A saboteur, a real honest to God spy in our midst? And they'd shot him?

"Careful. He could be armed."

Silence; more probing flashlights, then: "Crap!"

"What? What's goin' on?"

"A fuckin' deer. Rubinski, you shot a fuckin' deer."

Laughter. "Rubinski shot a deer. Out of season, too." More laughter. "One round, right in the heart. Sound-shot, too. Not bad, Rubinski. Didn't know you was such a good shooter."

"Shoulda halted when I yelled 'Halt.'" said Rubinski.

More laughter. It was a fine four-point buck. I was a bit put off to lose one of my pet deer, but I doubt if he could have survived the coming hunting season—even if he had heeded Rubinski's command. In the morning we dressed it out. As venison, he made a delectable enemy.


That was Monday. Tuesday dawned bright, clear—and hot. That night for the first time in a week, a few thousand bats flew. They clung to the wire, wanting out to forage for the night.

They circled in the cave's mouth, squeaked and landed, clinging to the wire, fluttered back into the cave; more came. They were confused, but not overly upset, seeming to accept the new condition with less agitation than I expected. I sat in the darkness near the cave's mouth listening to their uneasy chatter, switching on my flashlight when I wanted to take a look. I listened to their lament for a couple of hours. When I went to bed it was hard to get to sleep. At dawn, all had returned into the earth. The cave mouth was quiet and deserted. It seemed no different than any other morning.

Another hot day was in the making. Noon. The sun burned down on the meadows and scrub brush. I was anxious. I wished to hell Doc would get back.

That afternoon when I went into the cave to check Wiswell's instruments, I stared with worry at the graph of the recording thermometer near the mouth. Its needle was tracing a sharp upward curve; the temperature was climbing even within the relatively stable cave. I climbed down deeper into the chamber. At the midpoint yesterday the cavern had seemed nearly unpopulated; now when I shined my flashlight upward I saw squirming bats by the millions—they covered the walls and ceiling with seething draperies. Rugh was right. There were enough small cracks and grottos branching off from the main cave for the whole colony to disappear from view. Now they were on the move again. Clearly, there would be a major flight tonight. If the screens weren't in place to hold them in, the whole colony would sally forth, possibly not to return until spring.

The flight started on schedule an hour before dark. I brought a lantern and watched them flutter against the screens. The cave was alive: masses of bats were milling in the spacious entrance chamber. More and more landed against the wire; others landed on the backs of ones already there and hung on, packing up against the screens. The wire sagged under their weight but held them in. The sound created by all of those small discontented animals, upset by the strange situation, was overwhelming. Millions of leathery wings, millions of shrill tiny voices, all amplified by the echoes of the cave. Even the marine guards, totally disinterested in the bats, came and stood around for awhile, awed by the spectacle.

Except for the guards, who lived in their remote worlds, doing their duty, three hours on, nine hours off, I was alone. And I was frightened. The consequences of keeping the bats confined in this state of high agitation could be extreme. I saw that some were flying head-on into the wire and killing themselves, but I knew that a few hundred dead had no real consequence when seen against the millions. But I had another restless night, wishing Doc would return and get on with his test.

Again, in the morning, all the bats had retired back into the depths of the cave. I scooped up several hundred carcasses from beneath the wire and buried them. Then I drove into Bandera and tried to get Doc on the phone in Washington. I couldn't reach him, couldn't even find a place to leave a message, and my nervousness grew. It was another day of hot Texas Indian summer. All afternoon the sun beat down out of a cloudless sky, heating up the earth, heating up the cave, heating up my apprehensions.

This evening the bats began to fly an hour earlier than usual.

Clearly, they wanted out—now. The bats had spent the past two nights in a state of frenetic activity, not the torpid condition of semi-hibernation which required no sustenance, and they had to eat. With their rapid rate of metabolism and small bodily reserve of energy they couldn't go for an extended period in this highly active state and survive. Starvation would quickly weaken and kill them.

Again that night I sat by the screen in lanternlight watching the bats pack up against the wire. I saw that more were falling to the ground and dying than the night before—a lot more. Bats hung from the wire in a solid squirming curtain more than a foot deep. As more flew in and landed on the mass, others which couldn't hold the weight of many dropped off, giving the whole seething mass the appearance of waves surging against a cliff and falling back. I was frightened, horrified, moved nearly to tears.

My orders had been specific. I had been left with no room for personal judgment, for my appraisal of a situation on which I could draw an analytical conclusion. I was a soldier, and although I didn't know a lot about soldiering, I did know that as such I was expected to carry out orders—to the letter—without question—that was the soldier's code, wasn't it?

I sat gloomily in the lanternlight and watched the bats mass against the screen, knowing that in the morning thousands would be dead. They couldn't survive another night of this frenetic keyed-up activity. They were too frail; most, if not all, would die. How many? A million? Five, ten million? We had no accurate census, so there was no way to know. But a population that had lived in Ney Cave for untold centuries would be wiped out. I was faced with a lesson familiar to naturalists—one can't arbitrarily impose human wishes on the natural world without dire consequences. Even the effect on the human population of this part of the world would be extreme. The insects of the night, mosquitoes particularly, would increase manyfold—by the ton!

But that serious consequence didn't even occur to me at the time. It was the prospect of all this impending death that overwhelmed me. It wasn't just my opinion—the looming calamity was an obvious fact. It was about to happen. I pictured the pile of dead bats. It could fill the mouth of the cave—fifteen feet high!

I was but a nineteen-year-old boy. The grave import of making a decision contrary to my orders was simply too great a verdict for my experience. I was terrified by what I knew I ought to do. But there was no other way. Crying with emotion, I went to the panels and pulled them down and the bats surged free. They poured forth in their millions, and, having made the decision at last, I felt the huge load of responsibility suddenly vanish. I knew I had done the right thing.

I sat up all night by the cave mouth waiting to hear the whistle of diving bats' wings as they returned to their daytime roost. I never heard it. They didn't come back. All day the cave was as still as a catacomb.

The bats would return in the spring, of course, after their southern vacation, but that would be too late for Doc's funnel-capture experiment.

When Adams arrived back at Ney Cave expecting to conduct his test and learned what I had done, he was beside himself with anger. In Washington he had made a commitment to report back on the imminent test, and my action would cause him extreme embarrassment. But what, I asked, would the reaction be if he had to report that we'd just killed ten million bats, as I was sure we would have done if I'd kept them confined for another foodless night? Doc in his fury wouldn't listen to my reasoning. I had deliberately disregarded his orders, he fumed. The deer killed by the guards hadn't been a saboteur, but I was damned with this appalling epithet. Doc could not be mollified. He demanded that I write a full report on the incident, and he almost seemed to expect my letter to be presented in the form of a confession.

It took me all day to compose my statement. So serious were Adams's accusations that I wanted to be sure I had everything right. The danger of official charges of treason was real. When finally my statement was finished and Doc read my words they seemed to have more meaning to him than when I had spoken them. Or perhaps by day's end he had simply cooled off and realized that I had done the right thing. After all, he hadn't seen that squeaking mass of desperate life struggling to survive. If he had, I'm sure he would have reacted the same as I did, probably quicker. No one could do otherwise.

I was forgiven, but the funnel test was put on hold until the bats would return in the spring. The Bracken Cave colony disappeared even as the enclosing panels were being completed. Either they got the word from their brothers and headed south with their kin from Ney or they crawled deep into grottos where they couldn't be seen and turned out the lights for the winter.

Still, from the colonies of millions, there were always a few, perhaps the rugged individualists, like Doc, who didn't follow the pattern set by the masses. Thus, although the great percentage of bats in our two caves were unavailable, either gone or hidden away, several thousand remained easily accessible, plenty to carry out all tests but the one with the funnel. They hung in torpid clumps where they could be picked from the ceilings like bunches of grapes from a vine.

I didn't feel like a traitor, and I *knew* I wasn't a hero. At least I was completely vindicated for my actions by the senior mammalogist and Wiswell. But I knew that I hadn't helped Doc—at the very time when he needed all the help he could get.

# 19

## *Dugway*

IT WAS A LONG TIME LATER that I began to think of myself as a character in a story. One never does until the pieces come together to have some grander meaning. A lot of holes never did get plugged up—for example, what role did the Benish brothers play in our drama? Maybe it was only the words of Frank Benish comparing a girl to an insect that von Bloeker repeated with a personal slant that had led to our big fistfight. But I found when I looked back in a certain way on that part of my life I could see that every event had a meaning or a reason and that all the odds and ends, when put together, were arranged just as if they'd happened the way they did for a dramatic purpose.

Like General Kabrich's order that came only one day short of two years since I had looked up into the faces of the cowboys on Santa Rosa Island and heard the words: "Pearl Harbor's been bombed":

December 6, 1943

SUBJECT: ADAMS' PLAN

TO: The Commanding Officer, Dugway Proving Ground, Tooele, Utah.

1. It is requested that a test be scheduled, if possible, on the Adams' Plan for 15 December 1943. Small delayed-action incendiary units are to be placed in position by hand, [and] static tested in the interiors of Japanese type buildings. . . . Close watch will be kept on the action of the units so that the buildings will not be seriously damaged or destroyed. . . .

2. All munitions, materiel, and handling equipment will be furnished by the National Defense Research Committee and the Marine Corps. . . .

3. Dr. Louis F. Fieser of Harvard will travel by commercial

airline from the East to observe the test. Lt. Colonel R. H. Rhoads, U.S. Marine Corps, who is in charge of development work on this plan for the Navy, will fly up in a Marine plane from the Marine Corps Air Station, El Centro. It is anticipated that Dr. W. G. Young of California will be present.

By order of the Chief of the Chemical Warfare Service.

W. C. Kabrich, Brigadier General, C.W.S.
Chief, Technical Division

Three days later, General Kabrich expanded his directive to include testing of the bats as well as the bomb:

The primary purpose of the present test is to check on the fire-starting efficiency of the present small special-type incendiary units placed by hand in Japanese-type buildings. It is also planned that a small number of units will be attached to the carriers, which will be released inside the Japanese buildings to determine the action of the carrier, and the effect of ignition of the incendiary unit upon the carrier.

The result of the last-mentioned test would seem to be a foregone conclusion. There could be but one effect—the quick cremation of the carrier.

But in spite of that slight anomaly, there was momentous import in Kabrich's orders. This test would be a turning point, whichever way it went, in the fortunes of Project X-Ray. It was to be the major test of the incendiary, now the most dubious element and the one most beset with design difficulties in the overall plan.

The other item of importance in Kabrich's directive was that the name Dr. Lytle S. Adams was conspicuously absent from the list of brass requested to attend. The father of the Adams Plan, the inventor of Project X-Ray, apparently was not invited. The omission was not a simple oversight. Not only was Doc's name absent from the list of experts and observers, but it did not appear on the muster of personnel who would carry out the legwork, we the noncoms of Project X-Ray. And there was no Authorization for Civilian Travel on Military Aircraft, a form required for Doc and Bobby Herold to get aboard the R-5-o. They often flew in our marine Lodestar and each time the permission had been issued routinely. This time no authorization accompanied our unit travel orders, and the omission was significant.

It was clear that Adams and his aide-de-camp had been forsaken.

Fletch and I plucked enough torpid bats off the ceilings of Ney Cave to fill four carrying boxes, loaded them into our jeep, and met Captains Leigh and Smith and the R-5-0 at Hondo Air Force Base. We tied down the boxes to the floor of the plane with cargo straps and took off for El Centro to pick up Colonel Rhoads en route to Utah. Eddie Herold, Williams, and the Benish brothers stayed behind to man the cave contingents in Texas.

Our commander was ill with the flu when we arrived at El Centro, but he dragged himself to the plane and as soon as we were airborne collapsed prone on a row of parachute packs laid out on the starboard bench. Fletch, von Bloeker, Wiswell, and I sat opposite, as far as we could get from Rhoads, not only because of his virus but because we suspected him of complicity in (if not the management of) Doc's ouster.

The early part of the flight over the California desert was dull and gave me time to contemplate our state of affairs.

We had all felt the growing tension between Adams and the brass, and Bobby had kept us in the picture, so it was no great surprise that Doc had become an outcast. But the method by which the others had turned him into *persona non grata* was unexpected. No matter what those at the executive level thought of Adams, even if one could grant that his visionary contribution to the project had now been fully achieved, his inventiveness satisfied, and his usefulness finished, there was no excuse for the method used to dispose of him. They hoped that by ignoring Adams he would simply go away like the carcass of a run-over dog stinking on the highway that no one wanted to pick up and get rid of properly—that the crows and vultures would eat him and he would disappear.

Doc was subjected to the classic "silent treatment." For the past couple of weeks, and forever henceforth, Adams was not present at executive meetings and was not advised of developments whether official or nonofficial; he was not consulted, not sent copies of memos, not invited to conferences, not advised that get-togethers were to be or had taken place. Whether or not this strategy was the result of a plot participated in by all the senior members of Project X-Ray we could not know. There are no official minutes of any meeting on record which even hint at such collusion. But the similar treatment that Doc received from all hands strongly suggests such a conspiracy. Otherwise, it would seem unlikely that all persons involved could suddenly, simultaneously, come up with the identical harsh method of brush-off. The only reference to be found in the archives regarding Doc's dismissal, if it can be called such, is a single sentence written long after his effective sacking. On January 11,

1944, WCL (Lothrop) wrote in a summary memo of a top-level conference: "The purpose of the meeting was to discuss the 'Adams Plan' now rechristened 'X-Ray' since Dr. Adams' departure from the work."

Even this sentence was spurious since the project's name change had actually taken place months ago when the Marine Corps took over. Was it WCL's way of putting into the record in a rather indirect way an event of momentous but embarrassing import—the dismissal of Lytle Adams?

Was the procedure the result of an oversight, of everyone thinking that someone else would thank Adams for his contribution and deal with the dirty work, with a pat on the back, at least, by way of good-bye? Or was it what it appeared to be, a callous way to forestall an embarrassing situation, with no one brave enough to face Adams with the truth? My respect for all of those men in the high executive level flew out the window with Doc's dream.

Doc's mistakes were not shenanigans intended to defraud and did not deserve such demeaning treatment. Even then I had immature inklings of the mature truth later expressed by a statesman of great worldly experience: "I realized that people in high positions were not necessarily always motivated by wisdom and concern for the common cause, but in fact could be motivated by other less desirable emotions, like vanity, ambition and a desire to score a point off somebody."*

This is perhaps an obvious human insight, but for me it was written nearly fifty years too late, for at my time of young idealism Doc's experience was *my* experience, and an enduring lesson in cynicism.

As I reflected on Doc's situation, I realized how simple it had been to oust him. Since Doc had no truly official role, was not in the military, had no contract with any agency, and was not on anyone's payroll, he didn't have to be dismissed, sacked, or even notified that his services were no longer desired. He had only to be ignored, and the situation was dealt with in this ugly way.

My reflections were brought to a halt by a sudden lurch of the plane. We were somewhere around the southern end of the Wasatch Mountains and the Lodestar had flown into an area of unstable air. We

---

*Interview with senior U.N. official Sir Brian Urquhart, *Time*, December 5, 1988.

began to be buffeted roughly in our seats. Those of us sitting on the benches cinched up our seat belts. Rhoads in his illness, lying on his back with eyes closed and arms folded across his chest like a mummy, didn't move; either he was feeling too miserable to care or was sound asleep.

The buffeting grew worse: the plane pitched and yawed, dropped and rose with short quick movements. I thought I should awaken the colonel and caution him about fastening his seat belt, but he seemed to be okay and I let it go.

Then we hit a tremendous air pocket and the plane dropped with sickening weightlessness. We in our belts merely felt a falling sensation; the straps held us to our seats. But I couldn't believe what was happening to our colonel. Suddenly he had levitated. Like a magician's shill he lay prone, stiff as a board, totally unsupported, as if suspended on an invisible plank by unseen wires. He seemed to hang in midair without props, in comfortable rest, for an incredible time. I was transfixed. Then the plane hit the bottom of its fall with a jolt and began its equally rapid ascent. Rhoads and the plane came back together like the clap of giant hands. *Wham!* Dust flew from the parachute packs.

Then we hit the next gap in unstable air and he was levitated again. Sustained in rigid repose, he still did not move. His composure seemed absolute, the stuff of Marine Corps officers. Probably he was only stunned by his first hard landing. But in its second fall through space the plane shifted sideways, and the next time it hit bottom Rhoads and the parachute cushions were not in their former alignment. He collided against the hard metal floor with a thump that shook the plane. Both pilots looked back wide-eyed through the compartment door and saw the colonel in his best Marine Corps greens, half-conscious, trying against gravity and the continuing jolts of the plane to pick himself up and retain a decorum befitting his rank. He was not successful, and none of us on the benches leaped out of our seats to assist our leader.

We landed at Dugway late in the afternoon. Testing would begin tomorrow morning. While everyone else retired to the comfort of base accommodations, I was left behind to look after the bats in the plane. The officer who met us, and with whom the others departed for their cozy bedrooms, advised me that the temperature was expected to fall to the mid-20s F during the night. This was a contingency for which we had not been prepared. Our bat containers were simple wooden boxes, footlocker-sized, beehivelike cases with vertical panels of burlap on which the bats could hang. They were fine for Texas or California, but if Dugway temperatures were to drop as low as expected, there was grave danger the bats would freeze. In spite of the irony, someone had to stand by to make sure the bats survived freezing tonight—to be cremated tomorrow.

As junior member, I was elected to be nocturnal manager of temperature control. I asked Leigh to park the R-5-0 close to a hangar where I could plug in a couple of extension electrical cords and with warm light bulbs, shielded with wads of metal foil crinkled around the globes to prevent the bats from burning themselves prematurely and to keep it comfortably dark within their sleeping place, I assured myself that the animals would have a comfortable rest. With a blanket provided by base supply wrapped around my shoulders, I began my night's vigil. By two A.M., the bats were doing fine, but I was freezing. The metal skin of the plane had grown so cold that a damp finger touched to its surface stuck like Krazy Glue. I latched the airplane door tightly in flight mode to shut out the cold draft from outside, but the effect was like locking myself inside a deep freezer. A glacial stillness as icy as Antarctic winter lay a hoarfrost over everything, inside and outside the ship. I constructed a cocoon of stacked parachute packs and wriggled within like a white grub, feeling as if I was crawling into my final polar coffin. I lay doubled up inside my igloo of chutes, teeth chattering, gooseflesh prickling; I couldn't stop shivering. In my half-numbed frozen state I almost envied the bats' fate of tomorrow. Recalling Robert Service's lively ballad, I tried to amuse myself by mumbling enviously the immortal words of the Yukon's Sam McGee, spoken from his blazing funeral pyre as consuming flames licked at his body: "This is the first time I've been warm in years." I knew just what he meant. Oh, for a fire—even Sam's crematorium.

Unable to bear lying still any longer, I wriggled out of the coffin and paced up and down the ship, stamping my feet on the brittle metal floor to keep my blood circulating, my frosty breath billowing in clouds.

To check on the bats again I opened their door. In their snug boxes they looked up in irritated reaction to the flashlight's sudden glare. With their odd pug noses and curiously shaped ears they seemed to be smiling and, with a chorus of complaining squeaks, said very clearly, "Close the door, you jerk!"

The next morning, I was told that the temperature had dropped to 14.9 degrees F.

A huge hot breakfast of pancakes, steaming coffee, bacon, and eggs stirred my sluggish blood to flow again. We faced the big day enthusiastically, heading out under cold cloudless skies for the remote Utah flats.

Dugway Proving Ground was a vast area of restricted entry. We drove for miles seeing no one, no sign of either people or habitation. The secret base was utilized for testing chiefly by the Chemical Warfare Service. As to the experiments other than our own, one could only guess. Years later, a rancher grazing sheep close outside the Proving Ground filed a lawsuit seeking restitution for losses to his flock killed by nerve gas, and the case was settled in his favor by the U.S. government.

Only once to my knowledge was the use of bats for anything more sinister than as carriers of incendiary bombs ever suggested, and no tests of the idea were ever undertaken, either at Dugway or anywhere else. When Admiral Furer wrote his denigrating letter to Stevenson of NDRC (saying that if one-ounce incendiaries were effective, they'd be using one-ounce rather than two-pound incendiary bombs), he also added the comment: "If we ever resort to biological warfare, it might be advisable to reopen the question of using bats as vectors." Fortunately, we never did turn to such methods, and Furer's idea went no further than that.

Far out in a remote area of the Proving Ground two remarkable installations had been constructed, simulated Japanese and German villages. These unpeopled towns were built of the materials, in the architecture, and in layout house to house in the most authentic way possible. Research for the construction and furnishings had been supervised by the most qualified anthropologists. The sterile towns stood several miles apart on the otherwise empty Utah plain, like abandoned movie sets picturing the aftermath of a devastating plague. Dust-devils swirled through the powdery lanes, curling high into the blue sky, and tumbleweeds rolled past the empty doors—as if the art director had made a mistake and built an old western ghost town with the wrong kind of houses.

I noted how much the Japanese village resembled the one along the shores of Osaka Bay described in the *Harper's* article that Adams had read to us months ago.

As I strolled through the deserted lanes and looked into empty windows, I visualized with awful clarity this place peopled in the way those authors had described their target villages. Crowded with life, the narrow aisles between buildings would be bustling with workers, children, families. People coming and going to the factories; hawkers, shoppers, kids playing games.

Casting aside that mental picture it was easy to imagine without emotional involvement the torching of this sterile village, which resembled nothing so much as a museum model in full scale. But when again I saw in my mind's eye the town as it really would be, my flesh crawled. I was very glad I was seeing it in this way, without people. I could watch our little incendiaries do their dirty work without hearing the screams, the cries of pain, the yells of hysteria, the clanging of the fire carts, the roar of burning paper and wood, the sobs of mothers and fathers and sons and daughters.

What were we doing?

Were we all crazy?

Had the whole world gone mad?

Major Evan A. Lewis, director of Incendiary Testing at Dugway, in charge of conducting the tests for CWS and of gathering and evaluating statistics, was given the unusual instruction "to make a personal and disinterested analysis" of the results. The wording of the order seemed most pointed, implying that General Kabrich might suspect our more biased chemist of writing a less than straightforward abstract of the tests.

Major Lewis and his squad of men arrived at the test site armed with clipboards and pens. He was not encouraging when he told us in his formal idiom, later to be written into his report, that "because of past and present cold weather, the moisture content of the wood in these unheated buildings is higher than would normally be found under actual conditions." Therefore, he said, the successful firestarts could not be expected to approach those if the weather was normal—hot and dry. If the buildings were affected by the unusual cold and moisture, our bats would be even more upset by this extreme condition. Nevertheless, we prepared to carry out the tests. We were, after all, somewhat used to adversity.

For the first tests we attached bombs to bats and released them by hand inside buildings. The statisticians watched our animals crawl into cracks and corners, dragging along their incendiaries, and recorded the fires that resulted by entering on their pads one of a number of categories recognized by incendiary experts. I secured a copy of the Bible of incendiary personnel, the training manual called *Fire*, with the subtitle, *Combustion and Destruction*. The pages describing fire categories for the purpose of statistical analysis were explicit in detail:

> *CLASS A* fires are those fires which are beyond the control of the householder equipped with a pump tank and would there-

fore require the attention of professional fire-fighters and appli-
ances. Since the locations of fire departments in various towns
differs widely this *CLASS A* has been subdivided into three
groups.

A-*1* is a fire which is beyond the householder's control at or
before two minutes elapsed time from the start of the fire.

A-2 is beyond control between two and four minutes.

A-3 is beyond control between four and six minutes.

Since I was not particularly inclined to pyromania, there was
the distinct danger of becoming bored with reading through the
complete listing of all classes of fires, so, skipping through "B" and
"C" to the final entry, I found: *CLASS D*, "all fires that don't start
because of incendiary malfunction." I thought it interesting that to
a fire statistician a fire that doesn't start is not called a nonfire, but
is still listed as a *CLASS D* fire. That is positive thinking with a
capital *P*.

In a way, the Dugway tests were quite dull for us in the bat
unit. Since Adams's departure, it wasn't fun anymore. Doc had always added a zest to any occasion. Fletch didn't get to chase across
the country following flying bats pell-mell with an admiral and a
colonel hanging on with gritted teeth and white knuckles. And we
weren't allowed to burn down any airfields. General Kabrich had
made sure that incident wouldn't be repeated. Two shiny red fire
pumpers were standing by at Dugway to prevent just such a contingency. We didn't even get to show off our hardware to best advantage
or exhibit the performance of vectors in any exciting ways. The bat
testing had all been done enough times with enough satisfactory
results to make more demonstrations redundant. The Dugway tests
were really Fieser's show—but the results achieved applied to all of
us. Our greatest satisfaction came not from the doing, but from the
reports that resulted. WCL (Lothrop) summarized the various statistics in his notes reporting a top-level conference held at NDRC
Headquarters in Washington.

> LFF [Fieser] described the tests performed at Dugway. . . . [It]
> had been demonstrated that the small unit is satisfactory as an
> incendiary which could be improved by the use of thicker gel
> than the present 8%. . . . LFF then gave calculations which he
> had made showing that on a weight basis X-Ray is more effective
> than any of the standard incendiary bombs.

Fieser's report then delved with considerable technical jargon into the fire-starting capabilities of the three types of standard incendiary bombs currently in use as compared to the bat bomb. The memo continued: "Expressed in another way, the regular bombs would give probably 167 to 400 fires per bomb load where X-Ray would give 3625 to 4748 fires." That was a considerable difference, with the vast superiority of the bat bomb as expressed by statistics a heartening surprise. Even the "disinterested report" of Major Lewis, chief of Incendiary Testing at Dugway, although hardly as glowing as that of NDRC, was definitely positive.

> A reasonable number of destructive fires can be started in spite of the extremely small size of the units. The main advantage of the units would seem to be their placement [by the bats] within the enemy structures without the knowledge of the householder or fire watchers, thus allowing the fire to establish itself before being discovered.

Then came the most significant words yet written regarding Doc Adams's strange invention. The NDRC report said, "It was concluded that X-Ray is an effective weapon."

The fact that NDRC approved the Dugway tests so resoundingly and Chemical Warfare Service had received a report of such high approval from its observer made it seem as if Project X-Ray might soon be on the agenda for an actual operation.

Colonel Rhoads's report on Dugway, on the other hand, was tucked rather obscurely into an extensive overview on the status of the project as a whole, an in-depth six-page document addressed to the Director of Aviation Planning, U.S. Navy. Von Bloeker, who was handed the report in scribbled form with instructions to type it up and put the periods and commas in the right places, was alternately shocked, amused, and concerned as he read through the draft. To Rhoads, Dugway was apparently just another in a long series of tests and merited no more notice than any other. He was looking at the project as a whole; in spite of our enthusiasm about the success in Utah, in the broader view the colonel's seemingly level-headed insight might have been proper. But, like everyone else, Rhoads had his personal prejudices. This was his first official attack based on a grudge of his own.

V. B. chuckled at his first reading of one statement, then its curious ambiguity caused him to consider its import more seriously. The colonel's statement concerning Dugway rang with off-the-wall undertones: "No attempt has been made by Project X-Ray personnel to evaluate the results of the [Dugway] tests, since no one attached to the project has had any previous experience with incendiaries."

Dr. Louis Fieser was considered by some, including officers of the Chemical Warfare Service, to be America's most distinguished and learned researcher in the development and testing of incendiary bombs. As a faculty member of the Harvard Chemistry Department, consultant to the Army CWS, and fellow of the civilian advisory group NDRC, he had developed or improved upon and tested several of the standard incendiaries currently in use in fire-bombing Germany and Japanese-held Pacific islands. The bat bomb was but one of half a dozen incendiary projects for the military in which he was involved at the time.

In view of Fieser's impressive background and the fact that his detailed analysis of the Dugway test was clipped to Rhoads's overview, the colonel's extraordinary statement could mean but one of two things. Either Rhoads had not read or had not absorbed Fieser's report, an extremely unlikely possibility, or Rhoads did not consider Fieser, in spite of his close connection with the project from the inception, to be a member of Project X-Ray.

Von Bloeker puzzled over the colonel's meaning, trying to read between the lines of such an obviously pointed statement, so totally out of touch with the facts as v. B. saw them.

One reading of Fieser's report on Dugway suggested the unlikely possibility that Rhoads was unhappy with the chemist for his failure to write a statement that would be clear to an incendiary layman. The colonel knew that not everyone down the line who would be concerned with Project X-Ray at this important time in its development would have Fieser's fascination with incendiary statistics. The facts and figures were all a good contribution, but without a clear summary to hit the high points the total effect was lost in obfuscating detail. One surely had to be alert and blessed with a technical mind fine-tuned to the proper scientific frequency to assimilate Fieser's material with any sense of clarity.

"It has always been my notion," said von Bloeker, "that after one scans the same page of text three times, one should be either asleep or able to understand essentially what was written. If you read the same material four times without comprehension, then you've *got* to be snoring."

Although Fieser's report was an obstacle course of numerical comparisons, bomb-designer's jargon, and confusing text, when one finally cleared the last hurdle the prize was worth the effort.

Based on prior testing it was known that six clusters of conventional M60 incendiary bombs weighing 3,270 pounds would start 160 fires. The statistical results of the Dugway tests showed that the same weight of bat bombs (twenty-five to thirty-two shells or about half a plane-load) would start 4,768 fires.

Fieser's report concluded with a strongly upbeat statement:

> The computations have been made on a very conservative basis without the considerations of the very great advantage of the element of complete surprise and the very widespread destruction. The Dugway tests have demonstrated that very small incendiaries when properly delivered are effective in setting fire to the inflammable type of structure found in Japan. Thus every effort should be made to work out the various details required for effecting efficient delivery.

Was it possible, von Bloeker wondered, that Colonel Rhoads found Fieser's long and highly technical analysis to be totally incomprehensible? More likely, knowing Rhoads's capacity for impatience, he simply got bored with the language before he got to the crux. If he'd had someone pull out the pertinent sentence, the one that said the small bat incendiary had been proved to have the potential for setting many times more fires than any of the standard incendiary bombs currently in use, maybe he would have felt differently. But to say, after reading that document full of technical detail and incendiary jargon, that no one connected with Project X-Ray was qualified to make a judgment of the Dugway tests "since no one attached to the project has had any previous experience with incendiaries" was a strange statement indeed.

Von Bloeker considered the second and more believable—if no more logical—of the possible reasons for Rhoads's disclaimer. Was it thinkable that the colonel considered Fieser and the NDRC, as civilian auxiliaries, to be outside the preferred inner circle of the military? Was it conceivable that, after being with the project from the beginning, Fieser's civilian status now excluded him from the X-Ray club? If Fieser was an alien, he held all the scientific rank of a Spock on the starship *Enterprise* and to chuck him out in mid-flight hardly seemed prudent.

Rhoads's veto of Fieser as a member of the Project X-Ray team and his putdown of the chemist's report went even further. Because no Project X-Ray personnel were qualified to evaluate the Dugway tests, Rhoads said, "It is recommended that the Bureau of Ordinance be requested to review and coordinate the results of the tests of the incendiaries." In other words, the evaluations of the NDRC, Fieser, and the Chemical Warfare Service had been thrown out by the Marine Corps. Clearly, Rhoads was running the show on his own terms.

Rhoads's rejection of the optimistic report did not mean that the colonel held a negative attitude either toward the tests or toward the project as a whole. What he sought, marine that he was, was *Marine Corps* confirmation. Rhoads realized that X-Ray now had all the potential to become operational and was moving rapidly in that direction.

His main consideration in the latest maneuvering was that he saw Project X-Ray as being exclusively a military operation. If it was to be deployed, Rhoads knew *he* would be there and didn't want any civilian—particularly Fieser, whom he considered to be an annoying fussbudget—anywhere nearby when he started dropping real bombs on a real enemy. Rhoads's motives were simple; the marriage between NDRC and the Marine Corps had grown stale, and he wanted a divorce.

Rhoads's lengthy report on the overall status of X-Ray met the areas of development still to be proven or improved upon head-on, without dodging anything. The statements made by the colonel were noncommittal. He put forward the facts as he saw them, leaving inferences, along with most recommendations (such as the big one for actual deployment), to be made by someone else further up in the chain of command. Except for advocating that the Dugway test reports undergo scrutiny by an impartial board of review, Rhoads made only two other suggestions. "It is recommended that dispatch authority be granted to J. C. von Bloeker, mammalogist, and Ozro B. Wiswell, physiologist, of Project X-Ray, to submit the necessary forms for commissions in the Navy as Lt (jg) and Ensign (HC) respectively."* He also recommended that the other Army personnel (except for marines Fletcher and Williams, the entire remaining staff of X-Ray) "not be transferred to the Navy pending outcome of the [next] forced hibernation and weight-carrying tests."

We hadn't known that there were going to be more tests, nor had we been aware that our transfer into the Navy was being contemplated. But one military service was much the same as another to us—it was the project that mattered. Eddie celebrated the news

---

*Wiswell's commission was granted forthwith, but for reasons known only to Navy Headquarters von Bloeker's never came through.

by borrowing a swabbie's white cap and practiced in front of a mirror, trying it out at the most rakish angles, straight on, low over the left eye, low over the right eye, and tilted back. He very much liked it low over the left eye.

We saw Doc once more. He telephoned from Brawley saying he'd meet us in El Centro on his way back to Pennsylvania from Los Angeles. He and Bobby Herold were driving the now-derelict old Buick that had carried us all so far, using the last of some gasoline ration stamps left over from better times. He'd lost his visitor's privileges to the base, so we all met in the evening at the only hotel in El Centro, a rundown structure in the middle of town with a Chinese restaurant for a dining room.

We all sat at one big table with a food-stained tablecloth, and bowls of chop suey and fine noodles with chunks of chicken swimming through the seaweed were put before us by a Mexican waiter.

Doc wanted to hear about Dugway, and we told him all we knew. He seemed ambivalent about Fieser's new role, amused and troubled at the same time. That was the upbeat part of the evening—otherwise, our get-together had the character of a wake with the deceased all present and accounted for.

But the red dots that looked like they were painted on each of Bobby's cheeks had their old glow. "We picked up the usual crate of oranges at Doc's favorite fruit stand," he said, slurping his noodles. "This will be my last square meal till we get to Pennsylvania, so I'm stoking up."

An undisclosed important mission somewhere in the East had created the usual deadline and haste. The old urgency was still tugging at Doc. Although it was past ten, he was anxious to get on the road.

We walked outside and stood on the curb. "I'll be seeing you," Doc said and shook hands with us all. When he came to me, I said, "So long."

They climbed into the Buick, its back seat piled high with luggage and carton boxes, and Bobby turned the starter. The engine sounded as smooth as it had when it had carried us back and forth through so many nights and days to Texas. As inanimate objects sometimes do, the big black Buick had a personality. We'd all grown fond of it.

"Well, I guess we won't be seeing that old wreck again," said v. B. fondly. And we all knew he said the Buick—but was talking about Doc and Bobby.

"Yeah, it's just a worn-out bucket of bolts now," Fletch said. "I hope it gets them there."

Then Bobby tapped the horn as if to say "see you"; they turned out and purred into the road. We all stood on the sidewalk watching the red lights pull away. Then the car reached the bright lamp hung over the crossing of Fourth and Main and came into the glow, and the snow-white mop of Doc's head turned back. He watched us through the rear window as they pulled on through the light and I wondered what he was thinking. I had a pretty good idea that, whatever it was, it wasn't easy. At last, before they were gone, he waved. We all stood on the curb in the light of the Chinese restaurant and waved back.

While he was still looking back, the car plunged into darkness again outside the crossing light; its red lights began to get smaller. We watched the red dots sail away, disembodied points now, growing smaller and mixing with other lights until you couldn't tell one set of tail lights from another. Then I looked up into the sky, and I saw that it was another night of full moon. It was big and beautiful, a desert moon the color of a pale orange.

I realized that it was the same moon I'd seen that night months ago when I thought maybe I was never going to see another moon again, when I'd crawled out of the Devil's Sinkhole and collapsed on the ground and lay on my back looking up with such gratitude at the sky. I didn't feel the same now as I had then—I wasn't as tired and my feelings were of a different kind—but my heart was doing the same funny things.

# 20

# It's a Bit "Sticky" in El Centro

SOMEHOW TWO VERSIONS of the same memo have found their way into the archives of Project X-Ray. Their significance lies not in their similarities, but in their differences. One was the original handwritten draft from H. M. Chadwell of NDRC to his assistant, WCL, with instructions to have it typed up and distributed. That Chadwell completely trusted the editorial circumspection of his subordinate is evident in the frankness of the asides, obviously meant only for Lothrop's eyes. The memo, in part a written confirmation of verbal agreements made at a meeting between Colonel Rhoads and the incendiary specialists, brought to the fore in an obvious way the controversy involving NDRC, Fieser, and Rhoads. The marine colonel wanted to limit the contribution of the civilians to the development of the incendiary and time-control device. Then, so far as Rhoads was concerned, the scientists would have finished their job and could walk away. Fieser and NDRC, on the other hand, wanted to stay with the project up to and including its operational use. Their reasoning for this unusual stance is not clear; perhaps they felt they were better prepared to deal with any last-minute glitches. But to Rhoads this would mean opening the door to civilian interference in military matters, the mere notion of which caused the irascible colonel to stew with bitter indignation.

Chadwell's original eight-page message was written in an imperfect hand on stationery of the Hollywood Plaza Hotel, Hollywood Boulevard at Vine, under the letterhead slogan "The Smartest Rendezvous at the World's Most Famous Corner."

In both versions dated 10 February 1944, with copies of the edited version sent to Rhoads, Fieser, Dr. George A. Perley (of Leeds and Northrup), and Young, a daunting schedule was set. That this would include the final dress rehearsal and the next step beyond was made clear by the last item on the agenda, an order for the production of a million incendiary capsules with attached time-release pencils. One million units were not being ordered for a test. This was for a full-scale operation—the bat air raid on Japan.

The schedule as agreed to by all parties was to get underway in only two weeks. Deadlines were set for the manufacture and testing of newly modified adhesive capsules, for a final test involving 4,000 units, and May 1 was set as the date to begin manufacture of the million bat incendiaries.

The rapidly approaching deadlines were not fixed by arbitrary selection, but by the physiology of the bats. August through September were the months when the free-tails would be in prime physical condition to perform their task. The operation would have to take place in the early autumn of 1944.

But now that Doc was out, infighting had flared on a new front. Chadwell's revealing comments in his handwritten version, which did not make their way into the official missive, were scattered at random through the draft memo. The NDRC chief was open in speaking his mind with his assistant. After saying that "Rhoads wants Fieser and Young to cooperate in incendiary tests" but not in final operation, he went on to say:

> Relations are not too cordial—security very tight—at least that is used as excuse—I'm not sure. . . .
>
> Rhoads feels now that NDRC's responsibility stops with successful development of incendiary and time delay—he's responsible for rest of program. . . .
>
> When I get back we'd better review file to see if R's attitude now is in agreement with previous understanding. . . . It's a bit "sticky" in El Centro. *We'll have to talk it over*—Better not with Louis [Fieser] just at present. . . .
>
> For your info. only—they want this *in operation* in Aug. & Sept., and I'm afraid Col. R. doesn't realize the delays normally encountered in production of something like 1,000,000 items!
>
> H. M. Chadwell
> Chief, Division 19

After our usual low-level strafing attack on the town of Bandera, with the customary wing salute to the water tower, Leigh and Smith headed the Lodestar for Hondo, where our ground transport awaited. I rode back to Bandera in a jeep with Tim Holt. It was the first time I'd been alone with him since Doc's departure.

"Rhoads *had* to throw him out," Tim said. "The colonel was

in an impossible situation. He's been placed in total command, but Doc questioned every decision, always had what he thought was a better idea, always had some congressman friend or some general to call on and try to bring his influence into any equation. Doc was a politician, a promoter, and if he hadn't been good at it the project never would have come as far as it has. But he still thought of it as the Adams Plan, and it isn't anymore. It's like when you sell a treasured possession, a house you've built, and the new owners want to redecorate. You're offended by their poor taste, hate to see them cut down that rose bush that you've nursed and has grown so tall—but there's not a damned thing you can say. It's Project X-Ray now, and it's in the hands of the Marine Corps. Adams couldn't seem to understand that when the marines took over, they wanted a marine running the show."

"What's this about Rhoads threatening to have Doc thrown in jail?" I asked, referring to the latest rumor.

"He might do it, too. He's pissed enough."

"Why? What's going on?"

"Rhoads says that Doc can't keep his mouth shut. The colonel lives by the book, as we all know, and since the project is designated Top Secret, he figures nobody should even whisper about it. Its against the law; it's against the country; and it's against the Marine Corps. But Rhoads got some feedback that Adams had told some senator and his wife the whole story at a cocktail party. It rankled him so much that Rhoads said, 'If that old fart doesn't keep his trap shut, I'll have him put where he can't talk! In the brig!' He told Adams as much, but, knowing Doc, I wonder if he'll heed the word?"

"You backed Rhoads in giving Doc the axe," I said, accusingly.

"I had to," Holt said. "I love the old duck, too. But it was one or the other, Doc or Rhoads, couldn't be both. The project would have foundered. And at this stage of the game, it couldn't be Doc. The project's become what he wanted it to be, a military operation. It was his baby, but the child grew up and moved out of the house."

I saw the truth in what Holt said. I was able to forgive what I had considered his defection when he had sided with Rhoads and the chemists—who were now *número uno* on the colonel's hit list. Doc Adams, the visionary, was not Colonel Rhoads, the marine. Doc's inventiveness, his perseverance and dedication, had brought the project as far as these admirable qualities could carry it, but his role was completed. Rhoads stepped in like the commander he was and took a firm grasp on the project; even the technology was within his reach, and he had acted in the only way possible for

[ 219

him. Doc had been emotionally committed; Rhoads was involved professionally.

Up to a point, Adams had been able to bluff his way through. In his sometimes bumbling, always intuitive way, depending upon his incredible energy and savoir-faire, Doc had been able to cope; he alone had guided the Adams Plan from a crazy notion, through the labyrinth of government skepticism, to become Project X-Ray. Now he was out—and he'd be very well advised to keep his mouth shut about it. Colonel Rhoads wasn't kidding.

Only the method of his ouster remained a sore point with me— and that hurt like a boil.


Now that the virus of contention within Project X-Ray had become contagious, Doc Adams, poisoned by the disease, sank even deeper into the sickness. When he returned to Irwin, Pennsylvania, after many months of absence, he found his personal affairs in a mess. The IRS's claims for payment of back taxes had reached the point where some action must be taken immediately or his home and personal belongings would have to be liquidated to pay off the debt. The rich right hand of the government that Doc had imagined he was drawing from, to switch to the equally fat left-hand pocket, had suddenly become a dream. Either Doc had to get the reimbursement for his Adams Plan expenditures that he expected from the government or the government would cause him financial ruin. Because all of his business activities for the past two years had been classified as secret, and existing documentation was still confidential, it was as if there were no documents at all. Doc's indiscretion in talking to a senator about the project had been only his effort to get guidance or help in getting paid.

To substantiate his request for reimbursement and pay, using what letters prudence allowed and his diary as sources, Doc composed a detailed chronology to support his claim. He listed all major turning points in the saga of the Adams Plan and paid particular attention to meetings, personal conversations, telephone calls, and memos that would confirm his contention that he had been led to believe he would be paid. This chronology of evidence, his detailed documentation that the government owed him money, even in bare outline form, grew to a length of twelve single-spaced typewritten pages and consisted of forty-seven points illuminating the times during the past two years that his reimbursement or compensation had been discussed with supervisory brass or an important meeting had taken place confirming his claim that he had been working under government orders with the promise or expectation of being paid.

In this chronology, which is part of the Project X-Ray archives, one name occurs far more frequently than any other—Colonel Edwin E. Aldrin of General Staff, U.S. Army Air Forces.

Who was this Colonel Aldrin at the Pentagon whose name appears so often on Adams's list, but who had been totally unknown in the day-to-day activities of the working members of the project team? Years later, his son would be the second man to put foot on the moon, but that has nothing to do with the man whose name first appears in the Adams diary back on July 4, 1942, making Aldrin one of the original government people with whom Doc had been in contact. At that time, the colonel had been assigned to help Adams by Gen. Barney M. Giles of the President's Technical Staff. Aldrin's duties were to facilitate Adams's work, to "grease the rails," to assist Adams in every way possible. He arranged for Doc to be issued such hard-to-get items as gasoline ration stamps and automobile tires for the Buick, for the use of the dirigible hangar at Moffett Field where the first weight-carrying tests were done, and for anything else the inventor needed to carry ahead the preliminary work with greatest dispatch. Unfortunately, Doc also depended upon Aldrin to see that he got some money, and in this respect the colonel was not so efficient.

On October 7, 1942, Adams's notes read: "Aldrin urging that something be done about paying me. Informed that some way would be worked out, but [in the meanwhile] for me to carry on as best I could."

Several entries were made during November 1942 concerning Adams's role as technical advisor for the film unit. Various officers in the U.S. Army Signal Corps dealt with this situation, all with Aldrin's blessing. In fact, the whole obvious subterfuge of using a nonproducible training film as a source of funds for Adams seemed to be Aldrin's idea.

A Signal Corps contract for Adams's employment for the non-film as technical advisor was eventually drawn up, and a copy was sent to Aldrin for approval. Before the document was signed, however, it was revised. Instead of the standard pay scale of $50 per day plus expenses, Adams found a proposal that he be paid instead as "Associate Education Specialist (Visual)." The grade called for a pay rate of $3,200 per annum. When Adams objected to Aldrin about the changed downscale rate of pay, "the colonel suggested it was better than nothing and advised me to accept it as a temporary means of support."

In January 1943, long after Adams's appointment with the film unit had been revoked, he received a letter from a Capt. T. D. Yates of the Signal Corps. "Your papers are now at the Civil Service Commission awaiting their authority. As soon as the authority is obtained you will be placed on our PAYROLL"—this after he was no longer working with the Signal Corps film unit. It never happened.

More letters assuring Doc of payment were written and orders for salaries and reimbursements were issued, but the payments never came. January 22, 1943: "After you have been placed on our payroll you will receive a check twice a month." January 23, 1943: "In lieu of subsistence, a flat per diem of six dollars per day is authorized." "Travel is authorized by personally owned automobile, and reimbursement at the rate of four cents per mile authorized as being more economical and more advantageous to the Government."

Colonel Aldrin was privy to most of the confusion—indeed, he may have caused it. Former Signal Corps authorizations to reimburse Adams were deemed invalid. Since the plan to have Adams paid as a film advisor fell through, Aldrin wrote to him: "If you want to get travel paid, you will have to get on the pay roll. When we get the directive from General Anderson as I explained to you, the project will be presented to the NDRC and possibly California [Institute of] Technology will be designated the contracting agency. If and when that happens, arrangements [for pay] can be made directly with them."

But when Cal Tech did not materialize as the contractor, the stalling continued: "I trust that you will be able to carry on until this whole question can be settled to your satisfaction. E. E. Aldrin."

Months went by. Adams was so deeply involved in pulling the project together that he couldn't spend a lot of time hassling over getting paid. Still, he made a few halfhearted attempts. "General McClelland is very anxious to get this project into the proper channel. He wants to help you get back your expenses in any way possible. We are working on it to see what we can do about it . . . E. E. Aldrin."

"I wish you would be patient and bear with me while we get this program set up, because as it is now shaping up to be worth all delay. . . . Please take these comments as my own personal point of view. I think you can read what I mean. E. E. Aldrin."

Then a new name appeared in the financial brushoff: "Lt. Col. Homer A. Boushay of this Headquarters is expecting to be in Los Angeles between July 20 and 24, and will contact you relative to your personal financial status. General Barney M. Giles."

Later, Doc wrote to General Giles: "You advised me that Col.

Boushay was on his way to the West Coast and that you would request him to contact me. I have heard nothing from him to date. L. S. Adams."

And so it went. Just as Adams got the cold shoulder as the inventor of Project X-Ray, he now got the runaround from the paymasters of the government. In spite of the promises, half-promises, and documentation, he eventually received only $1,600 from the government. Then he sold the old family home in Irwin to pay off the debt claimed by the IRS.

Adams was broke, but he was not broken.

On February 1, 1944, only a few days after the new development and testing schedule that would terminate with the plan for ordering a million incendiaries was agreed upon, Navy Captains Teller and H. B. Temple, under the direction of Admiral McCann, chief of Naval Operations, paid a surprise visit to Project X-Ray Headquarters in El Centro, where they met with Colonel Rhoads. The purpose of the captains' trip from Washington was to discuss the progress report Rhoads had addressed to the director of Aviation Planning and to "examine all items and equipment and bats, and to discuss the present status and future program for the development of [Project X-Ray]."

It seems that the two captains arrived with a decision already made as to what they would find and what their recommendation for the future would be. The subsequent report of their deliberation treated the scheduled NDRC fine-tuning of the incendiary designs as if they were serious fundamental project changes.

> Upon reviewing all test data to date, it was found that the following work must be accomplished or facts must be established by test.
> A. New design and production of incendiary igniter.
> B. New design of incendiary capsule.
> C. New method of attaching incendiary and capsule to bat.
> D. New design of safety device which will arm the incendiary upon release of the bat.

The improvement of the design elements that remained to be done was presented by the captains as a far more daunting challenge than was actually the case. All proposed changes were merely refinements, a polish of the existing designs—all modifications were already well in hand, and some had even been completed. The report of the captains' inspection erroneously gives the impression that it was the intention of Fieser and NDRC completely to restructure the hardware—to start all over again because of a need for radically new features.

The captains' statement went on to say that not only must the hardware design begin again from scratch but, given the new components that would inevitably evolve from this procedure, all prior testing with the bats would become obsolete and would require repeating with the new materials.

Both positions were patently untrue. The modification in the capsule's shape, for example, was only an attempt to make the bomb ride more easily with the bat. The capsule's weight—which was the critical factor—would be exactly the same, so all load-carrying tests were still valid. The captains listed four problems they expected to encounter with bats equipped with the new hardware:

> E. Ability of bat to control glide while carrying new type incendiary pencil and capsule.
> F. Ability of the bat to crawl into favorable locations when encumbered with pay load.
> G. Percentage of bats which will carry pay load into favorable location in actual attack conditions.
> H. Maximum practical period of induced hibernation following which bats will perform properly.

Here it was again, the same old list, now made to seem imperative because of hardware merely being improved upon to increase the bats' already satisfactory performance. If any aspect of the new designs didn't come up to expectations we could always fall back to the original proven specifications. The captains had approached the subject as if to justify a plan already decided upon.

There is, however, another possible scenario. In view of Rhoads's tottering relationship with the chemists, one is tempted to wonder if the captains' report, following their meeting with Colonel Rhoads, could have been the result of a ploy by the colonel to get rid of Fieser and NDRC that backfired.

Did the captains come to El Centro with their minds already made up? Or did Rhoads, in a gambit to rid the marines of the civilian presence, color the meeting with an exaggerated picture of mechanical changes that he knew were only minor and that he could fix himself? If this was his motive, it boomeranged with a resounding shock.

As for the actual designs of the new hardware, Fieser and Perley were already far ahead of schedule and now had most of the problems solved. Fieser wrote to Rhoads that he had discovered "an extremely simple and apparently satisfactory method of attaching the incendiary to the bat with adhesive. The operation takes but a moment and seems to produce a very firm and uniform attachment to the fur."

Adhesive was a much simpler and faster method of attachment, with less chances for error, an innovation so obvious that it caused us to wonder why we hadn't chosen this method in the first place (although it must be remembered that the technology of adhesives was far more primitive then). The original surgical clip, which had been seized upon as the preferred method of attachment because it simulated a baby bat's teeth gripping the fur of its mother's breast and thus seemed to mimic nature, employed a short link of string between bat and bomb. The idea had been that the bat, having flown down and crawled into its place of concealment, would chew through the string before ignition, thus sparing the bat. But the system had several weaknesses. The dangling bomb was an impedance to perfect flight, less like a tightly clinging baby bat than the conforming shape of the modified adhesive capsule now being developed by Fieser, and it was more difficult for the bat to crawl into crevices with the trailing bomb, which sometimes got hung up on corners. Also, the slower, more labor-intensive use of clips in attaching a million bombs to bats in as short a time as possible was a problem. Adhesive attachment was much faster.

Furthermore, there was no advantage to the bat in releasing it from cremation at the moment of ignition. Indeed, instant destruction was a more humane alternative than freedom in an environment in which the Mexican free-tailed bat could not possibly survive, a climate too hostile for this semitropical species, which would only die a lingering death.

Also moving rapidly ahead was the development of the new time-delay device. On February 16, weeks ahead of schedule, Perley of Leeds and Northrup sent off the new prototype pencil and had 100 more units under construction with the promise they would be ready in a week. Fieser described the unit to Rhoads as "a little gem."

Yet, with all of these developments rushing forward to meet the agreed-upon schedule, the following order was issued by Naval Operations. The decision had been ratified by Admiral McCann: "The Chief of Naval Operations has authorized the discontinuance of Project X-Ray."

So Holt had been wrong, after all, I thought. Doc Adams *was* a required element in this equation. Without his energy and belief, without his driving force, Project X-Ray had foundered on the very brink of execution.

The project itself went into that familiar state of suspended animation—hibernation—but it would take much more than a rise in temperature to bring back life to Doc's moribund baby. Yet in retrospect I doubt that even Adams with all his determination and skills at political maneuvering could have pulled the project out of decline this time. The reasons given for cancellation were too boldly excuses, obvious objections invented to hide the deep secret. Two Navy captains and an admiral, after one brief inspection and review, weren't so thick that they could unanimously agree to cancel the project for the half-baked reasons they put forward. No, there had to be more to it than that.

As a pointed aside, Harris M. Chadwell of NDRC, in a personal note of thanks to Fieser, Perley, and Young, advised them of the Navy's decision with the following remarks. It all had the tone of a mutual admiration society. " . . . it [has] been decided to terminate the X-Ray project. This has not been based on any shortcomings of the incendiary and time units developed by NDRC, but rather upon the shortcomings of the fundamental idea and the opportunity of getting sufficient reliable data in order to plan a timely operation."

In another letter officially advising NDRC of the Navy decision, Chadwell made this highly loaded statement to the detriment of the bat research and the aggrandizement of the mechanics: "This decision was . . . based on the large number of uncertainties that would have to be evaluated before an operation was definitely scheduled. These uncertainties involved the behavior of the animal, rather than the behavior of the technical units which NDRC had developed."

Chadwell must have made a selective reading of the captains' letter. Their basic objections had been to the idea of hardware redesign, from which evolved their belief in the need for reconfirmation of the bats' capabilities.

Nowhere in the archives is there any indication of a letter of thanks or even of a status report to the inventor, Lytle S. Adams.

The news, of course, exploded like a fragmentation bomb on those of us who had been doing the work. The order to discontinue research was quickly followed by instructions to clean up the structures at the bat caves and return the surroundings to their former pristine condition. The lid of secrecy was not lifted, so in that respect alone our work continued unchanged.

After the bonfires of scrap lumber from the cave structures had cooled, Colonel Rhoads decently offered to do his best to have us reassigned to units of our choice, based upon logical preferences or skills.

On my way back from Texas to my new assignment at Hamilton Field near San Francisco, I stopped by my parents' home in Glendale. From there it was but a short drive to Pasadena. I wanted to close properly the last page of the last chapter of Flamethrower.

At the old shingle church on California Street, I spoke with the rector; again he gave me permission to ascend the stairs into the attic and belfry. The familiar pungent odor of guano assailed my nose. I shined my flashlight overhead and saw that Flamethrower would not want for company. At least a dozen other mastiffs crowded the crack between roof joists where I had pulled him biting and protesting a year and a half ago. Now he was used to me and when I took him from his box and held him up toward the crack and the other bats he was passive. I didn't suppose that he had any affection for me, as I had for him, but at least he didn't bite me. He crawled into the crack, elbowing his way between squirming bodies, and was soon lost to view in the clump of similar gray shapes.

Flamethrower had done his part and his reward was simple—to return to his natural life with warm feelings and a pat on the back. I did for a bat what nobody at NDRC or the Armed Forces had the decency to do for Doc. It made me feel good—and it made Flamethrower feel good, too.

There was great speculation, of course, as to the true reasons for discontinuing Project X-Ray. None of us believed for a minute the explanation offered. We hardly recalled the story Doc had told months ago after one of his trips to Washington. At the time, he had belittled rumors he had heard of secret experiments with the tiny particles of matter called atoms.

Although it would be more than a year until the first successful test explosion of an atomic bomb at Trinity Site, the research in northern New Mexico already showed great promise and the breakthrough self-sustained nuclear chain reaction had been achieved a year and a half previously. A far superior munition to the bat bomb, at least in killing power, was approaching completion.

The first atomic bomb was exploded in a desolate part of the New Mexico desert not far from Carlsbad at 3 : 29 : 45 A.M. Mountain

War Time on July 16, 1945. The device was 4 1/2 feet wide, 10 1/2 feet long, and weighed 10,000 pounds. Twenty days later, a similar bomb was exploded over Hiroshima, Japan. It killed 78,000 men, women, and children outright, and other fatalities eventually approached 50,000, many having died after the explosion from leukemia. The immediate impact of the A-bomb injured another 37,000, and 13,000 more were missing. Over 60 percent of the city was destroyed. Nine days later, another A-bomb was exploded over Nagasaki, resulting in the surrender of Japan. The stunned country, which had never before heard Emperor Hirohito's voice, listened to the imperial surrender: "A new and most cruel bomb," the emperor said, had devastated Hiroshima and Nagasaki. "We have now resolved to pave the way for a grand peace . . . by enduring the unendurable and suffering what is insufferable."

The terror wrought by these incredibly inhumane bombs stopped the war, frightened the entire population of the globe, and profoundly changed the world forever after.

Would the millions of living persons displaced by a successful deployment of the bat bomb have forced Japan to its knees? Project X-Ray could never have achieved the scope of death and destruction or the world upheaval wrought by the two atomic bombs exploded over Japan. But was the great devastation necessary to achieve the surrender of the emperor? Or would the burning of the three industrial cities in the crescent of Osaka Bay have done the job without the great loss of life?

That is a question that is only interesting to contemplate. There is no way to answer it. But somebody must have made the comparison and came up with the horrible answer that the whole world now knows so well. To this day, the true reasons for the cancellation of Project X-Ray remain mere speculation. There has never been official public comment beyond the smokescreen of the captains' report. All other documents that may have referred to the issue have been withdrawn from the file by order of the CIA.

In retrospect, I suppose it's farfetched to speculate that the bat bomb could have stopped the war. Were we merely groping in the dark, hoping to try anything that might change the tide? Perhaps it's absurd to imagine the victory of one great country over another brought about by little bats. Yet, however bizarre, it's interesting to contemplate the possibility. At least the process would have ended there; unlike the horrible alternative, it would not have proliferated. The notion brings a smile, not a shudder. It is amusing to visualize the great industrialized nations of the world squabbling over the international control of bat caves.

I held Arlie's callused cowboy-hard hand on our last night at the OST Cafe, knowing that I would never see her again. Fletch raised a foaming glass. "It's too bad Doc isn't here," he said through more than his usual blush, puffing and out of breath from a lively round of our favorite square dance. "He'd want to be with his boys in their final hour. Here's to him."

We all stood and blurted out personal sentimental tributes to our elderly absent friend. It was all a bit maudlin, but such was our mood.

Tim Holt, who alone among the officers was back in the drinking company of the enlisted corps, in a burst of eloquence spoke a moving soliloquy. I wondered if he had adapted the words from something he'd once learned for a film role, so perfect was his message, so touching. The brief improvisation and toast nearly brought us all to tears. Tim surely had a way with words.

Then von Bloeker, through misty eyes, said, "Let's give the old boy a call."

We trekked *en masse* to the phone booth and lined up along the curb. V. B. tracked down Doc at the Jacktown Hotel in Irwin, where he was holed-up courtesy of the reinstated manager, Bobby Herold.

The whole cadre and a few of Bandera's softhearted citizens took the phone in turns, thinking they would cheer up the old boy's despondent heart. But Doc didn't seem to need anyone to boost his spirits. Whether it was bravado or genuine dismissal of something tried, lost, and forgotten was hard to nail down. The greetings were welcome, but Doc's vibrant thoughts had already turned to his latest invention.

"Good of you to call," he said when I picked up the phone. "But listen, I want you to hear about a new project I'm working on—to turn the deserts green. Remember when we were looking for bats in Arizona, and we drove through those miles of burned-out country? That's what gave me the idea."

"That sounds great, Doc," I interrupted. "But listen, there's a line wants to say hello to you that's half a block long."

"Never mind. Never mind. I've got all night," he said, enthusiasm flowing like electricity through the wire. Doc was on a new roll and he wouldn't be distracted. "It's aerial seeding. I know what you'll say . . . they've tried shaking seeds out of an airplane before, and what happens? First thing, they fall on the ground, the sun burns them up, the birds eat them, bugs get them, harvester ants harvest them. Right? Never get a chance to germinate. So how do you lick that, eh? Well, the answer is simple. The Adams Aerial Pellet Seeding System. The seeds are molded into small soluble pellets, like aspirin pills. Except they contain, not acetylsalicylic acid, but a secret combination of vital nutrients, plus a humidifying agent to aid sprouting, and odor and taste inhibitors—ugh! They smell awful—birds won't touch them, bugs won't munch 'em. Hah! There's a sales slogan, if I ever heard one!

"Under the belly of the plane I hang the dispersal machine, round, like a wagon wheel hanging flat. The spokes are like rifle barrels, and it spins. You fly over the area to be seeded and it shoots out pellets like machine gun fire in all directions, tremendous distribution . . . "

"Doc," I finally got a word in. "It sounds wonderful. Listen, here's Fletch. There's still a line of guys halfway to the corner who want to wish you all the best. Your idea sounds great, Doc. Maybe after the war we'll all get together again and bomb the desert with seed pellets. Here's Fletch . . . "

We never mentioned bats or the Adams Plan. It was right that we shouldn't. Project X-Ray was finished. We all had new directions to go.

We had been a team, as different as the faces on dice, yet all the same; we were a crew and we were one. The anger we felt because of the snubbing of our leader needed an outlet—when von Bloeker and I had squared off, it brought us all closer together. My fight with my best friend might have been the most important role I played in the story. It was an outgrowth of everyone's frustration and sense of wrong, so it had been something more than just an ordinary Saturday night brawl, after all—it had been a cleansing. When Doc left, we worked on. We did our jobs—but without the inspiration of Doc's passion and belief, and it wasn't fun anymore.

Now the plot had come to an end, the final curtain of the last act had fallen, and I realized that this story I had been a part of was really about Doc. He had opened my eyes and given me a suspicion, at least, about many worldly things. Mostly, I thought, about what life really is and what to expect of it.

Shortly after the night we stood on the dusty street of Bandera and talked to Doc on the phone, his wife died. It was said that the strains of financial ruin and the disappointments of the Adams Plan contributed to the illness that killed her. A few years later, at the age of seventy-two, Doc married Rae Rambeau, who was about thirty-three, and resumed his practice of dentistry. They had three children. At the age of nearly seventy-seven, Adams fathered the last of his nine children, a boy forty-six years younger than Doc's eldest son. Some said this was the final confirmation of Doc's irresponsibility. Others say that producing a child at such an age was a last proof of Doc's eternal optimism and vitality.

In looking back, one might view the whole plan simply as a romantic notion, only valid because we were grasping at any straw to save our country from extermination. But bat incendiaries were more or less proven a year and a half before Hiroshima and their deployment might have slowed down the Japanese even if it didn't stop them. We were so close, it seems a pity that we didn't try.

I will never forget Tim Holt's words when he brought us news of the project's cancellation: "You know, the crazy thing is, I think it would have worked."

*Pearl Harbor Day, Santa Rosa Island. Fletch excavating jaw of a pygmy elephant. A short time later, cowboys told us we were at war.*

*(All photos by the author unless otherwise indicated.)*

*Von Bloeker, mentor and best friend—before the fisticuffs.*

*Fletcher dressed in the flashy Marine Corps blues that accentuated the dreariness of our Army olive drab uniforms.*

*Louis Fieser, incendiary chemist. (Photograph courtesy of U.S. Air Force)*

*Mexican free-tailed bat, the ultimate "living machine."*

*Fletch, Couffer, Bobby and Eddie Herold, Doc Adams, and the trusty Buick that would soon log its first 100,000 miles.*

*Fletch, Bobby and Eddie Herold, and the Buick: a sandy wash in the Arizona desert.*

*Camino del Diablo: the ancient track from Sonora was first used by Native Americans, then Jesuits, smugglers, illegal aliens, and the Border Patrol.*

*Court of the "Hanging Judge," Roy Bean, in west Texas.*

*Doc (on the right) made friends and fit into local society wherever he went, from befriending a desert rat to success in Washington diplomacy.*

*Fletch: the center of an unremarkable depression in a level plain suddenly opened into the sinkhole, a seemingly bottomless black pit (Medina Co., Texas).*

*It takes up to three hours for the bats of Ney Cave to complete the evening's emergence.*

*Frio Cave: the kiln where the Confederate Army burned guano to extract nitrogen, a fundamental element in the manufacture of gunpowder. Again a source of potash in World War I, Texas bats were used in three wars.*

*Bobby Herold, Adams, and Ray Williams loading bats into the "egg-crate" bomb trays. (Photograph courtesy of U.S. Air Force)*

*Tim Holt, bombardier, USAAF.*

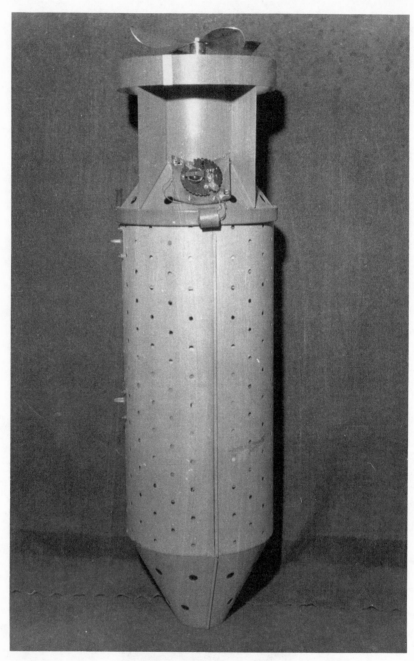

*Early model bat bombshell with mechanical opening device, later improved with altimeter switch. (Photograph courtesy of U.S. Navy)*

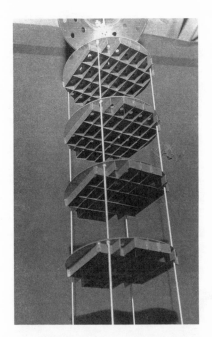

*"Egg-crate" trays: each bat dropped
from its private compartment onto
the roof of the tray below, which then
became its launching platform.
(Photograph courtesy of U.S. Navy)*

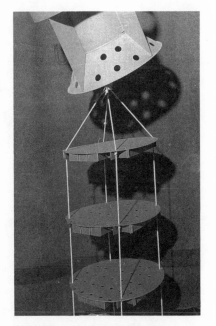

*The bat bomb trays hung from a
parachute on a chain after the bombshell split away.
(Photograph courtesy of U.S. Navy)*

*Chase plane with Doc aboard circles the deployed bomb.*
*(Photograph courtesy of U.S. Air Force)*

*The accidental incineration of Carlsbad Auxiliary Army Air Field by incendiary bats was both a high and a low in the fortunes of Project X-Ray. (Photograph courtesy of U.S. Air Force)*

*(Photographs below and on opposite page courtesy of Denny Constantine)*

*Denny Constantine and a mastiff bat. If we could use this large rare species, we joked, it could carry a stick of dynamite rather than 17 grams of napalm.*

*Mexican free-tailed bats carpet the ceilings of Frio Cave. By measuring one-foot squares, counting the number of bats in a square, and multiplying by the number of squares, Constantine developed a system for estimating the total bat populations of caves. Researchers calculated the bats of Frio Cave at ten million, Bracken Cave at twenty million.*

Mexican free-tailed bats, Frio Cave, Texas. Males, females, and flightless young hang in separate areas at different seasons. These bats consume many tons of insects per year in Texas, helping to check the spread of insect-borne diseases and assisting agriculture by limiting the use of dangerous chemical pesticides.

Bats begin to peel off the ceiling. In moments the air will be choked with flying bats and photography will become impossible.

*At the El Centro test site: Captain Hulls scatters the troops with a surprise attack.*

*Mark Benish, Patsy Batista, Eddie Herold, and Jack Couffer, assembling test structures. The frame was faced with plywood, with holes cut to simulate windows. After deployment from a B-25 bomber, the numbers of incendiary bats that flew into the structures were tallied and the hypothetical success of the mission was calculated.*

*Project X-Ray crew (left to right, back row): Captain Hulls, Ozro Wiswell,*
*"Doc" Savage, von Bloeker, Eddie Herold, Captain Leigh;*
*(front row) Jack Couffer, Captain Smith, Tim Holt, Bobby Herold.*

*Doc's son, Devil Bill Adams (named after an ancestral Mexican-American War hero), in Ney Cave, Texas, with screens in place for a test. (Photograph courtesy of U.S. Air Force)*

*Captain Leigh, Frank Benish, and Ray Williams in Ney Cave, Texas (cases are for carrying bats to a test).*

*Bracken Cave: dismantling the doors. We returned the caves to the same pristine condition in which we'd found them.*

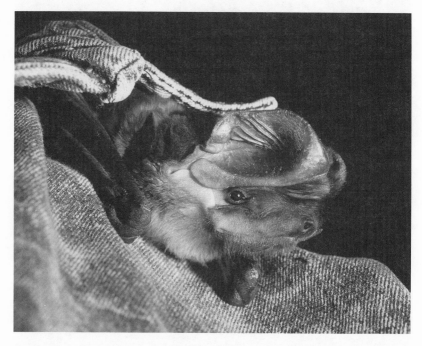

*Flamethrower rode like a living gargoyle on my shoulder, leering out from under my collar with whimsical curiosity. (Photography courtesy of Mike Couffer)*

# *Epilogue*

AFTER NEARLY FIFTY YEARS, it hasn't been easy to track down all of the project's major participants and come up with a complete post–bat bomb biography of each individual. Yet it seems fitting to try. Even in alphabetical order, Doc comes first.

Lytle S. Adams, as has already been told, shifted from the bat bomb project to a scheme for reseeding parts of the desert with pelletized seeds sprayed from an airplane. Fletch and Denny Constantine eventually joined him in Arizona for this endeavor, which ended badly— like his other inventions, seemingly good ideas in search of inspired realization.

I have already told of Doc's marriage to Rae Rambeau and the third family produced by that union. But another marriage came between. This was a short-lived affair, conceived through mutual misunderstanding—each partner mistakenly believing the other was wealthy. When the truth came clear, the arrangement was quickly and affably annulled.

After the collapse of the seeding project, Doc and Rae moved to Seattle, then to Moses Lake, Washington, where he resumed his practice of dental surgery. There Doc came up with one more invention that he tried unsuccessfully to get off the ground, a fried chicken vending machine. A good idea ahead of its time?

Adams and Rae retired to Tuscon, Arizona, where Doc died at the age of eighty-seven.

Somehow we had always regarded Patsy Batista's avowed underworld connections as farfetched, his singular way of self-glamorization, an alleged former profession too bizarre even for the bat men. Patsy's life after the project has been harder to score than others. Shortly after the war, he was visited in Chicago by both Fletch and Williams, so my report comes secondhand, from observers of moot probity.

Fletch and a buddy, both with fresh Marine Corps discharges in their pockets, were driving to Indiana and stopped off in Chicago to pay Patsy a visit. From a hotel room Fletch called Garrick's Lounge, a joint on the Loop where Patsy had said he hung out and was well known. Fletch says Garrick's Lounge was a famous place, The Cats and the Fiddle played there, and *On the Sunny Side of the Street* was their song. The phone receptionist was noncommittal, but Fletch left his name and hotel room number.

A short time later, Patsy knocked at the door accompanied by three hoods. Patsy came in; the hoods stayed in the hall.

Fletch's friend Gene was taking home a "liberated" Japanese pistol as a souvenir. He hadn't wanted to leave it in the car, so he'd brought it to their room, where it now lay in plain view on the table. "When Patsy saw that," Fletch said, "he flipped out, grabbed a towel from the wash room, picked up the pistol and wiped it off, wrapped it up, and tossed it to one of his friends in the hall. 'Get rid of it!' he said."

"What are you trying to do?" He glowered at Fletch. "Set me up?"

Awed by Fletch's buildup of the mobster he was about to meet, the unnerved owner of the pistol hadn't had time to say "spit" before his prized possession had disappeared into the depths of gangland.

When Patsy cooled off, he said that in Chi you go to jail for leaving a gat lying around, and he accused Fletch of trying to be a big shot. Fletch interpreted the episode as convincing evidence of Patsy's glorified role in the Chicago underworld.

A short time later, Williams contacted Doc's ex-driver at Garrick's Lounge, where to the strains of *On the Sunny Side of the Street* Ray proceeded to toss down a few too many old-fashioneds. He was well lubricated when Patsy took him to a Chinese restaurant for a meal. They hadn't been inside five minutes when two ugly-looking mugs showed up, produced big black guns, and began loudly and angrily to berate Patsy about something that Ray couldn't understand.

Williams was just drunk enough that he said to Pat, "If you don't like those guys, Patsy, just give me the word and I'll take those gats away from them and put 'em where the sun don't shine."

Probably not reacting to Ray's threat but for reasons of their own, the thugs took off. Pat hustled Ray out the back door.

"Where were they going?" Ray questioned.

"To ask somebody if it's okay to shoot me," Patsy said.

Ray says he lost his suitcase in Chicago, couldn't remember what hotel he'd left it at, and still wonders if the gangster episode was real or if it was a sideshow staged by Patsy for his benefit.

A woman called me recently and said she was a researcher for a TV show doing a piece on the bat bomb. She'd heard that Doc Adams had practiced dentistry in Irwin, Pennsylvania, and on the basis of that bit of information placed a blind call to Irwin and asked for Dr. Adams, a dentist. As we know from the preceding biography, our Doc Adams hadn't been near Irwin in many years, but by the fall of the dice there happened to be a dentist of that name in Irwin. He didn't know anything firsthand about the bat bomb, of course, but it happened that he had a patient who had been connected with the project. And this leads us to Mark Benish—about as implausible a connection as the one that originally brought him to us.

On the basis of this information, I called Mark, the only contact we've had since 1944. I learned that both Mark and Frank returned from the war to jobs they had left with Westinghouse. Frank died of leukemia a few years ago. Mark has been retired for fourteen years.

I finally got around to asking Mark why Adams had gotten him assigned to Project X-Ray. "When Doc's airmail pickup system was working," Mark said, "if any of the airfields were socked-in by fog or clouds, I'd drive the mail from one pickup point to another."

It seemed as good a recommendation as any. So at last we have that point cleared up.

After the war, Denny Constantine earned his doctorate at U.C. Davis and joined the U.S. Public Health Service at the Centers for Disease Control at Atlanta. He made milestone discoveries about bats and rabies and is today considered one of the world's authorities on the subject.

For reasons of his own, Doc had dissuaded Denny from entering the Armed Forces, but later, as a member of the Commissioned Corps of the U.S. Public Health Service, one of the Uniformed Services often incorporated into the Armed Forces, Constantine was detailed for ten years to the Navy. There he reached the rank of captain and was recommended for promotion to rear admiral shortly before he retired. Thus Doc missed by a few years the high-ranking

officer in his private corps he so hopelessly wished for yet so reck-
lessly acquired.

Denny retired in 1990 and lives near San Francisco, where he
now has time to continue research on bats and to write up years of
unpublished work.

Now we come in our alphabetical listing to Jack Couffer. Because I
know a good deal more about what happened to me than to the others, I could go on for pages telling exaggerated stories of my fabulous
life. But in the interests of brevity and honesty, I'll stifle the urge
and keep to a few bare facts.

I was transferred from the bat project to an Air Force Air Sea
Rescue Unit. As a sergeant, I was supposed to know something
about the military. To dodge the obvious fact that I didn't, I came to
my new unit with a letter saying I had never been properly trained
to that rank militarily. I suppose the point of this missive was to say
not to expect too much of me. In the Air Sea Rescue, we were Army
guys, but on shipboard we wore Navy clothes, including the white
hats—another eccentric outfit. We raced around in high-speed boats
chasing planes that crashed into the Pacific. But *rescue* I did not. On
my boat, we picked up only pieces, never a living downed pilot.

Later, I studied zoology at USC, switched to a major in cinema,
and have followed that work as a writer, director, cameraman, and
producer ever since. I am still working at it and split my time between homes in California and Kenya.

Louis F. Fieser went on with the development of more high explosive and incendiary bombs. In keeping with his specialty, among his
wartime publications was the offbeat handbook *Arson, an Instruction Manual.* By war's end, production of napalm—the development of which he had pioneered—reached a scale of 75 million
pounds per year: approximately 30 million M-69 napalm bombs
were produced.

A look at Fieser's list of accomplishments in *World Who's Who
in Science* reveals his incredible versatility—research in cancer and
chemotherapeutic studies, synthesized vitamin K-1, other work on
oxidation-reduction, quinones, aromatic chemistry, carcinogenic
hydroquinones, steroids, resin acids, napthquinone antimalarials,
cortisone, industrial products related to pharmaceuticals. He won
several Chemical Association awards and was a fellow of the National Academy of Sciences and a member of the Surgeon General's

advisory commission on smoking and health. Evidently Fieser's gift for massive correspondence never diminished: he published over 300 research papers. Curiously, his biography makes no mention of his work with incendiaries during the war.

After his distinguished teaching and research career, Fieser retired with his chemist wife to Belmont, Massachusetts, where he died in 1977.

Harry J. Fletcher was assigned as an aerial gunner to a marine air wing and served in the South Pacific. He was on Tinian in the Marianas when the atom bombs went off, which he sees as an ironic denouement because the island had also been designated as a possible takeoff site for the bat bombs.

Fletch worked on boats after the war, from Alaska to Mexico, Central America, the Caribbean, and the Mediterranean. He was employed for a time by the Mexican government in some kind of clandestine antidrug work. Fletch was laid low by a stroke a few years ago and now lives in semiretirement in southern California.

Bobby and Eddie Herold returned to Pennsylvania. A short time after getting his discharge from the Army, Eddie went into his garage, closed the door, started his car, and began to read a magazine he would never finish.

Bobby assumed his former post as manager of the Jacktown Hotel in Jeanette, where his friendly greetings delighted clientele for many years. In 1983 he suffered a stroke, a loss felt by all who had ever patronized that charming place, made gracious through Bobby's warm hospitality. He is now retired not far from Doc's old home in Irwin.

Tim Holt married the girl who accompanied him for a swim in the El Centro irrigation ditch after he'd dumped the colonel's car. Holt was only six years my senior, yet as my superior officer he assumed a curiously paternal role. It seemed to me that this war would go on forever, and it was Holt's questioning of my aim in life when the conflict was over that brought it home to me that there really *was* a future. I had not the slightest aspiration to participate in the motion picture world to which Tim would return. The idea was so far removed from my mind that I never discussed the subject with him. After the war ended, when I did study for a career in cinema, I would have liked to have met Tim again in my new role. But I was never to see him again. Tim died of a heart attack in 1973.

Jack C. von Bloeker, Jr., was assigned from the bat project to aerial gunnery school. Upon becoming qualified, he taught aerial gunnery and served in the Philippines. After the war, he taught zoology at Los Angeles City College, where for many years he enlightened students with his contagious passion for nature. He and his wife, Ona, retired to Green Valley, Arizona, where v. B. died in 1991.

Ray Williams shipped out to the Pacific theater as a marine reserve and followed the war from shipboard, always on the verge of landing, never making it. He sailed from Ulithi, a lonely atoll halfway between Guam and the Palau Islands, to Espírito Santo in the New Hebrides, then he was beached for the duration at Okinawa.

After the war, Ray and I pooled our savings and mustering-out pay and bought a commercial fishing boat. A couple of years later, I went back to school on the GI Bill. Williams stuck with fishing and is still operating his own lobster boat out of San Diego.

Following his transfer as a lieutenant, Ozro B. Wiswell undertook research for the Navy in human aviation physiology. After his discharge, he broadened his studies to other biological and anatomical subjects. He taught and wrote about human anatomy at the University of California, and in Japan and Brazil. His main research dealt with bone structure, calcium, and vitamin E, but he also continued his interest in biology and wrote about mice, rabbits, squirrel monkeys, and the giant South American land snail.

Ozro retired as associate professor of anatomy, emeritus, from The University of Texas (dental branch) in 1971. He is still married to lovely Viola and they had six children—four boys and two girls. They are retired and live in Houston.

There is something sad about collecting the statistics on friends known and cared for in the past, as affecting as the reunion of a high school class from long ago. I have been unable to glean anything about the others. From looking at the bare facts of our lives, I wonder if our youthful dreams were realized—I suspect in most cases they were. My own aspirations were perhaps exceeded, and for this

I owe a debt to Doc, from whom I learned much more than the Art of Confusion and that Old Grand-dad is the world's best bourbon. We were just a diverse group of guys, thrown together by the imponderables of the times—and by the whimsical inspiration of one incredible man.

# References

Allen, Glover Morrill. *Bats*. Cambridge, Mass.: Harvard University Press, 1940.

"Bats Away." *Newsweek*, Mar. 24, 1961.

Brophy, Leo P., Wyndham D. Miles, and Rexmond C. Cochrane. *The Chemical Warfare Service: From Laboratory to Field*. Series: United States Army in World War II. Washington, D.C.: Office of the Chief of Military History, Dept. of the Army, 1959.

Burns, Eugene, with George Scullin. "The U.S. Secret Weapon You've Never Heard of." *True Magazine*, July 1958, pp. 44–114.

Campbell, Charles A. R. *Bats, Mosquitoes and Dollars*. Boston: Stratford Company, 1952.

Constantine, Denny G. *Activity Patterns of the Mexican Free-tailed Bat*. Albuquerque: University of New Mexico Press, 1967.

———. "Health Precautions for Bat Researchers." In *Ecological and Behavioral Methods for the Study of Bats*, edited by T. H. Kunz, pp. 491–528. Washington, D.C.: Smithsonian Institution Press, 1988.

———. *Rabies Transmission by Air in Bat Caves*. Public Health Service Pub. No. 1617. Washington, D.C.: U.S. Govt. Printing Office, 1967.

Davis, Richard B., Clyde F. Herreid II, and Henry L. Short. "Mexican Free-tailed Bats in Texas." Texas A & M, *Ecological Monographs* 32 (1962): 311–346.

Fieser, Louis F. *The Scientific Method*. New York: Reinhold, 1964.

"Fifty Years of Flying High." *USAir* 11 (May 1989):5.

Griffin, Donald R. *Listening in the Dark: The Acoustic Orientation of Bats and Men*. New Haven: Yale University Press, 1958.

Griffin, Donald R., and Robert Galambos. "Obstacle Avoidance by Flying Bats." *Anatomical Record* 78 (1940):95.

———. "The Sensory Basis of Obstacle Avoidance by Flying Bats." *Journal of Experimental Zoology* 86 (1941):481–506.

"Incendiary Bats." *Life Magazine*, Feb. 1948.

Lovell, Stanley. *Of Spies and Stratagems*. Englewood Cliffs, N.J.: Prentice Hall, 1963, pp. 61–63.

McNichols, Charles L., and Clayton D. Carus. "One Way to Cripple Japan: The Inflammable Cities of Osaka Bay." *Harper's*, June 1942, pp. 29–36.

Mohr, Charles E. "Texas Bat Caves Served in Three Wars." *National Speleological Society Bulletin* 10 (1948):89–96. Washington, D.C.

Noyes, W. A., Jr., ed. *Chemistry, History of the Chemical Components of the NDRC*. Part 6: History of Division 19. Boston: Atlantic Monthly Press/Little, Brown & Co., 1948.

Ridenour, Louis N. "Bats in the Bomb Bay." *Atlantic* 178 (Dec. 1946):116–117.

Sherrod, Robert. *History of Marine Corps Aviation in World War II*. Washington, D.C.: Combat Forces Press, 1957.

Trimble, William F., and W. David Lewis. "Lytle S. Adams, the Apostle of Nonstop Airmail Pickup." *Technology and Culture* 29 (April 1988):247–265.

Tuttle, Merlin D. *America's Neighborhood Bats*. Austin: University of Texas Press, 1988.

Declassified government letters and documents quoted were obtained from the following offices:

1. Albert F. Simpson Historical Research Center, U.S. Air Force, Research Division, Maxwell AFB, AL 36112.
2. Center for Polar and Scientific Archives, National Archives and Records Service, Washington, DC 20408.
3. Department of the Navy, Headquarters, U.S. Marine Corps, History and Museums Division, Washington, DC 20380.
4. Department of the Navy, Navy Historical Center, Operational Archives Branch, Washington Navy Yard, Washington, DC 20374.
5. General Services Administration, Franklin D. Roosevelt Library, National Archives and Records Service, Hyde Park, NY 12538.
6. General Services Administration, National Archives and Records Service, Reference Branch NNGR, Washington, DC 20409.
7. General Services Administration, National Archives and Records Service, Records of the NDRC and Office of Scientific Research and Development, Science and Technological Division, Washington, DC 20408.
8. Modern Military Branch, National Archives and Records Service (Record Group 227), Washington, DC 20408.

# *Index*

Abrams, Allen, 145
Adams, Ida Mae, 23–24
Adams, Lytle S.: first meeting with, 4–5, 7; personality of, 4, 62, 93,
165, 231; as inventor, 5, 163–164, 229–230, 233; letters to Roosevelt, 5–9, 102; proposal for use of bats in WWII, 5–13; Roosevelt's memo concerning, 5; and incendiary chemicals for bat
bombs, 15, 17–18, 46; reaction to Chemical Warfare Service's
recommendation on, 15–19; project personnel assembled by, 21–
25; reaction to support from Army Air Forces, 21; and funding
of bat bomb project, 23, 98, 101, 220–222; and pet bat (Flamethrower), 29–31; view of military system, 32–34; and military
rank of staff, 33–34, 157–159, 166; weight and size-carrying tests
on bats, 48–51; and Kabrich's lack of support, 52–54; and search
for bat caves, 54–59, 62–75, 77–83; skills in the Art of Confusion, 56–57; reaction to Navy's rejection of Adams Plan, 59–
60; meeting with Chemical Warfare Service, 60–61, 76; on the
atomic bomb, 61; and sponsorship of bat bombs, 84–88; and need
for physiologist on staff, 88–89; and physiologist for Adams Plan,
93; on Osaka Bay, 95–97; and Fieser's desire for control of bat
bomb project, 98–100, 165–168, 179–180; and Batista, 103–105;
design of container shell for bat bombs, 108–110, 166; and Carlsbad test of bat bombs, 113–120; and hibernation tests, 126; and
Young, 145, 148, 165, 167, 168; and Rhoads, 157–159; financial
problems of, 164–165, 185, 196, 220–222, 230–231; criticisms
of, 184–186; and funnel method for capture of bats, 194–195,
196, 200–201; dismissal of, 203–205, 218–220; final meeting of
staff with, 215–216; and discontinuance of Project X-Ray, 226;
and greening of the deserts, 229–230, 233; life after Project X-Ray,
229–231, 233; death of wife, 230–231; children of, 231; marriage
to Rae Rambeau, 231, 233; death of, 233

Adams Plan: proposal for use of bats in WWII, 5–13, 85; questions concerning, 13–15, 18, 25–26, 53–54; reaction of Chemical Warfare Service to, 15–16; support from Army Air Forces, 20–21, 25–26; staff of, 21–25, 38, 41–42, 45–48, 88–89, 92–94, 104–105, 106, 124; funding for, 23, 98, 101; headquarters and barracks for staff of, 23–25; clothing of staff of, 24–25, 39–40; leisure activities of staff of, 24–25, 40–41; security used by, 38–39; encounters with military law by staff of, 40–41, 42–44; chemists on staff of, 41–42, 45–48, 60; letters of introduction for staff of, 41; salary of staff, 43; weight and size-carrying tests for, 48–51; setback from Kabrich, 52–54; and search for bat caves, 54–59, 62–75, 77–83; Navy's reactions to, 59–60, 146–148; and forest fires, 76; sponsorship of, 84–88; Stevenson's idea for releasing bats from submarines, 84–85; physiologist on staff of, 88–89, 92–94; Fieser's interest in control of, 98–100; official approval of, 98; Muroc tests of bat bombs, 100–101, 105–110; Carlsbad test of bat bombs, 113–120; Lothrop's involvement in, 120–123; high-altitude pressure test of bats, 123, 124–125; negative attitude of the National Defense Research Council on, 145–146; renamed Project X-Ray, 147–148. See also Project X-Ray
Adhesive for bat bombs, 224–225
Air Force. See Army Air Forces
Aldrin, Col. Edwin E., 221–222
Anderson, General, 222
Anson, Col. O. A., 87
Army Air Forces, 12, 14, 20–21, 25–26, 52, 53, 59
Arnold, Gen. Hap, 20, 41
Atomic bomb, 61, 227–228

Bandera, 77–79, 126–143, 148–149, 160–161, 170–171, 174–178, 180–184, 229–230
Bat bombs: Adams's proposal concerning, 5–13, 17–19; ethical issues concerning, 7–9; incendiary chemicals for, 15, 17–18, 46, 89–90, 113–114; weight and size-carrying tests for, 48–51; and forest fires, 76; incendiary device for, 88, 89–90; napalm as incendiary for, 89–90, 113–114; Muroc tests of, 100–101, 105–110; manufacturing of, for Muroc tests, 107, 108–110; container shell for, 108–110, 166; method of deployment of, 109–110; safety device for, 110; Carlsbad test of, 113–120; high-altitude pressure test of, 123, 124–125; time-delay device for, 144–145, 173, 225; demonstration of, for Marine Corps, 152, 155–156; Dugway tests of, 202–216; adhesive for, 224–225. See also Adams Plan; Project X-Ray

Bat caves, 54–60, 62–75, 79–83, 91–92, 126, 129–137, 149, 174, 187–193, 195–201, 204

Bat guano, 76, 77, 82–83, 91, 92, 127, 129–132, 174, 188, 193, 227

Batista, Patricio (Patsy), 103–105, 107–108, 126, 151, 161–162, 233–235

Bats: spotted bat, 2; symbolism of, 2; mastiff bat, 27–31; as pet (Flame-thrower), 27–31, 55, 128–129, 142, 149–150, 162–163, 175, 227; information in reference books on, 35–38; weight-carrying abilities of, 35, 45–46, 48–51; echo-location ability of, 36–38; species of, 36, 45; Mexican free-tail bats, 45, 48–49, 129–137, 193–194; in Carlsbad Caverns, 48, 55, 87, 91, 105, 123–124; diet of, 48, 191; flights of, 48, 55, 81–82, 92, 133–137, 187–188, 197–201; search for bat caves, 54–59, 62–75, 77–83; in Bracken Cave, 55, 91–92, 126, 187–188, 196, 200; in Ney Cave, 55, 80–83, 91, 126, 129–137, 188, 196, 197–201; canyon bats (*Pipistrellus*), 58; *Leptonycteris* species of, 58; temperature constraints of, 60–61; predators of, 81, 91–92; parasites of, 82–83, 129–132, 192–193; release from submarines, 84–85; *Mormoops* species of, 92; high-altitude pressure test of, 123, 124–125; hibernation tests of, 126–143, 149, 188–189, 193–196; *Myotis thysanodes*, 127–128; as pet (Princess), 127–129, 142, 149–150, 162–163; determination of number of, 187–188; and rabies, 189–193; vampire bats, 191; funnel method of capture of, 194–195, 196, 200–201; migration of, 195, 196

Bean, Roy, 59

Benish, Frank, 38, 61, 126, 151, 202, 204, 235

Benish, Mark, 38, 126, 151, 204, 235

Blandy, Rear Adm. W. H. P., 147

Bombs. *See* Atomic bomb; Bat bombs

Border Patrol, 57, 58

Boushay, Lt. Col. Homer A., 222–223

Bracken Cave, 55, 91–92, 126, 149, 187–188, 196, 200

Brown, Col. W. G., 86

Campbell, Charles A. R., 60

Canyon bats, 58

Capone, Al, 104, 162

Carlsbad Caverns, 48, 55, 87, 91, 105, 123–124

Carlsbad test of bat bombs, 113–120

Carr, Capt. Wiley, 122, 167, 180

Cave exploration, 62–63

Caves. *See* Bat caves

Chadwell, Harris M., 42, 145, 179–180, 217–218, 226

Chemical Warfare Service: objections to Adams Plan, 15–19, 52–54, 59, 86; support for Adams Plan, 20, 25–26, 98, 99, 101; Fieser's contacts with, 42, 166; Adams's meeting with, 60–61, 76; and Muroc tests of bat bombs, 100; and Carlsbad test of bat bombs, 113; Peake in Technical Division of, 123; support of Project X-Ray, 173, 211

Conant, James B., 42, 84–87, 173

Constantine, Denny, 124, 129–134, 188, 189–193, 233, 235–236

Couffer, Jack: and Pearl Harbor bombing, 1–2; work at Los Angeles County Museum, 1–3, 12; first meeting with Adams, 4–5; drafted by Army, 4; Army basic training of, 16–17; assignment to bat bomb project, 21; clothing worn by, 24–25, 39; pet bat (Flame-thrower) of, 27–31, 55, 128–129, 142, 149–150, 162–163, 175, 227; military rank of, 33, 34; encounters with military law, 40–41, 42–44; salary of, 43; character assessment method of, 47; weight and size-carrying tests on bats, 48–51; and search for bat caves, 54–59, 62–75, 77–83, 91–92; in Bandera, 77–79, 137–143, 148–149, 161, 174–178, 229–230; on bat guano, 94; at Muroc tests, 105, 106–112; sexual experience of, 110–112; and Carlsbad test of bat bombs, 113–120; and hibernation tests, 126–143; pet bat (Princess) of, 127–129, 142, 149–150, 162–163; and Arlie, 138, 140, 161, 182–183, 186–187, 229; and cowboys, 138–141; and pet tiger (Top Sarge), 142–143; introduction to Rhoads, 151; and flight with Hulls, 152–155; and marines, 175–178; and fist-fight with von Bloeker, 181–184, 202, 230; relationship with von Bloeker, 181–182; and counting of bats, 187–188; and marine guard's shooting of a deer, 196–197; decision to take down containment doors at Ney Cave, 197–201; at Dugway tests, 204–216; final meeting with Adams, 215–216; and Holt's criticisms of Adams, 218–220; reassignment to Hamilton Field, California, 227; life after Project X-Ray, 236

Cowboys, 138–141

Craig, Colonel, 26

Crosby, Bing, 107, 110

Crosby, Larry, 107, 110

Crosby Company, 107, 108, 109, 110, 166

Curtiss, Glenn, 5

CWS. *See* Chemical Warfare Service

Deer, shooting of, 196–197

DeHaven, Gen. Louis, 113, 121, 146

Donovan, Col. William J., 102

Du Pont, Richard, 5, 163
Dugway tests, 202–216

Eisenhower, Dwight D., 40

Fawcett, Lt. Col. M. A., 179, 180
Fieser, Louis F.: as chemist for Adams Plan, 41–42, 45–48, 51, 60; incendiary projects of, 42, 99, 212; personality of, 47, 99; photograph of, 47; and incendiary device for bat bomb, 88, 89–90; and control of bat bomb project, 98–100, 165–168, 179–180; funding for, 98; and Muroc tests of bat bombs, 100–101, 106–110; and safety device for bat bombs, 110; and Carlsbad test of bat bombs, 113–120; and Lothrop, 120–123; and time-delay device for bat bomb, 144–145, 173, 225; and Young, 145; under Navy supervision, 147–148; and Dugway tests, 202–203, 210–214; and Rhoads, 211–214, 217, 224; adhesive for incendiary mechanisms, 224–225; and discontinuance of Project X-Ray, 226; life after Project X-Ray, 236–237
Flamethrower (pet bat), 27–31, 55, 128–129, 142, 149–150, 162–163, 175, 227
Fletcher, Harry J.: work in Los Angeles County Museum, 3; as Marine Corps member, 22–23, 147; as member of bat bomb project, 22–23; clothing worn by, 24–25, 39, 151; living arrangements of, 24; and pet bat (Flamethrower), 28; weight and size-carrying tests on bats, 49; skills in the Art of Confusion, 56–57; and search for bat caves, 59, 62, 64–75; uniform of, 93; supervisor of, 106; and Carlsbad test of bat bombs, 113, 114, 115, 118; and bat collecting in California, 123–124; and high-altitude pressure test of bats, 124–125; and hibernation tests, 126–127, 133; and pet tiger (Top Sarge), 142–143, 169–172; introduction to Rhoads, 151; demonstration of bat bombs for Marine Corps, 155–156; and Rhoads's staff car, 155; in Bandera, 160, 161; and counting of bats, 188; at Dugway tests, 204; final meeting with Adams, 216; and discontinuance of Project X-Ray, 229, 230; life after Project X-Ray, 233, 234–235, 237
Frey, Jack, 86, 87
Frio Cave, 92, 189
Funnel-capture experiment, 194–195, 196, 200–201
Furer, Adm. J. A., 59, 84, 85, 208

Galambos, Robert, 37
George, Jay-R, 138–140

Gerdes, Ben, 149, 175
Giles, Gen. Barney M., 221, 222–223
Griffin, Donald R., 10–14, 35–37, 45–46, 49, 50, 86–87
Guano, 76, 77, 82–83, 91, 92, 127, 129–132, 174, 188, 193, 227

Herold, Bobby: as member of bat bomb team, 21–22, 48, 49, 54; as ad-
    jutant to Adams, 54, 59, 93, 204; and pet bat (Flamethrower), 55;
    and search for bat caves, 78; and Muroc tests, 105; and Carlsbad
    test of bat bombs, 115–116; and Art of Confusion, 120; and hi-
    bernation tests, 126; absent from Dugway tests, 203; final meet-
    ing of staff with, 215–216; and discontinuance of Project X-Ray,
    229; life after Project X-Ray, 237
Herold, Eddie: as member of bat bomb team, 21–22; sexual experience
    of, 39, 94, 111; uniform worn by, 39; weight and size-carrying
    tests on bats, 49; and search for bat caves, 58, 62, 65, 67, 71, 72,
    78, 79; on bat guano, 94; and Muroc tests, 105; and Carlsbad test
    of bat bombs, 113; and hibernation tests, 126; introduction to
    Rhoads, 151; and counting of bats, 187–188; at Texas bat caves,
    204; and Dugway tests, 214–215; life after Project X-Ray, 237
Hibernation tests of bats, 126–143, 149, 188–189, 193–196
Hiroshima, 228, 231
Holland, Col. Harvey, 86, 87–88
Holt, Jack, 105, 140
Holt, Tim: as actor, 105, 140, 161–162; father of, 105, 140; as flight
    officer, 105–106, 150; on staff of Adams Plan, 105–106, 156; and
    Carlsbad tests of bat bombs, 113, 114; in Bandera, 126, 140–141;
    and cowboys, 140–141; and nickname for Wiswell, 149; introduc-
    tions of staff to Rhoads, 150–151; accident with Rhoads's staff
    car, 155; criticisms of Adams, 184–186, 218–220; on discontinu-
    ance of Project X-Ray, 229, 231; life after Project X-Ray, 237–238
Hovde, Frederick L., 35, 51, 85–87
Hubbard, Chuck, 160
Hufferd, Col. R. W., 86
Hulls, Captain, 150, 152–156
Huston, John, 105

Japan: view of, during WWII, 6–9; and incendiary balloons, 76; Osaka
    Bay in, 95–97, 208; houses in, 96; atomic bombs exploded in,
    228, 231

Kabrich, Gen. W. C.: vacillations concerning bat bombs, 20, 52–54, 76,
    86, 98, 123, 166; Adams's meeting with, 60; directive concerning

time-delay device, 144, 146, 173; and Dugway tests, 202–203, 209, 210
King, Admiral, 113
Knox, Frank, 146
Kobe, 96–97
Kyoto, 96–97

Leeds and Northrup Company, 144, 145, 147, 148, 166, 173, 217, 225
Leigh, Capt. S. R., 156, 160, 172, 204, 218
*Leptonycteris* species of bats, 58
Lewis, Maj. Evan A., 209
Lothrop, Warren C., 120–123, 144–145, 205, 210, 217
Lovell, Stanley, 145

McCain, Adm. J. S., 155
McCann, Admiral, 223, 225
McClelland, Gen. H. M., 88, 98, 100, 101, 110, 113, 126
McIntyre, M. H., 102
March Field Air Force Base, 42–44
Marine Corps, 113, 147–148, 152, 155–156, 166, 175–178, 196–197, 214
Mastiff bats, 27–31
Mexican free-tail bats, 45, 48–49, 129–137, 193–194
Milliken, Robert, 18
Miyaki, Toya, 96
Montgomery, Field Marshal, 40
*Mormoops* species of bats, 92
Morrell, Col. J. C., 60
Muroc tests of bat bombs, 100–101, 105–110
*Myotis thysanodes,* 127–128

Nagasaki, 228
Napalm, 89–90, 113–114
National Defense Research Committee: decisions about Adams Plan, 10, 31, 86–88, 98, 99, 145, 211; purpose of, 10; objections to Adams Plan, 35, 59, 84, 98, 145; Fieser's contact with, 41, 42, 45, 90, 101, 166; and Stevenson's proposal for bat release from submarines, 84–85; funding for Fieser from, 101; approval of Project X-Ray, 211; controversy with Rhoads, 217, 218; and discontinuance of Project X-Ray, 226
National Inventors Council, 14, 17, 20, 52, 60, 76
Navy Department, 59, 60, 84, 85, 113, 146

NDRC. *See* National Defense Research Committee
Ney Cave, 55, 80–83, 91, 126, 129–137, 149, 174, 188, 196, 197–201, 204

Office of Strategic Services, 102, 145, 166
Osaka Bay, 95–97, 208
OSS. *See* Office of Strategic Services
OST Cafe, 77–79, 126, 137–138, 140–141, 148–149, 170, 175, 181–184, 229

Parasites of bats, 82–83, 129–132, 192–193
Peake, Col. Millard F., 123
Pearl Harbor bombing, 1–2, 8, 202
Perley, George A., 217, 224–225, 226
Pets: Flamethrower (bat), 27–31, 55, 128–129, 142, 149–150, 162–163, 175, 227; Princess (bat), 127–129, 142, 149–150, 162–163; Top Sarge (tiger), 142–143, 149, 169–172
Petty, George, 148
Photographers: of Carlsbad test, 117–118; of bat colony in Ney Cave, 129–137
*Pipistrellus* species of bats, 58
Predators of bats, 81, 91–92
Princess (pet bat), 127–129, 142, 149–150, 162–163
Project X-Ray: Rhoads as commanding officer of, 149, 150–151, 160, 181; demonstration of, for Marine Corps, 152, 155–156; military rank for staff of, 157–159; Fieser's interest in control of, 165–168, 179–180; Wiswell's design of artificial environment for hibernation of bats, 173–174; personnel problems of, 184–186; hibernation experiments, 188–189; funnel method of capture of bats, 194–195, 196, 200–201; Dugway tests, 202–216; Adams's dismissal from, 203–205, 218–220; Rhoads's evaluation of, 211–214; staff of, 214–215; controversy between Fieser and Rhoads, 217, 218; schedule for, 217–218; improvement of design elements for, 223–226; discontinuance of, 225–231. *See also* Adams Plan

Rabies, 189–193
Rambeau, Rae, 231, 233
Randolph, Jennings, 5
Rhoads, Lt. Col. R. H. (Dusty): as commanding officer of Project X-Ray, 146–147, 149, 150–151, 160, 181; introduction to staff of Project X-Ray, 150–151; on uniforms, 151, 181; accident with staff car of, 155; and test of bat bombs for Marine Corps, 156; on military ranks of Project X-Ray staff, 157–159; and Fieser, 165–166, 211–

214, 217, 224; and pet tiger (Top Sarge), 169–170, 172; and fistfight between von Bloeker and Couffer, 184; and personnel problems of Project X-Ray, 185–186; and number of bats, 187, 188; and Dugway tests, 203, 204–206, 211–214; dismissal of Adams, 218–220; progress reports for Project X-Ray, 223; and discontinuance of Project X-Ray, 227
Roosevelt, Eleanor, 5
Roosevelt, Franklin D., 4–7, 8, 10, 102, 164, 184
Rugh, Emil, 76, 77–83, 91–92, 127, 174, 188, 195, 198

Savage, "Doc," 160
Signal Corps, 101, 113, 221–222
Smith, Capt. R. N., 150, 160, 204, 218
Smith, Gen. Holland, 146
Spallanzani, 37
Spelunking, 62–63
Spotted bats, 2
Stanley, Andrew Paul, 109, 110
Stevenson, Earl, 42, 76, 84, 87, 145–146, 208

Taylor, Thomas R., 16, 17, 18–19, 20, 60
Teller, Captain, 223
Temple, H. B., 223
Tiger, as pet (Top Sarge), 142–143, 149, 169–172
Tinajas Altas, 57–58
Tokyo, 96
Top Sarge (pet tiger), 142–143, 149, 169–172
Tschappat, Gen. W. H., 19
TWA, 86, 87

Vampire bats, 191
Von Bloeker, Jack C., Jr.: as bat authority, 2–3; on bat bomb proposal, 12–14; handwriting of, 13; enlistment in the Army, 21; and research problems to be solved, as identified by Air Force, 25–26; military training of, 31–32; military rank of, 33–34; on weight-carrying abilities of bats, 35, 45–46; security concerns of, 38–39; uniform worn by, 39–40; weight and size-carrying tests on bats, 49; and search for bat caves, 57, 58, 62, 65, 67, 71, 72, 75, 77–78, 79, 82, 91–92; on atomic bomb, 61; and physiologist for Adams Plan, 88–89, 92–94; and Carlsbad test of bat bombs, 114, 115, 118; and hibernation tests, 126; introduction to Rhoads, 150–151; and military rank of staff, 157–158, 159; as correspondent for biological unit, 167; and fistfight with Couffer, 181–184, 202,

230; relationship with Couffer, 181–182; and Dugway tests, 204, 211–212; commission in the Navy for, 214; final meeting with Adams, 215; and discontinuance of Project X-Ray, 229; life after Project X-Ray, 238

Von Bloeker, Ona, 238

Wiles, Capt. William G., 15–19, 52, 53, 54, 60, 86
Williams, Ray: as Marine Corps member, 22–23, 147; as member of bat bomb project, 22–23; weight and size-carrying tests on bats, 49; and search for bat caves, 62, 64, 65, 66, 71, 72, 82; supervisor of, 106; and Carlsbad test of bat bombs, 116, 118; and bat collecting in California, 123–124; and hibernation tests, 126; introduction to Rhoads, 151; demonstration of bat bombs for Marine Corps, 155; and Rhoads's staff car, 155; and marines, 178; and counting of bats, 188; at Texas bat caves, 204; life after Project X-Ray, 234–235, 238
Wiswell, Ozro B.: as physiologist of bat bomb project, 92–94, 101, 167; wife of, 94, 148–149, 238; and Batista, 107–108; and Muroc tests, 107–108; and Carlsbad test of bat bombs, 114; and hibernation tests, 126–127, 134, 149, 188–189, 193–196; in Bandera, 148–149; introduction to Rhoads, 151; and artificial environment for hibernation of bats, 173–174; support for Couffer's decision to allow bat flight, 201; at Dugway tests, 204; commission in the Navy for, 214; life after Project X-Ray, 238
Wiswell, Viola, 94, 148–149, 238

Yates, Capt. T. D., 222
Young, William: as chemist on bat bomb project, 45, 46, 47, 51, 60, 173; photograph of, 48; and Adams, 145, 148, 165, 167, 168; and Fieser, 145, 179; letter concerning criticisms of Adams, 184–186; and discontinuance of Project X-Ray, 226